THE AUTOBIOGRAPHY OF MEDGAR EVERS

THE AUTOBIOGRAPHY OF
MEDGAR
EVERS

A Hero's Life and Legacy Revealed Through His Writings, Letters, and Speeches

EDITED AND WITH COMMENTARIES BY

MYRLIE EVERS-WILLIAMS

AND

MANNING MARABLE

BASIC
CIVITAS
BOOKS

A Member of the Perseus Books Group
New York

Published by Basic Civitas Books
A Member of the Perseus Books Group

A Cataloging-in-Publication data record is available from the Library
of Congress.
ISBN 13: 978-0-465-02177-2
ISBN 0-465-02177-8

05 06 07 08 / 10 9 8 7 6 5 4 3 2 1

CONTENTS

CHAPTER II

TRIAL BY FIRE   47

CHAPTER III

WHY I LIVE IN MISSISSIPPI   85

Documents 24–34

(January 24, 1958–March 23, 1959)

CHAPTER IV

OUR NEED FOR POLITICAL PARTICIPATION   131

Documents 35–44

(May 21, 1959–March 22, 1960)

CHAPTER VI

TAKING FREEDOM FOR OURSELVES 213

CHAPTER VII

I SPEAK AS A NATIVE MISSISSIPPIAN 255

Documents 70–81
(November 7, 1962–June 10, 1963)

CHAPTER VIII

AFTER MEDGAR, NO MORE FEAR   291

Documents 82–89

PREFACE

MYRLIE EVERS-WILLIAMS

This book is a tribute to the forgotten heroes of the modern civil rights movement and to the man who contributed so much to the freedom struggle and to my life: Medgar Evers. Medgar was an integral part of the civil rights movement that began long before the media exposed America to the struggle of those who had embedded into their very being the hunger for justice and equality.

Those freedom fighters possessed raw courage and bravery enhanced by a generous dose of determination to secure these rights at all costs. They were aware that the ultimate price—the loss of life— might be that price. They did not seek recognition or glory. There was no glamour, just an unbreakable bond between those on the front lines. They were the "salt-of-the-earth," moving through their fear and placing all possessions, home, family, jobs, on the sacrificial plate of freedom.

Civil rights activists of the early '50s embraced spirituals as an enhancement to a sometimes flailing movement. The spirituals were food for the soul, a gauge of progress and exploding emotion that could be heard in mass meetings held in churches, and later expanding to auditoriums that held thousands. Songs such as, "I'll Keep On Inching Like an Old Inch Worm," "I Shall Not Be Moved,"

"Can't Let Nobody Turn Me Round," progressing to "We Shall Overcome," all filled the air with hope for a better day.

Negroes, the descriptive name used in the '50s, moved into three self-determined categories: the youth and the elders who boldly stepped to the drum beat of FREEDOM NOW; those who encouraged the slow, legal process; and the middle-class "don't rock the boat" mentality. The mix of ideologies sharpened the action plan for involvement and drew a wider national participation of activists.

However, as we revisit and analyze the history of the civil rights movement, too many of the early freedom soldiers are unknown, their contributions unrecognized. Yet it is through such heroic efforts displayed during the initial modern struggle that we enjoy the progress of today.

While touring a southern college campus before a lecture, I stopped along the way to dialogue with some students. I asked, "Do you know who Medgar Evers was?" A puzzled look crossed the faces of the students. They all agreed that they had never heard of him. One young man guessed, "Was he one of those old baseball players in the Negro League?" Another asked, "Did he play basketball?" I responded, "No, he was a civil rights leader in Mississippi until his assassination in 1963." They looked at me with a nano-second of discomfort, shrugged their shoulders, and walked away saying, "Never heard of him."

Although this incident happened two years ago, it is firmly embedded in my memory as is my almost frantic search for Medgar's inclusion in corporate booklets and calendars distributed during Black History Month (February); the search for more than a sentence about him in books on civil rights leaders.

Medgar Evers never craved recognition. Whenever I raised the issue, encouraging him to seek credit for his work, I was always met with an icy stare and firm voice saying, "It's not about me, it's about the mission and the little people."

Knowing Medgar's wishes, I am still moved today to see the quiet, strong, and steady force that he was recognized as—one of the indestructible foundations of the civil rights movement.

Is this wish only a selfish one? No. Our youth today are more in need than ever for excellent role models, for examples of strong, unselfish leadership. They must be able to make the link between the past, the present, and their future.

Inquiries are made on the lack of media coverage during the early '50s. In Mississippi, we lived behind the cotton curtain. The news of lynching, physical and mental brutality were made known to the larger American population via Western Union telegrams wired to the NAACP New York headquarters, then distributed in press release form directed to AP and other press sources. National television shows that irregularly included Lena Horne, Nat King Cole, and Roy Wilkins were always blacked out with no reason provided—simply a dark screen, until the offending guests departed. The demonstration and arrival of the Freedom Riders initiated a momentum in news coverage.

Only through dedicated research are the hidden gems of history past discovered for all to see. We are privileged to have internationally renowned history scholar Manning Marable assume the responsibility of shaping Medgar's life whereby we can more completely understand his time, his challenges, his dreams as well as those who worked with him.

As for me, after 40 years plus, I found memories rushing through my being as a flood, draining the life from my soul. As I reviewed Medgar's speeches with his hand written notations, photographs, love letters, his driver's license covered with dry blood from that fateful early morning of June 12, 1963, poll tax receipts to vote and numerous other artifacts, I realized that one never completely recovers from such a tragedy. But to use that horror as fuel to continue the unfinished work is the victory.

I was privy to emotional spillovers at home by a man who was extremely private. In anger and frustration, Medgar put his fist through the flimsy wall of our living room when Clyde Kennard died. What lingers most was the time he came home tired and defeated—bearing all of the weight of the movement of the NAACP in Mississippi. He sat on the arm of a chair in the living room, put his head in his hands, wiped away tears and said, "My people, my people. Will they ever be ready?" Within a moment, his resolve returned, and he answered his own question. "Yes, yes, we will be ready!"

Medgar Evers loved life, he loved his family, he was fully aware of the threats to end his life. He said at a mass rally days before his assassination, "If I die it will be for a good cause. Perhaps my death will do some good."

His family honors him. Through this book, may you get to know him—to remember him.

INTRODUCTION

A Servant-Leader of the People:
Medgar Wiley Evers (1925–1963)

MANNING MARABLE

In the popular American imagination, the historical period of 1954–1968 in the Black Freedom Movement—widely termed the "civil-rights movement"—is often characterized by charismatic African American political leadership. When the civil-rights struggle is discussed, one immediately thinks of the soaring language and powerful personality of Dr. Martin Luther King Jr., and for good reason. King personified for millions of Americans the unfulfilled promise of American democracy; through his creative and savvy use of public discourse, he brought into sharp focus the burning issues at hand. King was the most prominent representative of his generation's charismatic-black-leadership tradition, but there were many others: Wyatt T. Walker, Ralph David Abernathy, Hosea Williams, Joseph Lowery, Fred Shuttlesworth, and the young Julian Bond and Jesse Jackson. In national politics, few possessed the oratorical skill or charisma of Harlem congressmember Adam Clayton Powell Jr. Within the black labor movement, the brilliant and persuasive language of both Asa Philip Randolph and the skillful organizer Bayard Rustin inspired and sustained the intense activism of millions of people.

These powerful personalities attracted much of the media attention and analysis about the civil-rights movement, then and even now. Yet at the local level, in hundreds of cities and towns, in thousands of neighborhood churches, schools, and community centers, another kind of black leadership was predominant. They rarely received the degree of media focus or scrutiny that the mostly male charismatic figures attracted. They labored tirelessly, making telephone calls, visiting people's homes, organizing community educational meetings, building support for the cause at the grassroots level. The speeches they delivered rarely were made before television cameras or for radio networks. They were only occasionally quoted in local newspaper accounts of civil rights–related events. Yet they were the foundation of the movement's successes.

Their undeserved obscurity and marginalization is partly derived from the politics of gender. As anyone who has seriously participated in grassroots, neighborhood organizing can attest, women are far more likely than males to emerge as the critical leaders in most working-class and poor neighborhoods. Women activists are far more prevalent than males in the building of civic capacity—whether within faith-based institutions or in groups engaged in educational reform, community safety, and/or public health. Day-to-day political-organizing work is rarely glamorous or exciting. Much of it is mundane, boring, and quite difficult: typing and processing letters; making numerous telephone calls; meeting frequently with small numbers of people at their homes; preparing and serving food; fundraising; finding places for people to sleep or to live; organizing childcare; driving people to and from meetings; negotiating with local ministers, businesses, and schools to obtain space for activities; sustaining communication between group members; and representing the interests and objectives of one's group to other constituencies and organizations. Added to all of this is the profoundly human dimension: the loss of time and intimacy with one's partner or spouse, children, family, and friends; the financial costs; the physical and emotional pressures; the burden of ostracism and harassment for advocating unpopular views. To be a "leader" in this context is to assume the burden of these necessary responsibilities and tasks. Within a society structured hierarchically by gender, women disproportionately assume these responsibilities. This was certainly the case within the Black Freedom Movement, especially in the patriarchal culture of the U.S. South in the mid-twentieth century.[1]

The general "story" of the Montgomery bus boycott of 1955–1956 usually mentions the courageous individual action of Rosa Parks, a respected, middle-aged seamstress whose arrest for refusing to surrender her seat to a white man on a segregated public bus was the spark that started the public protest. Yet the focus then concentrates on the public leadership of local black ministers such as Martin Luther King Jr. and Ralph David Abernathy, ignoring other individuals who actually did as much—or more—to make that boycott successful. A key figure in this regard was college professor Jo Ann Robinson. The Women's Political Council, an African American women's group chaired by Robinson, was instrumental in the planning and building of the boycott. After Parks's initial arrest, for example, Robinson mimeographed 35,000 handbills calling for a mass boycott of Montgomery's segregated buses overnight. Members of the Women's Political Council made enormous personal and financial sacrifices for nearly one year to win their victory over racism.[2]

Robinson epitomized what several authors have described as servant leadership, a model of civic engagement that seeks to inspire change through personal examples of sacrifice. The servant-leader achieves the goals of change by transforming how oppressed people perceive themselves, awakening the sense that by and through their own energies and actions they have the capacity to both resist oppression and achieve meaningful results.[3] Two excellent models of this type of transformative leadership who made enormous contributions to the modern Black Freedom Movement were Septima Clark and Ella Baker.

Born in South Carolina in 1898, Septima Clark established "citizenship schools" to teach poor and rural African Americans basic educational and home-economics skills, as well as the importance of becoming involved in civic affairs and voting. Impressed with the civic-engagement model Clark had established, the Southern Christian Leadership Conference (SCLC) adopted and promoted the notion of citizenship schools. Before long, Clark's citizenship schools had successfully trained tens of thousands of new community leaders, many of whom became influential in hundreds of local communities across the South. Clark rarely attracted public attention or the lavish praise of prominent national leaders in the civil-rights movement. But her personal sacrifice and dedicated effort in building local sites for black civic education made a profound difference in the success of the movement.[4]

Ella Baker's servant-leadership role in the movement's development, which has only recently been richly documented by historian Barbara Ransby, can hardly be overemphasized. Born in Norfolk, Virginia, in 1903, Baker began her career in public leadership as the head of the Young Negroes Cooperative League, which promoted cooperative black economic development. Joining the NAACP's staff in 1940, Baker rose to become the director of branch organizations. In 1957, Baker and Bayard Rustin organized the important Prayer Pilgrimage for Freedom at the Washington Mall on the third anniversary of the *Brown v. Board of Education* desegregation decision. Critical of the NAACP's bureaucratic structure and petty organizational infighting, in 1958 Baker agreed to accept a leading administrative role at King's SCLC headquarters in Atlanta. Baker again encountered a patriarchal structure, as leaders such as King and Abernathy routinely excluded females and young people from making important decisions. In February 1960, when Southern black college students initiated the sit-in movement, Baker supported their efforts to organize independently from the SCLC and to develop a model of activism that was genuinely democratic and fully participatory.[5]

Baker became convinced over her many years of activism within the Black Freedom Movement that a different kind of leadership was required to build and sustain a fundamental transformation in the lives of oppressed people. This would involve the elimination of the social distance that frequently set apart better-educated and more economically affluent Negro leaders and their white liberal allies from the masses of working-class and poor blacks. Political actions needed to invite the participation and perspectives of all sectors of the community, not simply those who possessed the material resources and other socioeconomic advantages of middle-class status. Exclusionary practices such as relegating women to the margins of decisionmaking, Baker recognized, also had to be contested and replaced by more egalitarian, participatory approaches for addressing people's problems. Baker described this general approach toward political organizing as fostering "group-centered leadership" rather than building "leader-centered groups." The group-centered leader is a facilitator who seeks to inspire others to become involved in political activities through personal example and dedicated service.[6]

The unique leadership characteristics of the nearly invisible and underappreciated women servant-leaders were also present in Medgar Wiley Evers. In most standard textbooks of African American history, Evers is either barely mentioned or completely ignored. In the third edition of August Meier and Elliott Rudwick's *From Plantation to Ghetto*, Evers is not cited.[7] More recent studies of the Black Freedom Movement generally mention Evers, but only as the victim of assassination, or as a relatively obscure leader referenced in connection with his nearly decade-long role as the NAACP's field secretary in Mississippi. For instance, Jeffrey O.G. Ogbar's excellent study, *Black Power: Radical Politics and African American Identity*, refers to Evers's murder only as an event that pushed local NAACP chapters "to greater militancy by more firmly and boldly affirming their rights to self-defense."[8] Barbara Ransby's outstanding biography of Baker goes somewhat further, mentioning that Medgar Evers and another Mississippi-based civil-rights leader, Aaron Henry, "never fully agreed with the NAACP leaders in New York not to form alliances with other civil rights groups, and both men worked closely with the SCLC and other groups on particular campaigns." Ransby also briefly mentions that Evers's "assassination sent anger and fear ricocheting through movement circles and elevated Evers to the status of a national martyr."[9] Joanne Grant's *Ella Baker: Freedom Bound* only mentions Evers among a list of civil-rights martyrs.[10] In Chana Kai Lee's *For Freedom's Sake: The Life of Fannie Lou Hamer*, Evers is referenced only twice, without any substantive comment about his central role in building the Freedom Movement's foundations in Mississippi.[11]

Even in memoirs and commentaries by veterans of civil-rights struggles, Evers barely merits any attention. For example, in *Lay Bare The Heart*, the autobiography of Congress of Racial Equality leader James Farmer, Evers's name appears only twice. One reference is among a list of civil-rights activists who were killed; the other citation has Evers stating that the Freedom Rides of 1961 were "a bad idea and hoped we wouldn't come to Mississippi."[12]

A modest body of literature and films about Medgar Evers and his personal sacrifices to the struggle for freedom nevertheless has managed to keep his legacy alive. Chief among these sources is, of course, Myrlie Evers-Williams's inspirational account with William Peters, *For Us, The Living*, published in 1967.[13] Former Mississippi civil-rights activist John R. Salter discussed Evers's role and many contributions to the movement in his 1979 book, *Jackson, Mississippi: An American Chronicle of Struggle and Schism*.[14] Four years later, an adaptation of *For Us, The Living* written by actor/activist Ossie Davis made its way to television. Directed by Michael Schultz, the film featured actor Howard Rollins Jr. as Evers, alongside actors Irene Cara, Paul Winfield, and Laurence Fishburne.[15]

In Mississippi, African Americans continued to push for greater civic recognition of Evers. In 1987, Mirtes Gregory, a businesswoman and civic leader in Jackson, initiated a campaign to build an honorific statue of Evers. Local supporters organized an effective fundraising campaign that attracted donations from thousands of individuals. On June 28, 1992, a life-sized bronze statue of Evers was unveiled at the Medgar Evers Public Library in Jackson.[16] In 1988, the Afro-American Studies Program at the University of Mississippi, in conjunction with the Mississippi Network for Black History and Heritage, produced a commemorative booklet, "Remembering Medgar Evers . . . For A New Generation." Describing Evers as an "unsung hero," the booklet praised the civil-rights leader for leaving "a powerful legacy of faithful and selfless service and of fearless sacrifice, a common legacy of all Mississippians regardless of race. . . .

There are those who will argue that we should try and forget the turmoil of the 1950s and 1960s, to forget the struggle to achieve democracy, to forget Medgar Evers," the booklet's author, scholar Ronald Bailey, related. "But those who fail to remember history are doomed to repeat it. . . . Medgar is symbolic of the very best of what Black people, what Mississippi, and what the United States can produce."[17]

The courageous effort of Myrlie Evers-Williams in calling for the conviction of her late husband's assassin, white supremacist Byron De La Beckwith, provoked a new generation of Mississippi prosecutors in the late 1980s to re-examine the nearly thirty-year-old murder case. On December 17, 1990, Beckwith was finally arrested for Evers's murder. After a two-week trial, a jury of four whites and eight African Americans found Beckwith guilty. In 1997, the Mississippi Supreme Court upheld Beckwith's murder conviction.[18] Beckwith's conviction led to an increase in public awareness of and interest in Medgar Evers. Within a few years, several new books on Evers appeared, including Adam Nossiter's *Of Long Memory: Mississippi and the Murder of Medgar Evers*, Jennie Brown's *Medgar Evers*, Reed Massengill's *Portrait of a Racist: The Man Who Killed Medgar Evers?* and Maryanne Vollers's *Ghosts of Mississippi: The True Story*.[19] Filmmakers initiated new projects dealing with the Evers assassination. In 1994, Home Box Office aired an investigative report, *Southern Justice: The Murder of Medgar Evers*, narrated by civil-rights leader Julian Bond.[20] Columbia Pictures and Castle Rock Entertainment two years later produced a major multi-million-dollar feature film on Evers's murder and its legal aftermath: *Ghosts of Mississippi*, directed by Rob Reiner. Based on Vollers's book, the film starred Alec Baldwin, Whoopi Goldberg, and James Woods.[21] While *Ghosts of Mississippi* was an informative and entertaining film, it ironically failed to explain the content of Evers's political ideas and actions, or why Beckwith and other white racists feared and hated the civil-rights leader. Evers is a ghost in his own film, because the audience cannot hear him in his own words.

In the late 1990s, Myrlie Evers-Williams, who at that time also served as the national chair of the NAACP, founded a nonprofit organization, the Medgar Evers Institute (MEI), with the goal of preserving and advancing the heritage of Evers. In 2002, MEI, in conjunction with Communications Arts Company, produced a video documentary, *The Legacy of Medgar and Myrlie Evers*. MEI hosted youth leadership-training conferences, public lectures, and other educational events in Mississippi.[22] Local elected officials finally began to express their appreciation of and active support for Myrlie's efforts. In March 2003, the Mississippi state legislature issued resolutions honoring the historic contributions of both Medgar and Myrlie Evers. A commemoration marking the fortieth anniversary of Evers's assassination, held at Arlington National Cemetery on June 12, 2003, was attended by Myrlie, Mississippi senator Trent Lott, and Mississippi congressmembers Bennie Thompson and Chip Pickering. Members of the Mississippi congressional delegation successfully moved a joint resolution adopted by the U.S. Congress, declaring the week of June 9–16, 2003, the Medgar Wiley Evers National Week of Remembrance.[23]

This book, developed in partnership with Myrlie Evers-Williams, is part of this larger effort to preserve and promote the ideas and example of servant-leaders such as Medgar Wiley Evers, whose dedication in the face of racist intimidation and violence made it possible for millions of Americans to achieve their constitutional rights. The best interpreter and observer of the difficult struggles in Mississippi in which Evers was engaged is Evers himself. Through his own voice, and in his own words—in memoranda, telegram messages, personal notes, transcribed public speeches, fragments of written texts—the true dignity and dedication of the man becomes crystal clear. Evers personally eschewed the limelight, modestly preferring that others bask in public recognition while he labored on the sidelines. Most people who had encountered Evers didn't "think that Medgar had any gumption at all," Supreme Court Justice Thurgood Marshall reminisced in 1977. "And that's how he got so much accomplished. People underplayed him. He had more courage than anybody I've ever run across."[24] Perhaps now, a half century removed from Evers's initial appointment as NAACP field secretary in Mississippi, his model of servant-leadership will come to the forefront of public memory and appreciation.

CHAPTER I

BRING

JUSTICE

SURE

Documents 1–11
(December 1954–December 1955)

Go Down, Old Hannah

. . . I say, get up dead man

Well, well, well

Help me carry my row

Help me carry my row

I say, get up dead man

Help me carry my row

Well my row so grassy

Well, well, well

I can't hardly go

Can't hardly go

Well my row so grassy

I can't hardly go.

I say, go down old Hannah . . .

Don't rise no more . . .

If you rise in the mornin' . . .

Bring judgment sure . . .

Traditional song, recorded by African American prisoners, 1964–1966.[1]

THE TRUE ORIGINS of Medgar Wiley Evers's political life can be traced back to the Mississippi state constitutional convention of 1832. The delegates at the convention adopted the principle of "universal white manhood suffrage," eliminating all property qualifications on the franchise.[2] The state's small free-black population, while permitted to own property, was excluded from voting. After the Civil War and the abolition of slavery, Mississippi experienced a brief period of democracy, as black males won the right to vote. White racists launched retaliatory violence against African American elected officials and voters, culminating in the overthrow of Reconstruction in 1875. In 1876, the Democratic-controlled state legislature gave local voting registrars the authority to demand "complete and correct answers" for blacks seeking to establish their qualifications to vote.[3] A series of repressive laws was passed, designed to roll back the gains African Americans had achieved since slavery's demise. Among the most outrageous was Mississippi's so-called "Pig Law," which defined the theft of a farm animal worth ten dollars or more a crime of grand larceny, punishable by up to five years in prison. The Pig Law increased the state's prison population by over 300 percent in less than five years, providing involuntary convict laborers for work on Mississippi Delta plantations.[4]

The legal and political regime of white supremacy was, however, not established until 1890, when the state held a new constitutional convention. Delegates adopted a series of provisions deliberately designed to exclude African Americans from voting, including the poll tax and literacy tests.[5] Blacks were also kept from the polls through outright violence and lynchings. Between 1882 and 1927, 517 African Americans were lynched in the state of Mississippi, the highest number in the nation for any state during this period.[6]

A backward, repressive political culture rooted in violence was firmly consolidated by the early twentieth century, making "Mississippi" symbolic for everything undemocratic and oppressive in the U.S. South. In 1949, noted Southern political scientist V.O. Key Jr. observed critically that Mississippi had to be considered "in a class by itself. . . . Yet Mississippi only manifests in accentuated form the darker political strains that run throughout the South. On the surface at least," Key added, "the beginning and end of Mississippi politics is the Negro. He has no hand in the voting, no part in factional maneuvers, no seats in the legislature; nevertheless, he fixes the tone—so far as the outside world is concerned—of Mississippi politics."[7] The state's most notorious practitioner of racist politics in the first half of the twentieth century was Theodore Bilbo. Elected Mississippi governor in 1915 and 1927, and elected three times to the U.S. Senate—in 1934, 1940, and 1946—Bilbo bragged that "the best way to keep the nigger from voting" was to visit him "the night before election."[8]

This was the oppressive world of white domination and black subordination into which Medgar Wiley Evers was born on July 2, 1925, in Decatur, Mississippi, the child of James and Jesse Evers. James was employed as a stacker at a Decatur sawmill; his wife, Jesse, took in laundry and ironing for local white families. The Evers family was never well-to-do, yet it managed to acquire land and a modest degree of security. Jesse was a devout Christian, extremely active in the Church of God in Christ, and her piety and deep faith had an effect on all of her children. James attended one of the town's Baptist churches, serving as a deacon of the congregation. Both parents preached to their children about the importance of self-reliance, pride, and self-respect, values directly contradicting the "customary" values that African Americans were expected to assume. As a child, Medgar was taught that during Reconstruction, his maternal great-grandfather had killed two white men in a dispute and had managed to avoid white retaliation by escaping from town.[9]

James Evers was frequently called "Crazy Jim" by local whites, partially because he adamantly refused to step off the sidewalk in deference to whites as they passed. "He had a reputation of being mean," Myrlie Evers-Williams now relates. "You didn't mess with him. *Nobody.*" James Evers would constantly preach to his children: "My family *will* be able to walk on the sidewalk. [Whites] will treat them with dignity. They will be able to register to vote."[10] The senior Evers emphasized that Negroes should never be apologetic or ashamed of who they were as black people; they should never attempt to negate or deny their black heritage and culture. These were lessons that profoundly affected young Medgar and formed the foundations of his core personal and emerging political identity.

Young Medgar was especially close to his brother Charles, three years his senior. It was Charles who gave Medgar his nickname, "Lope," because of the stride in his walk. Educated in racially segregated public schools in Decatur and Newton, Mississippi, Medgar was forced to walk twelve miles each day. Both he and Charles bitterly resented seeing neighborhood white children being transported on school buses to local public schools, while they had no choice except to walk. Medgar's childhood was typical for an African American youngster in his community, but something seemed to set him apart, even then. Years later, Jesse confided to Myrlie that when Medgar was a boy, he would sometimes "pull away and go up under the house," thinking to himself. "Sometimes I would go out and look for him, and he would just be leaning against one of the posts [in the yard] . . . just thinking . . . It's just the way he is."[11] Medgar constantly dreamed about things that were difficult to explain to others.

When Medgar was about fourteen years old, a neighborhood friend of his father's got into trouble, supposedly for "sassing a white woman" at the local fairground. The black man promptly was apprehended and brutally beaten to death. The lynching had a profound impact on Medgar's feelings about the racist conditions that surrounded him and his entire family. He was determined to escape the omnipresent pain and fear that Jim Crow segregation imposed on every black person.

As a teenager, he sought ways to assert himself. According to Myrlie, in high school young Medgar was a zoot-suiter, wearing oversized suit coats and baggy slacks, the hip style also favored at the time by young Malcolm Little, who would later become better known as Malcolm X. Medgar often wore a large, stylish hat, tilted to the side. "His vocabulary" at the time, Myrlie adds, "was a little on the raunchy side."[12] In 1943, Medgar prematurely left high school and, lying about his age, followed his brother Charles into the army.

Medgar served in a racially segregated army field battalion in both England and France during World War II. During his stationing in France, he became close friends with a French family, and became romantically involved with one of the family's daughters. Medgar was unaccustomed to being treated like a full human being by whites, and his experience must have affected him deeply. Medgar questioned whether he should even return to Mississippi. "He was very much in love," Myrlie states. Medgar learned to feel deep affection for "someone of another color and could see past the color." But once he made the decision to return to the segregated South, the idea of coming home with a French bride made absolutely no sense. The majority of the United States at that time, including Mississippi, had made interracial marriage a crime. Despite his decision, Medgar privately kept his precious photographs and letters of his French romantic acquaintance for years, destroying them only when he married Myrlie Beasley.[13]

In 1944, the U.S. Supreme Court in *Smith v. Allwright* had outlawed the "white primary" election, which in the solidly Democratic South was a principal means of disfranchising black voters. In 1946, the Mississippi state legislature passed a law exempting returning soldiers from paying the poll tax. Without pausing to realize that there were over 80,000 black Mississippians who had served in America's armed forces during World War II, the legislature's actions almost overnight created thousands of highly motivated black potential voters in the state. Returning from Europe, Medgar and Charles were determined to cast their first votes in their hometown of Decatur in the Democratic primary election. Bilbo was on the ballot, running for reelection to the U.S. Senate, but he had several opponents. Election day was set for July 2, 1946—Medgar's twenty-first birthday.

Medgar, Charles, and four other black World War II veterans walked to the county courthouse. Word about their plans to vote had spread, and Decatur's main streets were nearly vacant. A cluster of about twenty well-armed, angry white men stood at the courthouse entrance. According to Charles Evers, they held "shotguns, rifles and pistols. . . . We stood on the courthouse steps, eyeballing each other." Whites who recognized Medgar and Charles and who knew and respected their parents urged them to leave before violence erupted. The county sheriff, watching the confrontation, did nothing to assist the blacks in voting. Indeed, the sheriff "wasn't going to let us vote, but he didn't try to beat us or arrest us," Charles Evers recalls. "He knew he might have to kill us first, and he didn't want to do that." Finally, it was Medgar who decided that it was not worth the bloodshed that would be necessary to try to vote. "Come on, Charlie, let's go," Medgar stated. "We'll get them next time." As they departed, one enraged racist yelled, "You damn Evers niggers going to get all the niggers in Decatur killed."[14] Although Medgar and Charles were denied the right to vote that day, several thousand African Americans had been permitted to vote throughout the state. This was only a tiny fraction, less than 1 percent, of an estimated 350,000 black Mississippians of voting age.

Medgar enrolled in Mississippi's black Alcorn College (later Alcorn State University) in 1947, and soon became one of the most well-respected and popular students on the campus. A business major, Medgar excelled in both track and football. He edited Alcorn College's student newspaper for two years. Medgar received national recognition by being named in the *Who's Who in American Colleges*. During his college years, Medgar continued his personal habit of extensive reading, expanding his explorations to literature, especially poetry. He also deepened his interest in and commitment to political activism.

In 1947, with his brother Charles, he met a prominent African American physician, Dr. T. R. M. Howard, who owned property in the Mississippi Delta. Howard advocated for blacks to begin asserting themselves as an economic and political force. Howard's arguments certainly made much political sense to Medgar, and his obvious affluence added to his local prestige among Mississippi blacks. As Myrlie recalls, Howard was flashy, flamboyant, and self-assertive: "Big laugh, big flirt." He had started a small life-insurance company to provide coverage for working-class and poor black families as an alternative to the exploitative practices of white-owned companies. Howard constantly stressed that all African Americans, no matter how impoverished, should be given some degree of security and respect.[15]

Medgar's first encounter with newly arrived freshman Myrlie Beasley says much about the self-confidence of the young man. Myrlie had been raised in a strict, conservative, black-middle-class household in Vicksburg, Mississippi. Before her departure to attend college at Alcorn, her grandmother and aunt sternly warned her, "Baby, now don't you get involved with any veterans!" Soon after arriving on campus, with a small group of other female students, she encountered a cluster of Alcorn football players. One of the players made eye contact with the seventeen-year-old Myrlie and confidently walked over to her. Myrlie was standing against a utility pole. "You need to stop leaning on that light pole," Medgar said with a smile. "You might get shocked." Myrlie recalls: "[He wasn't] cute, but attractive . . . I tossed my hair. I was intrigued by him that very moment. . . . My poor grandmother and aunt! Before they could get a mile away from dropping me off, my fate had been sealed with a veteran."[16]

Medgar and Myrlie began to see each other socially. Medgar boldly began to plan the young woman's entire future life, much to her consternation. One day Medgar announced to her, "I'm going to make you into the woman I want you to be. . . . [You're] going to be the mother of [my] children." Myrlie may have been only seventeen years old, but she boldly responded, "You don't know me. . . . You haven't kissed me, you haven't even held my hand!" Myrlie reflects now: "Where in the heck is this guy coming from, you know? And I asked him about this . . . he said, 'I'll let you know when I do'"[17]

Young Myrlie Beasley soon became the object of Medgar's romantic attention, but he made it plain that she would have to make some changes. He constantly quizzed her about whether she had read certain books or articles. He appreciated literature and frequently in his everyday conversation displayed a remarkable vocabulary. "I can't tell you how many times during our courtship I excused myself to get to my room and pull out my dictionary," Myrlie recalls, in order to understand what Medgar had just said. He displayed a deep awareness of national and global events, and even at this early stage of his life, held a strong set of political beliefs. Medgar detested Negroes who were embarrassed or ashamed about the color of their own skin. Decades before "Black is Beautiful!" became a popular political slogan, Medgar had embraced his blackness, and encouraged Myrlie to do the same. "Wear your hair nappy," Medgar advised Myrlie, referring to a more natural hairstyle for black women. "I learned from Medgar, who said, 'Be yourself,'" she says. He also taught her never to accept white racism and discrimination. If Mississippi whites were clearly for something, regardless of what the issue was, one could be certain that Medgar Evers was against it.[18]

In late 1951, at the Mount Heron Baptist Church in Vicksburg, Mississippi, Myrlie Beasley and Medgar Wiley Evers were married. Both families expressed serious reservations about the marriage. Myrlie had not yet graduated from college, and her family had hoped that she would pursue a successful career in the arts. Medgar's brother Charles and his parents were less than entirely happy with Medgar's choice of a life partner. Charles had proposed to his younger brother that "they become rich landholders in Mississippi. . . . Medgar's community of Decatur was very, very upset," Myrlie remembers. "One of their very special sons [was] marrying a girl from Vicksburg." Local blacks complained, "Aren't any of our girls here good enough?"[19] Despite these reservations, the young couple was in love, so both families were reconciled to the inevitable. The young couple moved into married student quarters on the campus during the early months of 1952. Medgar completed his degree work that Spring, and received his undergraduate diploma in May 1952.

Medgar accepted a position as an insurance salesman with the Magnolia Mutual Insurance Company, owned by Howard. The couple would have to relocate, however, to Mound Bayou, the historic all-black town founded in the Delta by Isaiah T. Montgomery back in 1887.

In 1952, the Evers household moved to Mound Bayou, and Medgar began to travel extensively throughout the Delta, visiting hundreds of impoverished homes to sell life-insurance policies. Although he had been raised in Mississippi, Medgar could scarcely believe the incredible poverty and backwardness of the Delta region. "That [experience] gave him his real taste of poverty on the plantations," Myrlie now reflects. "He said to me, 'At least I can call these people 'Mr. and Mrs.' I can give them a sense of dignity. I can help them when they need to escape.'" Sharecroppers who owed their landlords incredible sums of money, which they could never hope to repay, simply would vanish from their shanties in the middle of the night, fleeing to Memphis and then, frequently, to freedom in the north. Medgar courageously decided to assist them.

When Howard and others came up with an idea for expressing their protest to segregation codes—an automobile bumper sticker which clearly stated, "Don't buy gas where you can't use the restroom"—Medgar enthusiastically endorsed the campaign.[20] "If you used one of the bumper stickers on your car, you were taking your life in your hands," Myrlie recalls. "Either [you were] beaten, your car damaged, fired if people knew where you worked . . . [only] a few people [would] do it. Medgar was one of the ones." At first Myrlie urged her husband not to jeopardize their safety by participating in the symbolic protest campaign. "But I loved the idea of it," she says.[21]

When Howard decided to establish a local civil-rights advocacy organization, the Regional Council of Negro Leadership (RCNL), in 1952, Medgar became a founding member. By 1953 he was assisting rural blacks to register to vote, and promoting memberships in the NAACP. During his years in Mound Bayou, Medgar continued to read extensively, especially about the emerging independence struggles that were erupting in Africa and the Caribbean. Medgar became particularly interested in the Mau Mau uprising against British colonialism in Kenya. The imprisoned leader of Kenyan anti-colonial resistance, Jomo Kenyatta, came to personify black militancy in Medgar's eyes. Africans employed revolutionary violence to combat white minority rule in East Africa; Medgar pondered whether the same radical resistance should be used by oppressed blacks in the Mississippi Delta against their white oppressors. "Why not really cross the line? we wondered," Charles Evers recalled about his brother and himself, writing in 1997. "Why not create a Mau Mau in Mississippi? Each time whites killed a Negro, why not drive to another town, find a bad sheriff or cop, and kill him in a secret hit-and-run raid?" Charles Evers had become convinced that violence was the only answer, but his younger brother ultimately could not accept it as a strategy for Negroes: "We bought bullets, made some idle Mau Mau plans, but Medgar never had his heart in it."[22] Nevertheless, when Myrlie and Medgar had their first child, a boy, he was named Darrell Kenyatta Evers.

Unlike Dr. Martin Luther King, Jr., Medgar was not an advocate of "nonviolence" in the face of white terrorism. He purchased a rifle, and over the next years carried it with him in his automobile, in case he had to protect himself and his family. He concluded that "race war" was a very real possibility throughout the South's Black Belt region, if blacks collectively ever created a real political movement to resist their oppression. If white structural racism—the extensive socioeconomic institutions of white prejudice, power, and privilege—was relatively "permanent," what practical options or alternatives did African Americans have? Perhaps blacks should consider demanding a separate, all-black state of their own, based on a territorial separation between the races. Myrlie explains that Medgar believed "you must always be prepared for whatever comes our way. And we were talking about the guns, the arms, collecting what we would need to fight if by chance we ended up in a race war. Which he felt could possibly happen. . . . [If we] found ourselves in a separate part of America, how we would not be starved out, how we would be in a location where we would not be surrounded and wiped out at one time. . . . [H]e was thinking about building a nation . . . of black people."[23]

Between 1952 and 1954 a new generation of African American leadership emerged throughout Mississippi, impatient with the lack of progress in reforming the state's legal policies of rigid racial segregation. Prominent within this activist group was Amzie Moore [see Documents 3, 4, and 5]. Born in 1912, Moore had been involved in the "Black and Tan" faction of the Republican Party in Mississippi. After serving in the segregated armed forces during World War II, Moore helped Howard start the Regional Council of Negro Leadership. In Columbus, Mississippi, a strong civil-rights advocate was Dr. E. J. Stringer, an African American dentist who in 1954 was elected president of the state conferences of NAACP branch organizations. In Clarksdale, the key figure was Aaron Henry. Another World War II veteran, Henry had been the first African American in Coahoma County to cast a ballot in the Democratic Party's primary election. In 1954 Henry was elected president of the Clarksdale NAACP branch. In Belzoni, the Reverend George Lee and grocery store proprietor Gus Counts organized an NAACP branch in 1953–1954. Lee was also a prominent RCNL officer. These grassroots local leaders were successful in assisting growing numbers of Mississippi blacks to register to vote. Lee even openly gave sermons predicting "the day when the Black people of the Delta were going to elect somebody to the United States Congress."[24]

It was in this hopeful, changing political environment in the fall of 1953 that Medgar Evers made the fateful decision to apply for admission to the University of Mississippi Law School. Myrlie immediately thought her husband's idea was "selfish and foolish." She was pregnant again, and financially the couple was especially vulnerable. An application to the University of Mississippi by a Negro would spark tremendous public controversy. "It would highlight [Medgar's] existence in Mound Bayou and his work that he was doing on kind of a secret basis on the plantations [with poor black tenant farmers]," Myrlie later explained. Evers's parents also strongly disagreed with their son's decision. During an emotional family discussion, Medgar became "so upset he turned over his chair when he got up from the table and walked out." He accused "all of us of being short on 'long-term wisdom', of not being able to see beyond 'the immediate complications.' . . . But we couldn't see down the road the benefits of his breaking down the barrier at Ole Miss."[25]

On January 16, 1954, Medgar submitted his formal application to attend the University of Mississippi Law School [see Document 1]. A white neighbor from Medgar's hometown, Jim Tims, was an "Ole Miss" alumnus who had the courage to recommend him. But as Charles Evers relates: "Most local whites thought Medgar applying was an outrage. Mississippi state pride required that its best university be high-toned, and Ole Miss couldn't be high-toned with nigger students. Case closed."[26] In September 1954, the Mississippi Board of Higher Learning rejected Evers's application. Medgar immediately requested the support of the NAACP in filing a lawsuit against the University of Mississippi. Stringer and other local NAACP leaders had an alternative suggestion—that Evers accept a position as their state's first NAACP field secretary. Myrlie's immediate response upon learning of the offer was to admit that she was "scared to death, but if that's what you want to do, let's try, because it also means that we come as a package, and that I will have a job."[27] On November 24, 1954, Evers became the field secretary of the NAACP in Mississippi. The Evers family relocated from Mound Bayou to Jackson, where they moved to the segregated Maple Street Projects. In January 1955, Medgar and Myrlie opened the NAACP office in Jackson. Medgar was only twenty-nine years old, but he was confident that he was prepared to be an effective advocate for racial justice.[28]

On May 17, 1954, in the historic *Brown v. Board of Education* decision, the U.S. Supreme Court overturned the 1896 *Plessy v. Ferguson* precedent, which had established racial segregation in the nation's public schools. Armed with this legal triumph, NAACP national leaders urged their members in the South to petition their local school boards to abolish racial segregation. At the forty-fourth annual NAACP convention, held in Dallas, Texas, July 1–15, 1954, NAACP Legal Defense Fund Director Thurgood Marshall called for new desegregation litigation targeting public transportation, residential segregation, and municipal parks. On September 3, a group of 250 African American leaders throughout the state circulated a public statement endorsing public-school desegregation.[29]

Both Charles and Medgar Evers had reservations about the *Brown* decision and the general strategy of racial integration pursued by the NAACP. Charles Evers believed that "full, instant integration would fail," and thought that desegregation had to be gradually phased into schools over a twelve-year period.[30] The legality of school integration, and the probability that it would usher in the general desegregation of society, generated what historians now describe as "massive resistance," especially in the Deep South. In November 1954, in a special session, the Mississippi Statehouse passed a resolution calling for resistance to "any efforts to force integration" on the state. The legislature passed a "pupil placement law," providing for the individual assignment of students to specific schools. The measure also created new "administrative remedies" for students who disagreed with their school assignments. These educational devices were explicitly designed to make school desegregation extremely difficult, if not impossible. The legislature also tightened literacy requirements for voting, with the clear objective of eliminating blacks from the polls.[31]

In July 1954, in Sunflower County, Mississippi, a local plantation manager, Robert B. Patterson, along with several businessmen and public officials, formed a "Citizens' Council" dedicated to the preservation of white supremacy and militant resistance to school desegregation. By October 1954, twenty Mississippi counties had Citizens' Councils. In early 1955, during the same weeks that Medgar and Myrlie Evers were establishing the Jackson NAACP office, the Citizens' Council headquarters in Jackson opened. By August 1955, the state organization claimed Citizens' Councils in sixty-five of Mississippi's eighty-two counties, and a mass membership of 60,000. Mississippi blacks publicly identified with the NAACP and the cause of school desegregation quickly fell under severe attack.

On September 9, 1954, thirty NAACP members in Walthall County, Mississippi, were forced before a local grand jury for supporting school desegregation. On September 16, a local NAACP meeting in Amitie was disrupted by law-enforcement officers who seized the branch's records.[32] Blacks who signed school-desegregation petitions were routinely fired from their jobs, or had their mortgages or bank loans foreclosed. NAACP state president E. J. Stringer and his family were brutally harassed: His wife was fired, their liability insurance was canceled, they received multiple threatening telephone calls, and they were audited by the Internal Revenue Service.[33]

In Belzoni, in April 1955, there were several incidents of African American–owned business and automobile windows being smashed by whites. In one case, a note was left: "You niggers paying poll tax, this is just a token of what will happen to you." On the evening of May 7, local NAACP activist Reverend George Lee was murdered in his car; a gun blast tore off the lower left side of his face. Remarkably, the local sheriff claimed that Lee's death was merely a traffic fatality, and that lead pellets embedded in his face were "dental fillings." Evers and NAACP Southern Regional Director Ruby Hurley investigated Lee's murder, and learned that many local blacks were "terrified" by it. One to two thousand blacks nevertheless came to Lee's funeral, which had to be held outside to accommodate the number of mourners. The local campaign of racist terror, however, continued. On November 25, 1955, the former president of Belzoni's NAACP branch, Gus Courts, was shot twice, in the stomach and left arm [see Document 2].[34]

It was in this context of spiraling white vigilante violence that fourteen-year-old Emmett Till, a black Chicago teenager, was kidnapped and murdered in Money, Mississippi, on August 28, 1955 [see Document 7]. Till's murderers were arrested, tried, and declared not guilty by an all-white jury. Till's unforgivable offense was whistling at a white woman. The Till case, and the courageous decision by the dead boy's mother, Mamie Bradley, to publicize the brutality of his death, made Mississippi racism notorious throughout the world. Evers worked exhaustively on the Till murder, along with Aaron Henry, Amzie Moore, and Ruby Hurley [see Documents 5 and 8].

According to Charles Evers: "All four dressed like field hands and slid around the Delta, looking for criminal evidence, trying to convince folk who'd known Emmett Till to risk their lives by being legal witnesses. Whites harassed them, but they pressed on. Medgar wanted to shame all America with the story of Emmett Till. He wanted to make the civil rights struggle a mass movement."[35] In a 1968 oral-history interview, NAACP field organizer Howard Spence, who assisted on the Till investigation, declared: "Had it not been for Medgar Evers, who was NAACP secretary at the time . . . it would have just been another 'case' that's been forgot. . . . The Emmett Till case was the beginning of the Montgomery bus boycott. It was the beginning of a lot of incidents in the South that began to make the Negro aware of the fact that he would *have* to get out and expose himself to these racists—to these people that were gonna kill him."[36]

1 Medgar Evers, Assistant Field Secretary, NAACP, Memorandum

DECEMBER 1954
REPORT ON MISSISSIPPI

In 1954 there were a number of things that happened in Mississippi that we deem progress, and of course the unequaled leadership that the National Association for the Advancement of Colored People provided was unquestionably the reason for such. Certainly other organizations had their effects, particularly the Regional Council of Negro Leadership, but the unwavering position taken by the NAACP was phenomenal in Mississippi.

For the first time in the history of the University of Mississippi a Negro made a formal application to its School of Law. There had been no other formal application by a Negro to any "white" school in the state of Mississippi since Reconstruction.

The NAACP here was instrumental in getting the applicant for Ole Miss. Even though the applicant was not admitted his application is still pending for further consideration.

The governor of Mississippi . . . was told that 99 percent of the Negro population of Mississippi, which is 45 percent of the total 2,200,000, was in favor of voluntary continued segregation. Now, this happened after the historic decision of the U.S. Supreme Court of May 17, 1954.

Now to prove his theory, the governor decided to call in a cross-section of Mississippi Negro leadership for July 30, 1954, which naturally had to include the "radical" NAACP head, Dr. E. J. Stringer, whom the governor would have been most pleased not to have invited, since he had already called in his "good" Negro leaders and briefed them on just what he wanted from them. However, since Dr. Stringer was also endowed by God to use his thinking faculties in the case of emergencies, he immediately called for a statewide meeting of Negro leadership including the governor's good Negro leaders. Now the governor, with his groundwork laid, was caught in a rather precarious position when more than two hundred (200) Negroes, representing many civic, religious, and fraternal organizations turned out just five days prior to his meeting which had been scheduled for the same issue for discussion, but from a different point of view.

And on that momentous day, July 30, 1954, ninety-nine (99) out of one hundred (100) Negro leaders before the governor of Mississippi and his Legal Educational Advisory Committee, of which the governor is chairman, told him in no uncertain terms that they would have no part in any scheme to circumvent the U.S. Supreme Court's decision on segregation in the public schools, thereby immediately putting a public end to the propaganda that 99 percent of the Negroes in Mississippi favored continued segregation.

As a result of the governor's tremendous defeat here, he immediately retreated to an abolition plan which he had previously opposed most vigorously. The LEAC (Legal Educational Advisory Committee) drafted plans to abolish the public school which gives and was given (by the votes 2–1) by the Mississippi legislature the authority to abolish the public schools to preserve segregation.

CITIZENS' COUNCILS RISE

Now during this time, "grass roots" vigilante groups began to form which called themselves "Citizens' Councils" but more appropriately called by Hodding Carter, Editor and Publisher of the Delta Democrat Times, Greenville, Mississippi, as the "uptown" Ku Klux Klan because so many of the towns being members and holding key official positions. Possibly four (4) out of five (5) bank officials, presidents or vice, hold a key position in the Councils. Particularly is this true in the Delta counties where in some counties Negroes outnumber whites as much as 3–1 in population. Bolivar County is an example: there are 19,000 whites and 46,000 Negroes, and of course Bolivar County has one of the strongest Councils in the Delta.

Objective: "Keeping the Negro in his place."

1. Keep him out of white schools.
2. Keep the ballot out of his reach.
3. Keep him dependent.

Schools

It would be only natural that such would have to be carefully planned even to the last detail so as to keep Negroes out of the institutions of higher learning for whites. You must get five recommendations from graduates of the institution you hope to attend, who live in your immediate community.

Voting

To cut down on the increased interest of Negroes registering and voting, an amendment proposed in the legislature was passed in the regular off-year election balloting in November 1954. The measure gave the local circuit clerks authority to reject anyone who could not interpret the Constitution as he would have. However, it was made clear to whites that it would not apply to them, but to keep the Negro in his place.

Dependent

It is also the objective of the Council to keep from the Negro any job that pays him a decent salary, such as factory work and skilled labor jobs. Except for teachers who are "controlled" as far as his militancy is concerned, good jobs are rare for Negroes. Now any Negro who is not content with the status quo should either go north or be branded here as a "troublemaker" and have economic sanction declared on him. And, if such doesn't work, then there are other measures. The other measures have not yet been clearly defined. But such are the tactics of the Citizens' Councils.

These Councils did not have their beginning until U.S. Senator James O. Eastland, who incidentally lives only 18 miles from the birthplace (Indinola, Mississippi) of the Council, started his campaign for re-election to the U.S. Senate in which he stated that such a movement was soon to begin that would spread nationwide.

It is reliably believed that from Senator Eastland's statements of bigotry and activities the Councils had their beginning.

Emmett J. Stringer (1929–?)—Stringer grew up in the tightly knit black community of Mound Bayou, and was already a member of the NAACP before he was a teenager. He served in the army during the Second World War for five years, and after earning a degree from Meharry Medical College in Nashville, Tennessee, he began dental practice in Columbus, where he was active in community affairs as the chairman of the local NAACP branch and leader of the American Legion. John Dittmer, *Local People: The Struggle for Civil Rights in Mississippi* (Urbana: University of Illinois Press, 1994), 42.

Hodding Carter (1907–1972)—Newspaper editor, publisher, and author of numerous books, Carter earned a journalism degree from Columbia University in 1928 and founded *Delta-Democrat Times* by 1938. In 1955, he was censured by the Mississippi State Legislature for criticizing the White Citizens' Council. As a white journalist, he opposed racist violence and denial of opportunities for black people, but mostly supported segregation as an institution. In 1946 he received a Pulitzer Prize for his editorial attacking "racial mores" of Mississippi. Ann Waldron, *Hodding Carter: The Reconstruction of a Racist* (Chapel Hill: Algonquin Books, 1993)

James O. Eastland (1904–1986)—A Mississippi Democrat, Eastland was first elected to the U.S. Senate in 1942 and held the seat for next thirty-six years. He was a close ally of Senator Joseph McCarthy during the heyday of his anticommunist crusade, and became a nationally known figure during the civil-rights movement as one of the most vocal and vociferous supporters of segregation. He used his position as the chair of the Judiciary Committee to delay civil-rights bills and reveled in inflammatory and often murderous rhetoric, as when in 1954 he declared that the *Brown* decision "destroyed" the U.S. Constitution, and, two years later, predicted that the time would soon come to "abolish the Negro race." His political power came to be diminished in Mississippi as black political power increased at the local and state level, and he retired in 1978. "James O. Eastland, 81, Former U.S. Senator," *Chicago Tribune,* Feb. 20, 1986, pg. 10. *Biographical Directory of U.S. Congress,* "Eastland, James Oliver (1904–1986)," http://bioguide.congress.gov/scripts/biodisplay.pl?index=E000018.

---

*

2 Memorandum to Mr. Wilkins from Mr. Current

[Note: This document is missing several pages, noted by ellipses.]

DECEMBER 13, 1954

RE: REPORT ON MISSISSIPPI SITUATION

Pursuant to your instructions, the situation in Mississippi in which members of the NAACP and others have been allegedly subjected to pressures of various kinds, chiefly economic, were discussed at a meeting of the Southeast Regional Advisory Board, Saturday, December 11. We heard reports from Dr. T. R. M. Howard of Mound Bayou, President of the Regional Council of Negro Leadership; Mr. Medgar W. Evers, NAACP Field Secretary; and Mr. Charles Evers.

Dr. Howard stated that the situation in Mississippi is a little worse than in any other State in the United States. He blamed ignorance on the part of most white citizens and their determination to keep "this thing we are fighting for from coming to pass." He said he believed three-fourths of the white Mississippians would take up arms to preserve segregation and that the picture is not encouraging. However, he was not so sure that one year from now this attitude would prevail because he believes that six months or a year hence many attitudes will be changed.

Efforts to keep Negroes out of Universities: After Medgar W. Evers's application to the University of Mississippi, the regulations were changed to require that each student applying to state institutions must be recommended by five of the alumni.

Most serious thing we are facing: Dr. Howard mentioned that in the November election the constitutional amendment adopted to tighten voting qualifications similar to the Boswell Amendment is going to make it extremely difficult even for a Negro law school graduate to vote in Mississippi. Information had come to him that in the spring of 1955, the Board of Supervisors will call for new registrations. They are going to make an effort to purge the Negro voters from the list. Governor Hugh White of Mississippi informed Dr. Howard on July 23rd that there are only 22,000 registered Negro voters in the State of Mississippi. He was informed by the secretary of the state that between eight and ten thousand of them would not be able to vote because of the poll tax. The greatest problem he felt facing the Mississippi Negro is how the Mississippi Negro will get beyond the registrars.

Citizens Council also a problem: Dr. Howard also reported on the citizens councils which are intimidating Negroes in some parts of the state. He said they are organized in 35 of the 82 counties. The citizens council originated in Sunflower County (Indianola). The state president is Herman Moore, President of the Indianola Bank. Executive secretary of the council is a man named Patterson, former football star of the University of Mississippi.

[...]

Dr. Howard indicated that he had given considerable thought as to what can be and must be done immediately. To this end, he talked to Dr. Joseph J. E. Walker, Chairman of the Board of the Tri-State Bank at Memphis, as to using the facilities of this bank to lend emergency assistance to those in dire need. He also felt that Negro insurance companies and other businesses should make money available to assist Negroes in Mississippi.

REPORT OF MR. MEDGAR W. EVERS,
MISSISSIPPI FIELD SECRETARY

Mr. Evers reported on economic pressure in Mississippi as follows:

CASE 1: MR. GUS COURTS
61 1st Street
Belzoni, Mississippi
On or about September 1, 1954, Mr. Gus Courts, President of the local NAACP Branch and merchant, was called into the City Bank by the President of said bank, Mr. Paul Townsend, Jr. While there, Mr. Courts was asked many questions about his affiliation with the

NAACP and, in order that he should remain in good standing with the City Bank, he was told to step down as President of the local NAACP of which he did. Even after having done that, economic pressure on Mr. Courts has been more apparent. Also, there were supposed threats on Mr. Courts's life.

CASE 2: MR. FRED MYLES, MERCHANT
Belzoni, Mississippi

Mr. Myles, who is a relatively young Negro man, inherited the very good meat market business that his father had built over a number of years. Mr. Myles, Jr. is known as one of the best meat-cutters in the Belzoni area with a tremendous amount of white clientele, that is before he became active in the NAACP and a registered voter. When it became known to the Citizens Council that he was a qualified elector and a pro-desegregationist, they began a campaign of boycotting his business. During this period, the Mississippi Power and Light Company, after Mr. Myles was delinquent one day in payment of a bill, cut his lights off which caused quite a bit of spoilage of meat. And to make it more incredible, where normally the charge to restore the circuit or lights is one dollar, this time, it cost Mr. Myles one hundred dollars and, of course, the extra ninety-nine dollars has not been explained to him.

CASE 3: DR. T. R. M. HOWARD, PRESIDENT
Regional Council of Negro Leadership
Mound Bayou, Mississippi

Dr. T. R. M. Howard, a renowned physician, farmer, businessman, and humanitarian, who, because of his steadfast attitude against injustices toward Negroes, has recently been subjected to some Citizens Council–like tactics. To be pointed, Dr. Howard has several plots of land that he is in the process of becoming in complete ownership. However, the negotiable papers passed into the hands of a white insurance agent, Joe B. Lee, of Merigold, Mississippi, who is suspected of being a member of the Council, and who, since receiving the papers, has made unduly demands for immediate payment. Certain members of the Council have attempted to purchase all of Dr. Howard's papers from the Cleveland State Bank without success.

CASE 4: MR. CHARLES EVERS, BUSINESSMAN
Philadelphia, Mississippi

Mr. Charles Evers of Philadelphia, Mississippi, a non-compromising brother of Field Secretary Medgar Evers of Mississippi, has fallen victim to local economic pressure because of his influence in getting more than two hundred Negroes around Philadelphia to pay their poll taxes.

The first such pressure expressed itself in a denial to renew a lease on part of a building where Mr. Evers was operating a café. The second instance of apparent economic pressure came when a thunderous demand went out to the local radio station owner, where Mr. Evers was employed as a disc-jockey, demanding an immediate release of him which the owner refused then to do.

As it happened with Case #3, there were attempts made to purchase from under Mr. Evers his interest in a funeral home he is acquiring. After that was not successful, there were attempts to bribe his agents into quitting his employment. Then after about a year's effort, the citizens council was able, through boycotting the radio station and by refusal of local merchants to purchase the station owner's wholesale commodities, to apply enough pressure to the owner to compel a release of Mr. Evers.

CASE 5: MR. AMZIE MOORE
Cleveland, Mississippi

Mr. Moore is being pressured economically to the extent that immediate financial aid will be necessary to save his new service station and home. Mr. Moore has been active in the NAACP and the full amount of $6,000 on his mortgage is due December 18.

Dr. Howard felt that this was a good case for immediate assistance and was planning on taking it up with the Tri-State Bank immediately. In addition to being active in the NAACP, Mr. Moore helped to secure Negroes to register and vote.

In his report, Mr. Evers also cited the affidavit submitted by his brother Charles to the FBI through Daniel E. Byrd as a result of his inability to register. Although he has been paying poll tax for four years, the local registrars have refused to register him. The agent from Jackson came to investigate the complaint, but showed little interest in witnessing the refusal of the registrar to qualify Mr. Evers.

[...]

2. That the NAACP explore greater financial assistance to Negroes from the Federal Land Bank as well as the Federal Immediate Credit Bank of New Orleans to determine how much possible aid may be granted on an emergency and continuing basis to offset the pressures exerted by local financial institutions.

3. That investigations be launched of the surplus commodities situation in Mississippi to determine the conditions under which it operates and to determine whether discrimination is being practiced. Mr. Medgar Evers was instructed to get more information and pictures as well as other data on the operation of this program in order that a formal complaint might be drawn up.

4. That the matter of overcharge for restoration of power be taken up with the Mississippi Power and Light Company and with the Public Utilities Commission to ascertain whether this is a customary practice or whether it is a part of the economic pressure being exerted on Mississippi businessmen known to be active with the NAACP.

5. That the NAACP seek to dramatize the Mississippi situation, utilizing every possible arena, including feature articles in magazines, liberal newspapers, and possible use of radio and TV. In this connection, it was felt that the announcement of a large sum of money being made available to assist Negroes would have a dramatic appeal.

It was further suggested that a conference be sought with President Eisenhower, Herbert Brownell and Mississippi Negro leaders, including NAACP, to call the nation's attention to what is happening and to get pledges of assistance from the federal government on a top policy-making level.

6. That conference be held with the Department of Justice to find some way of dealing with failure of local agents because of their prejudicial attitudes to properly investigate cases called to their attention.

7. That study be given to setting up a commissary or cooperative to assist in the wholesale purchase of supplies and commodities throughout the State.

With reference to the first suggestion, the conference urged the National Board to act as quickly as possible in view of the fact that many mortgages are up for renewal in the month of December and many Negroes will lose their farms and properties before March unless immediate assistance is forthcoming.

Hugh Lawson White (1881–1965)—Forty-fifth and fifty-first governor of Mississippi, White's first administrations (1936–1940) focused on economic recovery of the state's industry and agriculture, and building statewide highways. In the early years of his second term (1952–1956), White tried to head off public-school desegregation by equalizing funding for white and black schools. After the 1954 Brown decision, however, his administration devoted resources and time to stop and delay school desegregation. David G. Sansing, "Hugh Lawson White: Forty-fifth and Fifty-first Governor of Mississippi: 1936–1940; 1952–1956," http://mshistory.k12.ms.us/features/feature48/governors/white.htm.

Charles Evers (1922–)—Brother of Medgar Evers, Charles became one of the important figures in Mississippi black politics and the civil-rights movement after Medgar's assassination in 1963. He grew up in Decatur and served in the U.S. army during the war. He studied and worked with Medgar until the mid-fifties, when he left for Chicago. He returned to Mississippi after Medgar was killed, and assumed the position of NAACP field secretary. In 1969 he was elected mayor of Fayette, becoming the first black elected official in the state since Reconstruction. He was re-elected in 1981 and ran for governor unsuccessfully. Charles joined the Republican Party, arguing that the Democratic Party had abandoned African American interests. Charles Evers, *Have No Fear: The Charles Evers Story* (New York: John Wiley & Sons, 1997)

T. R. M. Howard (1908–1976)—Originally from Kentucky, Howard moved to Mound Bayou in the early forties and became a successful physician, business entrepreneur, and charismatic political activist. In 1951 he founded the Regional Council of Negro Leadership in Cleveland and led the organization to vocally advocate black rights, particularly the right to vote. The RCLN attracted many existing local NAACP leaders and Howard played a role of political mentor to black youths such as Medgar who first worked for Howard's Magnolia Mutual Life Insurance. In 1957, however, Howard was forced to leave the state in the aftermath of the bloody terror campaign against black civil-rights activists. Dittmer, 32–33.

3 (1) Amzie Moore to Roy Wilkins

January 17, 1955
Amzie's Pan-Am Station
Highway No. 61 South
Cleveland, Mississippi

Mr. Roy Wilkins
Administrator, NAACP
20 W. 40th Street
New York 18, N.Y.

Dear Sir:

On January 3, 1955 I was elected president of Cleveland's Local Branch of the NAACP of Mississippi.

Since the above date several people have come to me asking about help with their farms and other things. I don't know what to tell them, I only know that I was turned down by the Tri-State Bank. I don't think it would be wise to tell them that.

I am sending you a letter from the Tri-State Bank addressed to me which is a reply to my application of January 6, 1955.

I need help, but I am not so worried about myself. I am thinking of all these people in this area who have been given hope by the newspaper reports.

May I hear from you soon? I am

Very truly yours,

Amzie Moore
507–1/2 N. Farish St.
Jackson, Mississippi

(2) Medgar Evers to Amzie Moore

January 27, 1955

Mr. Amzie Moore
Cleveland, Mississippi

Dear Mr. Moore:

In view of what you told me on January 23, 1955, I took the matter up with Mr. Current after our board meeting on Sunday night. Mr. Current suggested to me that I get full details from you and the Tri-State Bank of Memphis as to the reason for such actions. I would appreciate your furnishing me with the complete facts relative to your application. I have requested same from the Tri-State Bank.

The accumulation of such facts would make it possible to arrive at a conclusive point. Such information is needed as quickly as feasible.

Sincerely yours,

Medgar W. Evers
Asst. Field Secretary
Mississippi
MWE:mbe
cc: Mr. Gloster B. Current

(3) Medgar Evers to J.E. Walker, Tri-State Bank

January 27, 1955
Jackson, Mississippi

Tri-State Bank
385 Beale Street
Memphis, Tennessee
Attention: Dr. J. E. Walker

Dear Sir:

We would like from your office, in detail, the basis for which Mr. Amzie Moore's application, of Cleveland, Mississippi, for a loan was not approved. The National Office has requested complete information relative to Mr. Moore's disapproved loan. I would be most pleased to get such information as soon as possible.

In addition, please forward to this office, if it is your policy, application forms for real estate loans. We would appreciate your fullest cooperation in this matter.

Request for such application forms from Kileston, Mississippi should be in your office very soon. Your fullest consideration of such applications would be greatly appreciated.

Respectfully yours,

Medgar W. Evers
Asst. Field Secretary
Mississippi
cc: Mr. Gloster B. Current
Mr. Amzie Moore

(4) Gloster Current to Medgar Evers

February 1, 1955

Mr. Medgar W. Evers
Assistant Field Secretary NAACP
507–1/2 North Farish Street
Jackson, Mississippi

Dear Mr. Evers:

Thank you for sending me a copy of your letter of January 27th to Mr. Amzie Moore.

Enclosed are self-explanatory copies of correspondence between the Tri-State Bank, Mr. Moore and Mr. Wilkins. At the time I told you to get the information from Mr. Moore, I did not know Mr. Moore had written Mr. Wilkins whose reply clarifies the matter.

The bank has been following the procedure of notifying Mr. Wilkins about these matters and perhaps it might be best, before corresponding with them in the future about loans being turned down, that you find out from the National Office what has transpired.

Sincerely yours,

Gloster B. Current
Director of Branches

(5) Roy Wilkins to Amzie Moore

November 18, 1955

Dear Mr. Moore:

I have heard from the Tri-State Bank on their advancing you $1272 to take care of the second mortgage on your home in order to avert foreclosure. They said that payments have been arranged at the rate of $40 a month for 11 months with $832 as the final payment.

I have heard nothing from you on this matter. Did you receive the money? Was the foreclosure averted? Is the second mortgage now entirely removed from your home?

When I called Mr. Medgar Evers of our staff on the night of November 7 in connection with the speedy return of Rev. Moses Wright to Chicago after the Grand Jury hearing, he could hardly talk about the Wright matter because he was so impressed with the immediate danger to you in this foreclosure proceeding. He was so upset that even on his small salary, he wanted to offer some guarantee for you to get the money to save your home.

On the basis of his urgent recommendation, I telephoned Dr. Walker of the Tri-State Bank on November 8 and secured his consent to advance you the necessary sum. I did this on my personal responsibility contrary to the official policy of the Association only because it was represented to me that you were in dire danger of losing your property for want of something like $1200.

My Board of Directors is certain to reprimand me for this step and in all likelihood will hold me personally accountable for the transaction. Since this is so, I would like to have at least a word from you that you have received the money, that your home has been saved, and that you intend to take care of the obligation in a responsible manner.

Very sincerely yours,

Roy Wilkins
Executive Secretary

Amzie Moore (1911–?)—A World War II veteran and native of Grenada County, Moore was a founding member of the Regional Council of Negro Leadership, and served as NAACP leader in Cleveland, MS. Moore advised Robert Moses on voter registration in Cleveland in the early 1960s. Moore was widely known as the owner of various shops along Highway 61 which served as headquarters for civil-rights activists. See Howell Raines, *My Soul Is Rested: Movement Days in the Deep South Remembered* (New York: Penguin,

1977), 233–237; Charles Payne, *I've Got the Light of Freedom: The Organizing Tradition and the Mississippi Freedom Struggle* (Berkeley: University of California Press, 1995), 29–35.

Roy Wilkins (1901–1981)—Executive Secretary of the National Association for the Advancement of Colored People from 1955 to 1976. He joined the NAACP in the 1920s and became assistant secretary to executive secretary Walter Francis White. He edited the *Crisis* magazine between 1934 and 1949 after W. E. B. Du Bois resigned from the editorship. He took part in the 1963 March on Washington and the Selma to Montgomery March in 1965. See Wilkins, with Tom Mathews, *Standing Fast: The Autobiography of Roy Wilkins* (New York: Viking, 1982); Albin Krebs, "Roy Wilkins, 50-Year Veteran of Civil Rights Fight, Is Dead," *New York Times*, September 2, 1981, A1; Peter Levy, *The Civil Rights Movement* (Westport, Conn.: Greenwood, 1998), 145–147.

Gloster Bryant Current (1913–1997)—Current was active in the NAACP's youth council in Detroit during the mid-1930s and became the director of branches of the NAACP when Walter White brought him to New York in 1946. He remained in the post throughout most of his career with the Association, and was a member of the board of directors between 1978 and 1983. "Gloster Bryant Current, NAACP Stalwart," *New Crisis*, October 1997, Volume 104, issue 2, pg.45.

Joseph Edison Walker (1880–1958)—An influential figure in black business and politics in Memphis, Tennessee, Dr. Walker founded Universal Life Insurance Company in 1923 and Tri-State Bank in 1946 with his son, A. Maceo Walker. He also organized the Shelby County Democratic Club and led highly successful black-voter-registration campaigns. He was murdered in 1958 by a business associate over a financial dispute. Elizabeth Gritter, "Local Leaders and Community Soldiers: The Memphis Desegregation Movement, 1955–1961," Senior Honor's Thesis, American University, http://www.american.edu/honors/CurrentStudents/capstones/gritter.pdf. John N. Ingham and Lynne B. Feldman, *African American Business Leaders: a Biographical Dictionary* (Westport, Conn.: Greenwood Press, 1994).

✳

4 Medgar Evers to Lucille Black

July 20, 1955
Medgar Evers
Mississippi State Office
507–1/2 N. Farish Street
Jackson, Mississippi
Telephone Jackson 3–6906

Miss Lucille Black
Membership Secretary, NAACP
20 West 40th Street
New York 18, New York

Dear Miss Black:

In your letter of July 12 you brought to my attention the condition of the Meridian Branch and the need of giving it our immediate attention.

Prior to having received your letter, I had written to Mrs. Wynona Connor, secretary of the Branch, and asked her to call an executive meeting from which will be appointed a president for the unexpired term since the Constitution so provides. I have not heard officially from Mrs. Connor, however, Mr. Darden, who lives in Meridian and is a member of the branch informed me that a meeting was planned to appoint a president for the unexpired term.

I shall see to it that a branch of two hundred members in '54 shall not die in '55. I shall keep you up-to-date on the latest developments.

Yours truly,

Medgar W. Evers
Asst. Field Secretary
Mississippi

Lucille Black (1909–1975)—Black first joined the NAACP in 1927 as a typist for the Branch Department. In 1945 then–Executive Secretary Walter White appointed her membership secretary. Known as a highly effective organizer with intimate knowledge of NAACP branches nationwide, Black was responsible for coordinating membership drives. She is today regarded as one of the early pioneers of modern black feminist activism along with Ella Baker and Ruby Hurley, with whom Black was friends. "Lucille Black, Former Aide of the N.A.A.C.P., 66, Dies," *New York Times*, May 22, 1975, pg. 42.

Charles R. Darden (1911–1984)—Founder of the Meridian Negro Business and Professional League in 1946, Darden led the NAACP Meridian branch and its Youth League, and served as the State Conference president from 1955 to 1960. He worked for a jewel company that sold rings and pictures to black schools. He was part of the state delegation sent to the 1964 Democratic Party National Convention in Atlantic City. "Civil Rights Documentation Project: An Oral History with Evelyn Dorsey Polk," http://www.usm.edu/crdp/html/transcripts/polk_evelyn-dorsey.shtml.

5   (1) Henry Lee Moon to Medgar Evers

September 16, 1955

Dear Medgar:

A number of newspaper reporters are going to cover the Till murder trial in Summer. I have suggested to some who have spoken to me that they get in touch with you, with the president of our Greenwood branch, and also with Ruby Hurley who I understand will be at the trial. Any assistance and guidance that you can give to these gentlemen will be greatly appreciated.

Among those who will cover the trial are the following:

John Popham, *New York Times*
James Hicks, *Afro American*
Murray Kempton, *New York Post*
James Boyack, *Pittsburgh Courier*

James Desmond, *New York Daily News*

Bem Price, *Associated Press*

I know I can depend upon you to see that they get the right angles on the situation down there.

Sincerely,

Henry Lee Moon

Director, Public Relations

[A handwritten note at the bottom of this page indicates that the same letter was sent to Mr. Edward V. Cochran, president of the Greenwood branch, NAACP.]

(2) Evers to Moon

December 5, 1955

Mr. Henry Moon

Director, Public Relations, NAACP

20 West 40th Street

New York 18, New York

Dear Mr. Moon:

Thank you for the *New York Daily News* clippings you sent. I find them most interesting.

Do not ever think I am too busy to give information to those persons who are going to, some way or the other, help our cause down here. I refer to the number of newspaper men you have sent. Continue to send them on.

Yours truly,

Medgar W. Evers

Field Secretary

Emmett Till (1941–1955)—Emmett, known to his friends as "Bo," was born and raised in Chicago, and his life as a teenager was cut brutally short when he was murdered by a lynch mob in Mississippi, where his mother had sent him to stay with her relatives. The murder sparked outrage and focused the nation's eyes on Mississippi and the brutality of Southern lynching. Christopher Metress, ed., *The Lynching of Emmett Till: A Documentary Narrative* (Charlottesville: University of Virginia Press, 2002); Stephen J. Whitfield, *A Death in the Delta: The Story of Emmett Till* (Baltimore: Johns Hopkins University Press, 1991).

Henry Lee Moon (1901–1985)—A graduate of both Howard University and American University, where he studied journalism and public relations, Moon became the NAACP's public relations director in 1948 and edited *Crisis* magazine. During the civil-rights movement, Moon was the principal spokesman for the Association with the national media. He was also the author of *The Emerging Thought of W.E.B. Du Bois* (1973). "Henry Moon, at 84; Was Director of Public Relations for NAACP," *Boston Globe*, June 11, 1985, pg. 31.

John Popham (1910–1999)—Popham became the first Southern correspondent for the *New York Times* in 1948 and traveled extensively throughout the South covering the Emmett Till murder trial and the early stages of the civil-rights movement. In 1958 he became an editor of the *Chattanooga Times*, a position he kept until his retirement in 1977. Douglas Martin, "John Popham, 89, Dies; Journalist Was Noted for Perceptive Coverage of South," *New York Times*, December 14, 1999, B13.

James Hicks (1915–1986)—A decorated World War II veteran, Hicks joined the Baltimore *Afro-American* and the National Negro Press Association after the war. In 1955 he assumed the executive editorship of the New York *Amsterdam News*, covering the civil-rights movement, and became the first black war correspondent during the Korean War. In 1966 he resigned from the paper to serve as assistant commissioner of New York's State Division of Human Rights. After a brief return to the *Amsterdam News*, he became the editor of the *New York Voice*. "Black Newsman James Hicks Dies at 70," *Los Angeles Times*, January 23, 1986, 3.

Murray Kempton (1917–1997)—Kempton was born and grew up in Baltimore, Maryland, but he is best known as an influential reporter and columnist for the *New York Post*. In the 1930s he worked for the renowned journalist H. L. Mencken at the *Baltimore Evening News* and was briefly a radical labor organizer. After World War II, he began writing for the *Post*, covering the civil-rights movement and labor issues. During the 1970s he was briefly an editor for the *New Republic*. He won a Pulitzer Prize in 1985. His columns are collected in *America Comes of Middle Age: Columns 1950–1962* (Boston: Little Brown, 1963). See Godfry Hodgson, "Obituary: Murray Kempton: Left and Loved in New York," *The Guardian*, May 7, 1997, 15.

James Desmond (1908–1968)—Desmond was first employed by the Associated Press and other news organizations, and joined the *New York Daily News* during World War II as a specialist in state political affairs. He gained his reputation as an analyst of New York politics in his "Albany Line" columns. Desmond was close to then-governor of New York Nelson Rockefeller, and published *Nelson Rockefeller: A Political Biography*, in 1964. See "James Desmond Is Dead at 59: Political Writer for Daily News," *New York Times,* July 28, 1968, 31.

—————————————————————————————————————— *

6 Gloster B. Current to Medgar Evers

October 5, 1955

VIA AIRMAIL SPECIAL
Mr. Medgar W. Evers
Field Secretary, NAACP
1072 Lynch Street
Jackson, Mississippi

Dear Medgar:

In further reference to the meeting in St. Louis on Sunday, October 9, please advise the President of the local Branch, Mr. Hubert L. Brown (11 N. Jefferson, Suite 312) of your estimated time of arrival and where you will be stopping. The Branch will send you further details about the meeting which will be held at the Masonic Temple, 4525 Olive. Transportation from St. Louis to East St. Louis for the evening mass meeting is being arranged by Attorney Billy Jones, President of the Illinois State Conference NAACP.

In your talk, expound on the broader implications of what is happening in Mississippi, emphasizing what individual citizens can do. Do not be bitter, but factual as much as possible. Stress in the appeal the need for money to help NAACP fight injustice in Mississippi.

Keep up the good work.

Sincerely yours,

Gloster B. Current
Director of Branches
GBC/cs
Encs.

Billy Jones (1917–1987)—One of the civil-rights lawyers who worked on be-half of the NAACP, Jones in 1949 brought a federal suit to desegregate East St. Louis public schools. Later he was appointed a judge of the federal circuit court. A local elementary school is named in his honor. See "Children Help to Open Judge Jones School," *St. Louis Post-Dispatch*, September 24, 1990, 11.

---

7 Telegram to Roy Wilkins

October 27, 1955
WESTERN UNION TELEGRAM

Roy Wilkins
20 West 40 Street

11 YEAR OLD BENTON COUNTY NEGRO BOY FOUND MYSTERI-OUSLY DEAD. CAUSE OF DEATH UNKNOWN. WILL GIVE FULL REPORT LATER. FUNERAL FRIDAY OCT 28TH=

MEDGAR EVERS=

8 Medgar Evers, Memorandum

NOVEMBER 3, 1955
REPORT ON DEATH OF TIM L. HUDSON, TWELVE-YEAR-OLD
NEGRO YOUTH FOUND DEAD IN LAMAR, MISSISSIPPI

On Wednesday night, October 26 Mr. Simeon Booker of JET magazine called from Chicago, Illinois to inquire of the death of twelve-
year-old Tim L. Hudson of Lamar Community of Marshall County,
Mississippi. Until then there was no knowledge of the death of
young Hudson. Immediate contact with one of our local branches
in the general area revealed that the child had been found dead in
the driveway of the owner of the place on which young Hudson
lived with his grandparents as tenants.

My trip to Holly Springs, Mississippi where the body of young
Hudson was in the J. F. Brittenum and Son Funeral Home (colored) revealed that on the left side of his face there were bruises
and scars that appeared to have been the results of a possible severe beating. His left eye was black and apparently swollen, there
was an opening above the right eye on the forehead and according
to the undertaker it was a flesh wound.

My conversation with the grandfather, Mr. James Flemon, and
Mrs. Emma Dowdy, the mother, revealed that young Hudson's body
was not discovered from the time he left home Monday evening October 24 at about 6:00 P. M., until the next morning, October 25 at
about 6:30 A. M.

According to Mr. Flemon, his grandson had insisted on going over
to a cousin's house where a new well (water) was being installed.
After he did not consent for Tim to go, young Tim Hudson went toward the "big" house, the Hoxey Morgan house, which was the last
time the grandfather saw him alive. The boy's body was found between the barn and the house according to Mr. Flemon. I asked Mr.
Flemon if he thought that his grandson died accidentally, his reply

was "I do not know but my wife thinks that he was killed." He said the reason his wife thought so was because when a Mr. Elbert Skelton, Sr. pointed out the body to her he turned immediately and went into the house without saying anything further.

It is very strange that the boy could have been run over by a truck (as is alleged) so close (75 ft.) to the house without his possible cries from agony being noticeable.

The reluctance and reservation with which the grandfather talked indicated that he possibly knew more than he was telling.

The mother has requested NAACP assistance in the death of her son. She would like to file damage charges against the Roxy Morgan Plantation.

Respectfully submitted,

Medgar W. Evers

File Secretary/Mississippi

Simeon Booker—Booker was the first black full-time *Washington Post* reporter, from 1952 to 1954. He then moved to Chicago and began working for *Jet* magazine, and he vigorously covered and reported on the civil-rights movement, including the freedom rides and the murder of Emmett Till. His *Jet* column, "Ticker Parade," became a major feature of the magazine. In 1982 Booker was awarded the National Press Club's Fourth Estate Award. See Carolyn Dubose, "Newsman Simeon Booker Rounds out 20th Century with Honor," *Michigan Chronicle*, January 12, 2000, Vol. 63, no. 16, A7.

9 Transcript of a telephone conversation, Medgar Evers and Gloster B. Current

DECEMBER 8, 1955, 4:05 P.M.

INFORMATION RECEIVED FROM TELEPHONE CALL FROM

MEDGAR W. EVERS (CALLING FROM GREENWOOD, MISSISSIPPI,

EN ROUTE TO JACKSON)

Evers: Stated that he had just left the wife of C. Milton; talked with her briefly and she was very much disturbed. She is not feeling well, disturbed emotionally and is in bed. Her name is Beulah Milton, 29 years old and has four children: Dolores, age 5; Clinton, Jr., age 3; Vivian, age 2; and Kenneth, age 5 months. She was very much upset and tried to talk with her as much as possible. We got some pictures and will send them as soon as they are developed. She indicated that she did not want us (NAACP) but I told her that whatever we do for her would help all of us.

She got quite a number of sympathetic remarks from local white people. Reverend Harris of the Glendora Methodist Church gave her $60.00. The local Lions gave $26.00. Of course they all offered their sympathy.

Milton was 33 years old, World War II Vet and served in ETO. He received an honorable discharge, was well respected in the community.

I understand that his brother (Frank Milton) was put in jail for safety reasons the night Milton was killed. He was arrested for safety because shortly after the shooting the Milam boys came in town. Frank Milton has been released since then.

GBC: What's the story about the shooting?

Evers: Story is that when the man drove up he asked that his car be filled up. He told the white gas station owner to fill his gas tank. Lee McCarrh, owner of the gas station asked Milton to fill the gas tank. When Kimball came out of the gas station, (owner of the car) he told Milton that he did not want his car filled and told Milton he was going to kick his so and so. Milton said no he would not. Kimball went into the station and told McCarrh that he had a smart so and so. As he left the station, he told Milton, "I'm going to come back and kill you."

Kimball returned to the gas station. He had been gone long enough to go home and come back just as Milton was getting into his car to go home. Kimball shot him three or four times in the face. That is just about the story.

GBC: Did McCarr [sic] see the shooting?

Evers: Yes. It took place in front of the gas station. However, I did not talk to him. Milton's wife and Frank Milton were the only ones I talked with.

GBC: How is the family fixed?

Evers: They are not fixed too hot; not well at all.

GBC: How much money has the family received so far?

Evers: Only those figures I mentioned. I gave her $7.00 of my money and that is how I was able to get the pictures.

GBC: What is the family's address?

Evers: They live in the rural area. Mailing address is P. O. Box 274, Glendora, Mississippi—ten miles from Sumner.

GBC: How far is Glendora from Jackson?

Evers: About 120–30 miles.

GBC: Where is Kimball?

Evers: Kimball is still under arrest in Sumner charged with murder. The whole thing has the local citizenry up in arms. They are outraged. I will send you a full written report.

--- *

10 Roy Wilkins to Medgar Evers

December 21, 1955

Dear Mr. Evers:

Gloster talked with you and Mrs. Hurley yesterday about cooperation in the distribution of toys, food, and other articles collected by the Los Angeles Branch of the NAACP, now en route to Mississippi. Our best understanding is that these items are consigned to Mound Bayou, Miss. at the direction of Dr. T. R. M. Howard. I talked on the telephone yesterday with Dr. Howard who is in Los Angeles and he asked that the NAACP assist in the distribution. He seemed pleased when I told him that we already had talked with you and that you would help.

We wired you $500 today so you would have some cash for immediate operations. Enclosed is a check in the amount of $1,500, to give you a total sum of $2,000. We suggest that this money be placed into a special checking account, apart from your own personal account, and that you draw on it from time to time in such amounts as are convenient and necessary so that the bulk of the money at all times will be in a safe place.

The money is to be used first of all for the relief of families of NAACP members who have suffered hardship because of the signing of school petitions, but it is not to be limited to that and can be used for NAACP members who have suffered hardship because of their activities in behalf of our program. The money should be used to purchase clothing and shoes, especially for children, and other items of needed clothing. Also, for some back rent, grocery bills, medicine and doctor bills. Also, for items of food not covered by any shipments. Also (in your judgment) for some candy and toys for children.

Obviously all this cannot be done before Christmas. But some of it you will be able to do and your efforts can continue all through the holidays until you leave to come here for the Annual Meeting and a staff workshop.

I realize that we are placing quite a burden upon you, both physically and otherwise, but we have confidence in your judgment and we are certain you will see that the money is used wisely for the people for whom it is intended. We will make some additional money available, but, obviously, we cannot undertake a rescue operation for all the people in the area. First must come our members who have suffered directly as a result of their interest in and support of the NAACP.

I know I need not tell you that we wish an accounting of the money sent you. Because of the nature of the operation, it may not be possible to do this down to the very last penny, but we expect it to be reasonably accurate. If we were a social agency for relief and had a staff trained for that purpose, we would, of course, expect an exact accounting.

You may need some of this money to hire a truck for some operations or to purchase gasoline for a volunteer or volunteers who may offer the use of their cars in this operation. You would also take care of meals in such cases and incidental expenses.

The operation is in your hands. You know the territory and the people and we leave to you the determination of the promptest and most effective method of getting some relief to the people concerned.

With appreciation for the fine work you have done in your first year with us and with best wishes for the holiday season, I am,

Very sincerely yours,

Roy Wilkins,
Executive Secretary
Mr. Medgar Evers
1072 Lynch Street
Masonic Temple Building
Jackson, Miss.
RW/mdj
Enc.:
Air Mail Special Delivery

Ruby Hurley (1913–1980)—Southern regional director of the NAACP, Hurley was one of the few women to hold a national position within the organization at the time. In 1951 she moved from New York to Birmingham, Alabama, to open the first permanent NAACP office in the Deep South, and was one of the pioneering professional civil-rights workers in the South. Hurley was also deeply involved with the case of Autherine Lucy, the first black woman to attend the University of Alabama. Elizabeth Thompson, "Ruby Hurley," in Darlene Clark Hine, ed., *Black Women in America: An Historical Encyclopedia*, Volume 1 (Brooklyn, NY.: Carlson, 1993), 597–598; Barbara Ransby, *Ella Baker and the Black Freedom Movement: A Radical Democratic Vision* (Chapel Hill: University of North Carolina Press, 2003), 120–121.

11 Transcript of telephone conference call, Medgar Evers, Ruby Hurley, and Gloster B. Current

DATE: DECEMBER 27, 1955
SUBJECT: MURDER OF J. E. EVANSTON

Field Secretary Medgar Evers reported via conference telephone call that a Negro man between 65–70 years of age had been found in Long Lake, Tallahatchie County, Mississippi last Saturday, December 24, 1955. The victim was fished out of Long Lake about noonday. He had been missing 3 days prior to his being found. He was married, reportedly has no children, wife remains in Tutwiler, Mississippi (about 12 miles from Sumner). According to Evers's statement, Mr. Evanston was not an NAACP member; he reportedly attended the trial of the alleged murderers of Emmett Till. He was a teacher in the public elementary and high school at Merigold, Mississippi (approximately 35 miles southwest of Sumner). As yet the motive for the slaying is not known. Dr. Henry accompanied Evers to Clarksdale, Mississippi to help determine the cause of death.

—

Ruby Hurley stated that she had received reports of the alleged rape, assault, and robbery of a 60-year-old Negro woman. Two white men about 24–25 years old have been arrested. No further details are available.

—

Evers reported two gift lift trucks had arrived from the coast. The first truck arrived December 25 about 2:00 A.M. The second truck arrived about 4:00 P.M. of the same day. Approximately 4,000 persons have received items from the trucks. Distribution center— Mound Bayou Baptist Seminary. Gifts were distributed first to NAACP members who had experienced economic pressure and afterwards on a first come basis. The local citizens of Mound Bayou together with the American Legion had given excellent cooperation, Evers stated. He also reported that they had been advised that two more trucks were scheduled to depart for Mound Bayou on Wednesday, December 28, 1955.

✳

CHAPTER II

TRIAL

BY FIRE

Documents 12–23

(June 21, 1956–November 14, 1957)

"In 1857—99 years ago—the Supreme Court declared a Negro had no rights which a white man was bound to respect. That decision was reversed by the Civil War, yet today many whites are following the Dred Scott decision and ignoring all that has happened since. The present situation is squarely in the hands of the leaders of opinion in the South. Condemnation of the NAACP is a smokescreen. A plea for understanding based on defiance of constitutional government is a plea for anarchy and secession.

"The white people of the South must face up to the basic questions of law and citizenship under law. I, for one, do not for a minute underestimate the difficulties, real or imagined, which confront them in their soul searching. But in every question there are right and wrong sides, profitable ones and unprofitable ones, comfortable ones and uncomfortable ones, easy and difficult ones.

"The choice for them is not easy, but it must be made. Our people and our Association stand ready, as always, to help them arrive at a just decision.

"It is long past time to begin."

Roy Wilkins, 1956 address at NAACP Southeast Regional Convention, Charleston, South Carolina, February 24, 1956, published in Crisis, **Vol. 46 (April 1956), 197–201; 254–255.**

I N DECEMBER 1955, African Americans in Montgomery, Alabama, initiated a mass, nonviolent boycott against the policy of racial segregation on municipal buses. Although the woman who had initiated the public protests with her arrest, Rosa Parks, was a veteran NAACP activist, the mobilization was largely independent of the Association. A new, locally based group, the Montgomery Improvement Association, was established to mount the effort, and its young spokesman was the Reverend Dr. Martin Luther King Jr. The nonviolent, direct-action campaign achieved over 95 percent support among local blacks, many of whom had to walk miles to work and school. Throughout 1956, whites responded with police harassment, arrests of protest organizers, and bombings. In February 1956, state judge George C. Wallace in Montgomery even threatened to imprison FBI agents who had investigated blacks' charges that they were "barred from serving on grand juries."[1] The inspirational example of the Montgomery protest served as an exciting, new model of black resistance, and blacks in other cities soon followed. In May–June 1956, Florida A&M University students in Tallahassee started a local bus boycott. The following month Birmingham blacks, organized by the Reverend Fred Shuttlesworth, launched their own boycott. On November 13, 1956, the U.S. Supreme Court declared that racial segregation on public transportation was unconstitutional.[2]

Most white supremacists did not comprehend that the new black resistance strategy, the use of Gandhian nonviolence, represented a distinct break from the traditional reliance on litigation, voter registration, and civic education favored by the national NAACP. King and other activist African American ministers across the South had broken ranks with the more gradual approach of the Association. As far as they were concerned, the integrationist "enemy" was still the

NAACP. Across the South, segregationist state legislatures passed laws restricting and even outlawing the organization. NAACP local leaders became targets for threats, intimidation, loss of employment, and murder. Between 1955 and 1958, the NAACP lost 246 branch organizations across the South, and nearly 50,000 members.[3]

In Mississippi, several thousand NAACP members refused to renew their memberships. Negro public-school teachers, for example, were warned that NAACP membership was grounds for dismissal from employment. "On our street," Myrlie relates, when most blacks recognized Medgar "they would turn their backs, and even cross to the other side of the street or completely ignore us." When the young couple attended social events in Jackson, "Medgar would always take the mike and ask people to register" to vote. Some people began "booing," complaining, "Evers, can't you talk about anything else? Evers, sit down." People came up privately to Myrlie, complaining, "Can't you talk to him? Can't you get him not to do it?" Medgar didn't care. He would insist: "If I can get one person to go register and have a chance to vote, it doesn't matter. I don't care what they say to me."[4]

Medgar became privately impatient with the gradual strategy of the Association, and especially the apparent animosity of its national leadership—Executive Secretary Roy Wilkins, Director of Branches Gloster B. Current, and Thurgood Marshall—toward Dr. King and the new nonviolent protest movement [see Document 15]. To Charles Evers, Wilkins's hostility to King rested on the question of whether "the NAACP [should] march, boycott, and sit in? Martin said yes. Roy said no, keep the movement in the courts. Roy said direct action would only work where Negro boycotts could cripple the local economy." Moreover, at a personal level, according to Charles Evers, "Roy Wilkins was jealous of Martin. . . . Wilkins and Thurgood Marshall were damned if they would follow Martin's lead."[5]

As the documents in Chapter Two make clear, the Montgomery bus boycott and King deeply inspired Medgar, and he wanted to bring this new philosophy of nonviolent, direct-action protest to Mississippi. In 1956, he sought unsuccessfully to invite King to his state [see Document 13]. At the NAACP national convention in San Fran-

cisco in June 1956, in which Evers was a delegate, he had his first opportunity to meet King, who had been invited as a featured speaker.
Evers invited activist delegates back to his hotel room, according to
Charles Evers, "to talk about how the NAACP" could learn from the
Montgomery protests.[6] The delegates in Evers's hotel room ended
up drafting a three-page resolution endorsing the Montgomery bus
boycott. When Wilkins and Marshall learned about the resolution,
they were furious. Both men visited King in his hotel room late in
the evening, questioning his motives and strategy. Marshall was especially perplexed with a strategy that deliberately broke the law, something the NAACP had never done. Confronted with a "runaway
convention," Marshall and NAACP Legal Defense Fund Deputy Legal
Counsel Robert Carter finally persuaded Wilkins to permit the Fund
to take over the litigation struggle surrounding the Montgomery boycott. The next day, before nearly one thousand delegates, Wilkins announced that the Association would give "careful consideration" to
nonviolent protest as a civil-rights tactic. The final resolution adopted
by the convention declared, "The people of the civilized world have
been heartened by the effectiveness of the bus protest."[7]

Back in Mississippi, Evers dedicated himself to the difficult task of
documenting the repression of the African American community. In
Vicksburg, he reported to local members on the national convention;
in Belzoni, Yazoo, and other towns, he led discussions on how blacks
might avoid becoming vulnerable to economic pressure. Increasingly,
Medgar was asked to give public speeches to inspire and motivate fellow members. For example, on April 29, 1956, Evers spoke before the
Walthall City NAACP branch on "What We Are to Do Here to Gain
First-Class Citizenship"; at the American Legion convention in Indianola, he gave a talk encouraging NAACP membership; on September
22, he spoke at a conference sponsored by the Mississippi Methodist
Church on "race relations"; three days later, he met with the Progressive Voter League in Jackson to examine ways to increase the black
electorate. To travel around the state, Evers purchased a large Oldsmobile with a huge V-8 engine. The car served as both personal transportation and hotel, because most white-owned establishments in the

state would not permit blacks to spend the night. He learned not to frighten rural blacks by not taking written notes during his investigations of crimes and harassment. After these conversations, however, he would return to his automobile and take down handwritten notes of his conversations, trying to recall every detail. Evers routinely had to dress in rural, farm workers' clothing to escape detection.

In February 1957, Evers attended the Southern Christian Leadership Conference [SCLC] meeting held in New Orleans, which was organized primarily by Southern black ministers who had been inspired by King's example. Although Evers was not a charismatic speaker and was known primarily in NAACP circles inside Mississippi, he was elected assistant secretary to the prominent Baton Rouge civil-rights leader, the Reverend T. J. Jemison. Less than one month later, as the correspondence below indicates, Wilkins pressured Medgar to disassociate from King's new civil-rights movement. The national NAACP opposed extensive cooperation with black groups that were independent from their own organization. "Roy told Medgar to get right out of the SCLC," Charles Evers states. "Once an NAACP man, always an NAACP man. Medgar obeyed Roy and got out."[8]

Through the remaining months of 1957, Evers drove thousands of miles, crisscrossing Mississippi, encouraging blacks not to abandon the NAACP. The challenge was difficult. On March 6, he testified before a Hinds County grand jury on deplorable prison conditions for black prisoners; the next day he visited Yazoo City to discuss ways to revive the local branch that had been devastated by economic pressures; on April 7, he addressed the opening of a new branch in McComb; on July 28, Evers and Wilkins both attended the Gulfport branch opening; on August 11, he spoke in Vicksburg on "Man's Obligation to God and Man" [see Document 19]. In his first formal speaking engagement outside of his native state, Evers spoke at the Racine, Wisconsin, NAACP branch on July 6, 1957. By late 1957, Evers was acquiring a reputation as a solid and skillful local civil-rights leader in the Deep South. That November, Evers had sufficient confidence to inform the press that "total racial integration will be accomplished in Mississippi by 1963" [see Document 22].

12 Monthly Report: "June 3 Meeting," "Bundles for Freedom," "Membership Campaign," and "Branches Visited"

JUNE 21, 1956
ASSISTANT FIELD SECRETARY, MISSISSIPPI
MEDGAR W. EVERS

Pieces of mail received	58
Pieces of mail sent out	326
Branches visited	4
Miles traveled	462

JUNE 3 MEETING

The Mississippi State Conference of NAACP Branches had as their guest speaker our Executive Secretary, Mr. Roy Wilkins. The meeting was well attended with approximately 2600 persons present. Mr. Wilkins's speech was the chief topic of conversation for several days.

BUNDLES FOR FREEDOM

The Chicago Branch NAACP, as a result of their second appeal, sent to the Mississippi State Office, a van load of clothing and food for the families hit by economic pressure.

We were also the recipient of eight cartons of clothing, from the Civic Hostess Committee of Detroit, Michigan, Miss Barbara L. Simmons, President, and two other cartons from Maryland and New York.

MEMBERSHIP CAMPAIGN

Although the membership campaign in Jackson has officially ended, memberships are still coming in. Our next campaign will be kicked-off after the National Convention sometime in September or October. It is our hope that the membership goal of each branch will be attained at that time.

BRANCHES VISITED

I attended the American Legion Convention at Indianola, Mississippi on June 10, and gave a short address in behalf of the NAACP.

Emphasis was placed on the need for cooperation among civic organizations in this "fight for freedom" and first-class citizenship.

On June 19 I made a special trip to the Delta, principally, Belzoni and Yazoo City, to check on the welfare of the members, especially those who have experienced severe economic pressures.

In both towns the NAACP, as an organization, has about ceased operation except for memberships.

Respectfully submitted,

Medgar W. Evers
Field Secretary

---

13 **(1) Medgar Evers to Martin Luther King, Jr.**

July 31, 1956
Medgar Wiley Evers
Jackson, Mississippi

Rev. Martin L. King, Jr.
389 South Jackson Street
Montgomery, Alabama

Dear Rev. King:

I am quite sure you do not remember me, but I managed to shake your hand and introduce myself at the National Convention, as being the field secretary for the NAACP in the State of Mississippi, and, at which time, I asked if it were possible to have you come to Jackson to speak to our branch here. You said that you would consider it. I am therefore, at this time, inviting you to speak to us on the first or second Sunday in October, or *on any other date* that will be convenient for you.

We, the NAACP here, feel that your presence would do more to bring together our ministers and the people of Jackson than any other person or incident conceivable.

In a recent conversation with Dr. Allan Knight Chalmers, who visited Jackson, he mentioned your having been a ministerial student in his class at Boston University.

Please let me hear from you immediately, and may God bless you.

Respectfully yours,

Medgar W. Evers
Field Secretary
MWE:mes

(2) King to Evers

December 11, 1956
[*Montgomery, Alabama*]

Mr. Medgar W. Evers, Field Secretary
National Association for the Advancement of Colored People
Mississippi State Office
Masonic Temple Building
1072 Lynch Street, Room 7
Jackson, Mississippi

Dear Mr. Evers:

This is to acknowledge receipt of your letter of November 13, inviting me to address the Jackson, Mississippi Branch of the NAACP. First, I must apologize for being so tardy in my reply. Absence from the city and the accumulation of a flood of mail account for the delay.

I have considered your request very seriously. It seems, however, that my schedule is too uncertain at this point to make any definite commitment. I am negotiating at this time on the possibility of being out of the country for about two months in the late spring and early summer. I cannot accept any further engagements until this matter has been finally cleared up. I would suggest that you write me again around the first of February, and I can let you know then exactly whether or not I can come to Jackson. I wish it were possible to give you a definite answer at this time, but present conditions make it impossible.

It was a real pleasure having you in Montgomery yesterday. Your presence added much to the success of our meeting. You have my prayers and best wishes for continued success as you continue your struggle against the forces of evil and injustice in the state of Mississippi.

Yours very truly,

M.L. King, Jr.
Minister
MLE:mlb

(Dictated by Dr. King but transcribed and signed in his absence.)

Dr. Martin Luther King, Jr. (1929–1968)—The powerful leader of the Black Freedom Movement, King emerged as a national leader in Montgomery, as the head of the successful desegregation campaign of that city's municipal bus system in 1955–1956. He was a founder and president of Southern Christian Leadership Council from 1957 to 1968. He prominently participated in the 1963 March to Washington, and delivered the famed "I Have a Dream" speech. He was assassinated in 1968 in Memphis, Tennessee, where he was attempting to mobilize support for striking sanitation workers. See David Levering Lewis, *King: A Critical Biography* (New York: Praeger, 1970); David Garrow, *Bearing the Cross: Martin Luther King, Jr., and the Southern Christian Leadership Conference* (New Yor: Morrow, 1986); and Michael Dyson, *I May Not Get There with You: The True Martin Luther King*, Jr. (New York: Free Press, 2000).

Allan Knight Chalmers (1898–1972)—Reverend Chalmers was a dedicated leader in the Christian peace movement throughout his life, and was also a veteran in civil rights activities. Chalmers was professor of applied Christianity at Boston University School of Theology from 1948 to 1968, where he taught young Martin Luther King, Jr. King would later recall that Chalmers had a "passion for social justice" and faith in human possibility. See "Rev. Allan Chalmers, 74, Dies; Led the Broadway Tabernacle," *New York Times*, January 24, 1972, 31; and Martin Luther King, Jr., *Strides toward Freedom: The Montgomery Story* (New York: Harper & Row, 1958).

 14 Telegram to President Dwight D. Eisenhower

NEWS RELEASE
MISSISSIPPI STATE CONFERENCE OF NAACP BRANCHES

October 25, 1956
1072 West Lynch Street
Jackson, Mississippi

[In a telegram to the president of the United States, dated October 25, 1956, the Mississippi State Conference of NAACP Branches had this to say relative to free elections:]

Mr. President:

You have expressed your profound and very deep interest in free elections throughout the world, so much so you have invited Russians to come to this country to observe our system of free elections.

We call upon you, Mr. President, to send the Russian observers to Humphrey County, Mississippi, where The Reverend Mr. G. W. Lee was killed and Mr. Gus Courts was shot because they tried to vote as Americans. Send them to Jefferson-Davis County where more than one thousand persons, who have been qualified voters from three to ten years, were disfranchised because they were Negroes. Send them also to Hattiesburg, in Forrest County, where there are less than twenty-five Negroes registered when there are twelve thousand Negroes in the county.

Mr. President, we feel that a more accurate and objective view will be derived from a visit in these counties, and the majority of Mississippi counties where no Negroes are permitted to register and vote in our great democracy.

[...]

NAACP ASKS SOVIETS HERE
Associated Press
A Negro group suggested Thursday in a telegram to President Eisenhower that Russians in this country to observe the election campaign be sent to Mississippi "where no Negroes are permitted to register and vote."

The Mississippi state conference of NAACP branches said "a more accurate and objective view will be derived" if the Soviet group visits Mississippi.

"We call upon you ... to send the Russian observers to Humphreys county, Mississippi," where the NAACP charges two Negroes were shot for trying to vote, the telegram said.

"Send them to Jefferson Davis County where more than one thousand persons, who have been qualified voters from three to 10 years, were disfranchised because they were Negroes.

"Send them also to Hattiesburg in Forrest county, where there are less than 25 Negroes registered when there are 12,000 Negroes in the county."

L. M. Cox, Forrest county circuit clerk at Hattiesburg, was unavailable for comment.

James W. Daniels, Jefferson Davis county circuit clerk at Prentiss, said:

"No one here has been refused the right to vote because of race or color. They have been refused because they have failed to qualify under the laws of Mississippi."

The 1956 legislature, following a statewide vote, amended the constitution by establishing more severe qualifications for voter registration. They include interpretation of a section of the constitution to the satisfaction of the circuit clerk. There are no Negro circuit clerks in Mississippi.

When the bill was argued on the floor of the House of Representatives in 1955 and 1956, backers said the tighter regulations would help curb the Negro vote.

Dwight D. Eisenhower (1890–1969)—The thirty-fourth president of the United States (1953–1961). During World War II he commanded the Allied troops in North Africa (1942) and Normandy (1944). After the war he became the president of Columbia University, and then assumed the leadership role in the newly formed NATO force before running for president in 1952. A moderate Republican, his stance toward the civil-rights movement is best characterized as lukewarm. See Tom Wicker, *Dwight D. Eisenhower* (New York: Times Books, 2002); Robert Fredrick Burk, *The Eisenhower Administration and Black Civil Rights* (Knoxville: University of Tennessee Press, 1984).

George W. Lee (?–1955)—A Baptist minister serving in the Belzoni area, Reverend Lee was very active in the NAACP and efforts to register black voters in defiance of Jim Crow. In 1955, he was shot to death when his car was overtaken by a mob of white assassins. See Payne, 36–38; and Dittmer, 53–54.

15 (1) Roy Wilkins to Medgar Evers

December 18, 1956

Dear Mr. Evers:

Some months ago you submitted a brief opinion that some registration and voting work could be begun in some places in Mississippi.

We should like to begin a long-time program of education and training for registration and voting in several of the Southern states as a part of our continuing activity through the next two years.

Will you submit to us in some detail your observations and suggestions on what could be done in Mississippi—where and how? We should like some estimation of the climate of opinion, the people on whom you would depend to carry out the program locally and ways in which it could be started and carried forward.

This will not be a ballyhoo campaign, nor do we expect it to be statewide at the outset. We would like to get it quietly in operation in one or two selected localities and let it spread as we learn how to work it and as we develop more resources.

Please give this some thought and let me hear from you.

Very sincerely yours,

Roy Wilkins
Executive Secretary
Mr. Medgar Evers
1072 W. Lynch St.
Masonic Temple Building
Room 7
Jackson, Mississippi
rw/mdj

(2) Evers to Wilkins

December 28, 1956
National Association for the
Advancement of Colored People
20 West 40th Street, New York 18, N.Y.
Longacre 3–6890
Please direct reply to:
Medgar Evers
Mississippi State Office
Masonic Temple Building
1072 Lynch Street, Rm. 7
Jackson, Mississippi

Telephone Jackson 3–6906
Mr. Roy Wilkins
Executive Secretary
20 West 40th Street
New York 18, New York

Dear Mr. Wilkins:

I shall prepare a detailed report as to possible starting places for the "Program of Education and Training for Registration and Voting." It will take a few days for the gathering of material to make the report complete.

In the mean time, I would like to know more specifically what you meant by "the people on whom you would depend to carry out the program locally, and ways in which it could be started and carried forward?"

Respectfully yours,

Medgar W. Evers
Field Secretary
MWE:mes

(3) Evers to Wilkins

February 1, 1957
National Association for the
Advancement of Colored People
20 West 40th Street, New York 18, N.Y.
Longacre 3–6890
Please direct reply to:
Medgar Evers
Mississippi State Office
Masonic Temple Building
1072 Lynch Street, Rm. 7
Jackson, Mississippi

Telephone Jackson 3–6906
Mr. Roy Wilkins
Executive Secretary
20 West 40th Street
New York 18, New York

Dear Mr. Wilkins:

After giving your letter of December 18, 1956 careful study, I am herewith submitting a tentative report as to my point of view on the possibility of a program of education and training for registration and voting.

This report is to deal exclusively with the cities of Jackson and Meridian, Mississippi, as follows:

JACKSON, MISSISSIPPI
HINDS COUNTY, 48TH CITY, 75 PRECINCTS
1. Registrar
The Hinds County circuit clerk, Registrar H. T. Ashford has from the very beginning opposed the new voter amendment and steadfastly said, "I am going to register anyone that comes up here who can read and write," and to my knowledge no one has been turned away.

2. *Poll Tax*

As you know, Mississippi is one of the last "Frontier" states that is still holding on to the poll tax system as a subterfuge to voting. Consequently, we, the NAACP, Progressive Voters Leagues, Elks, and the American Legion, launched a "Pay Your Poll Tax Campaign" to get as many persons to pay their poll tax as possible so as to take advantage of the "present forces" in the office of the registrar. We have had a very healthy response from local citizens.

3. *Number of Registered Voters—City of Jackson*

There was an overall total of 32,697 voters in Jackson November 6, 1956 according to the circuit clerk of which 3,946 were Negro.

4. *Number of Negroes in City*

There are 47,000 or more.

5. *Future Plans*

Our most immediate plan now, since our "Poll Tax Program" ended with the deadline (January 1–February 1), is to put on a campaign for registration. We hope to accomplish this similar to the program of our Poll Tax, except that in addition to the use of the telephone, radio, television, and correspondence, our plans call for "Register Now" bumper stickers, to be used on some 5,000 or more automobiles in the city for a given period of time.

We are anticipating an additional 2,000 registered voters (Negro) in 1957.

6. *Climate of Opinion*

Contrary to the southern pet expression "the time ain't ripe", the time is ripe, for in this particular area we can get even our ultra-conservative Negroes to voice a positive reply when you ask them to pay their poll tax and register. Even our city teachers are getting into the act, generously without any reservations.

7. *Precincts*

The formation of precinct leaders and organizations are also a part of our immediate goals.

MERIDIAN, MISSISSIPPI

Statistical data was not immediately available on Meridian, however, it is understood that the registrar there could be placed in the same category with the Hinds County, Jackson clerk.

These two areas mentioned would be the ones that I would suggest that we start in to get the fastest and most effective results.

I shall report periodically on our progress.

Oh! I enjoyed my visit to your home very much. Warmest regards to Mrs. Wilkins.

Sincerely yours,

Medgar W. Evers
Field Secretary
MWE:mes

(4) Wilkins to Evers

[Reproduced from the Collections of the Manuscript Division, Library of Congress]

February 8, 1957

Mr. Medgar W. Evers
Field Secretary
Mississippi State Office
Masonic Temple Building
1072 Lynch Street, Room 7
Jackson, Mississippi

Dear Mr. Evers:

Thanks for your letter of February 1 on the registration and vote campaign in Jackson and Meridian.

You may count on assistance from this office if we understand clearly how the work is being carried on from day to day and what phases of the program require help. I gather from your letter that a cooperative effort is being made by several organizations, including the NAACP. How are expenses being met? Who is paying for the printing of materials? Are volunteers being enlisted to make personal contacts with individual citizens—that is, is any door to door work being done? Are speakers appearing before group meetings and is literature being distributed? Is any effort being made to teach people about the questions they will be asked and about the answers that should be given? I assume the churches are being used to the fullest.

What kinds of leaflets are being used? Is any mail campaign to individual homes being used? Is it planned to use block meetings in neighborhoods? Just how are you going about carrying out the program?

We are anxious to have the NAACP participate fully in this effort and to make its contribution, along with the other organizations toward the expenses of an effective educational campaign. I will appreciate hearing more details from you.

Very sincerely yours,

Roy Wilkins
Executive Secretary

P.S. This is a most important campaign. We are interested in a steady increase in the number of registered voters, not in spectacular spurts. I hope you will keep the necessary records, so that methods may be made more efficient as we go from year to year. You can assure the other groups that we intend to cooperate on a continuing plan of education and registration.

(5) Evers to Wilkins

March 11, 1957

Mr. Roy Wilkins
Executive Secretary
20 West 40th Street
New York 18, New York

Dear Mr. Wilkins:

The fourteenth of February I motored to New Orleans for the Southern Leadership Conference, of which I am certain you have read a great deal about. While at this conference I was elected assistant secretary, with the responsibility to assist the secretary, Rev. T. J. Jemison of Baton Rouge, Louisiana.

While I was completely unaware of the fact that I might have been violating the policy of the NAACP for having taken such a responsibility, I was nevertheless sincere in trying to do what I possibly could to bring first-class citizenship to our section of the country as hurriedly as possible. However, it is not my intention to run counter to the policies of our organization. I would appreciate very much your opinion on the matter.

While in Atlanta, attending the Southeast Regional Meeting, I had the opportunity to be in conference with Mrs. Hurley and Mr. Current relative to this same question, at which time Mr. Current suggested that I write to you.

I would appreciate an early reply from your office.

Sincerely yours,

Medgar W. Evers
Field Secretary
MWE:mes
cc: Mr. Gloster B. Current
Director of Branches

T. J. Jemison (b. 1919)—Leader and organizer of the Baton Rouge bus-boycott movement in 1953 while serving as the pastor of the Mt. Zion Baptist Church. The protest mobilization came in reaction to the city parish council's partial desegregation ordinance that was not enforced. The boycott lasted for only two weeks, but its partial success represented an important precedent, leading to the 1955 Montgomery bus boycott led by Dr. Martin Luther King, Jr. See Adon D. Morris, *The Origins of the Civil Rights Movement: Black Communities Organizing for Change* (New York: Free Press, 1984), 17–25.

16 Medgar Evers to William Stratton, Governor of Illinois

March 20, 1957
1072 W. Lynch Street
Jackson, Mississippi

The Honorable William Stratton
The Governor of Illinois
Springfield, Illinois

Sir:

The following atrocities have been committed against Negroes in Mississippi during the past two years:

1. In May of 1955, Rev. G. W. Lee of Belzoni, Mississippi was ambushed and shot gunned to death because of his activities in trying to get Negroes to register and vote.
2. In August of 1955 the most infamous crime committed against Negroes was perpetrated against fourteen year old Emmett Till of Chicago, Ill. who was alleged to have wolf whistled at a white woman and was taken out at gun point and lynched.
3. In September 1955, about a month later, an eleven year old boy was mysteriously killed near the barnyard of his landlord.

4. In August 1955 Lamar Smith of Brookhaven, Mississippi was shot to death in broad daylight on the lawn of the courthouse in Lincoln County. Three white men were involved.

5. Also in 1955 a young Negro filling station attendant, who was alleged to have been smart, was shot down by an enraged white man in Glendora, Mississippi, simply because he asked the white man if he knew exactly how many gallons of gasoline he wanted.

6. In November 1955 Mr. Gus Courts was ambushed by a white assailant as he made change in his store. Provocation was alleged to have been the activities in which Mr. Courts had engaged. He was a member of the local branch of the NAACP, and an active citizen in getting Negroes to register and vote.

In none of the above incidents has there been a conviction. Only in two instances were arrests made, and in those cases there was no conviction.

This information is sent to you at the request of Attorney William Henry Huff for your information.

It is doubtful however, with evidence to point in that direction, that if this young man, Olin Little, is returned to Mississippi justice will be done.

Respectfully yours,

Medgar W. Evers
Field Secretary
Mississippi State NAACP
MWE:mes

William Stratton (1914–2001)—A Republican governor of Illinois, Stratton became the youngest state governor when he replaced Adlai Stevenson in 1953. He is known for building the Illinois highway system and considered himself a "progressive Republican." In 1955 he requested that the FBI investigate the Emmett Till murder, and was the first governor to appoint an African American to the governor's cabinet. He served two terms in office. See Noah Isackson and James Janega, "Populist Governor Built State's Highway System," *Chicago Tribune*, March 4, 2001, 1; "U.S. Turns Down Stratton's Plea for Till Inquiry," *Chicago Daily Tribune*, December 6, 1955, pg. 16.

Lamar Smith (?–1955)—A World War II veteran and a farmer in Brookhaven, Smith was active in organizing voter registration efforts. Three men were arrested for his murder but were never convicted. See Payne, 239; and Dittmer, 54.

17 Monthly Report: "The Alcorn Situation," "Report on Branch Activities," and "Hinds County Grand Jury Hearing"

MARCH 25, 1957

THE ALCORN SITUATION

March 3, while I attended the Southeast Regional Conference in Atlanta, Georgia, Professor Clennon King, an instructor of History at Alcorn A&M College, began a series of articles, the first of which ridiculed and castigated the NAACP, Supreme Court justices, etc., which led to a complete boycott of the school's facilities by its 570 students. The papers immediately charged the NAACP with creating the disturbance at Alcorn College and the board issued an ultimatum demanding that the students cease their boycott by noon Friday, March 8, or face expulsion.

The student body refused to return to classes on the grounds that Professor King had not been dismissed, and consequently at 11:55 a.m. on the morning of Friday, March 8 the president of the students (Ernest McEwen) read a statement that the entire student body had approved agreeing unanimously to withdraw, rather than be expelled. This of course shocked the very foundation that the white supremacists thought they had reinforced so very substantially. (Imagine Negro students defying an ultimatum issued by a Board of Trustees in the State of Mississippi who happened to be white!)

The students began immediately packing their clothes to leave the campus. On Friday night many of the students were en route home.

It was my good fortune "accidentally" to meet Ernest McEwen, president of the student council, at the Trailway Bus Station, at which time we talked at length and arranged a future meeting together in Jackson. By Saturday morning all of some 530 students, who were then on the campus (approximately forty were away practice teaching), had made their departure for their various homes.

The Board of Trustees of the Institution of Higher Learning, J. D. Boyd, present president, and J. R. Otis, outgoing president, met in an emergency session Saturday, March 9, at which time Dr. Otis was immediately dismissed (though he had already resigned effective April 1), and Boyd was given authority to bring the school back to normal, with dictatorial powers to admit or deny students whom he felt would or would not "conform" to the general welfare of Alcorn College and the State of Mississippi. On Monday the word had gotten around through the newspapers that students would be readmitted to Alcorn even though they had been expelled. Most of the students have returned to classes, but McEwen, President of the student council, A. J. Fielder and Mason Denham, members of the council, and others who were alleged leaders, have been denied the privilege to reenter.

[. . .]

REPORT ON BRANCH ACTIVITIES

There is an apparent decline in the activities of many of our branches, in fact we are losing some of them which stems from fear of economic reprisals, physical intimidations and the like. It is our design to absorb much of this loss from our smaller branches into our larger ones. We are still faced, especially in the smaller areas, with a great degree of intimidation tactics which ultimately make our smaller branches somewhat inoperative.

HINDS COUNTY GRAND JURY HEARING

The testimony of Mrs. Beatrice Young before the Senate Subcommittee on Constitutional Rights February 28, 1957, along with many other charges of police brutality in the Hinds County Jail, have brought forth a Hinds County Grand Jury investigation of the treatment of prisoners in the jail. Mrs. Young was summoned at 10:00 a.m. Wednesday, March 6, 1957 to appear before the Grand Jury the same afternoon at 2:00 p.m. She got in touch with her lawyer, Attorney R. J. Brown, who advised and accompanied her to the hearing.

While I knew that I could not be in on the Grand Jury hearing *per se*, I thought my sitting in the corridor with the others would be all right, however, my presence was recognized by some of the law enforcement officers, and while I sat talking with Dr. Miller, Mrs. Young's sister and niece who had also been summoned to appear, I was served a summons to come before the Grand Jury immediately (even before Dr. Miller who had been there some two hours before me). I was instructed under the penalty of contempt of the Grand Jury should I reveal before a period of six months the questions asked at this hearing, so such a revelation will have to wait until a period of time.

It is indicative that our organization in Jackson is being felt more and more. Our news in most instances makes the front page and not in the Negro page.

Respectfully submitted,

Medgar W. Evers
Field Secretary
MWE:mes

Clennon King (1920–2000)—Professor of history at Alcorn College, later known as the "Black Don Quixote" for his flamboyant activities. In 1958 King attempted briefly to enroll at the University of Mississippi. See Russell Barrette, *Integration at Ole Miss* (Chicago: Quadrangle Books, 1965), 33; and Katagiri, 41–43; and Michael Yockel, "Clennon King, Nutty Racial Provocateur," *New York Press*, 3/8/2000–3/14/2000, Volume 13, Issue 10, available online, http://www.nypress.com/13/10/news&columns/obit.cfm.

*

18 Medgar W. Evers, Introduction of Congressman Charles C. Diggs, Jr.

MAY 19, 1957
JACKSON, MISSISSIPPI

Introduction of Congressman Charles C. Diggs, Jr. by Mr. Medgar W. Evers, Field Secretary of Mississippi, on Sunday, May 19, 1957 at the Masonic Temple Auditorium, Jackson, Mississippi, 3:00 P.M., in celebration of the Third Anniversary of May 17, 1954 Supreme Court Decision. Sponsor— Jackson Branch NAACP.

In the year 1776 these words were written and spoken by a great American. "We hold these truths to be self evident . . . that all men are created equal." We read in our history books of such great Negro Americans as Hiram R. Revels and B.K. Bruce, United States Senators from the State of Mississippi; John R. Lynch and Joseph H. Rainey, Negro Congressmen from the States of Mississippi and South Carolina, respectively, but today, ladies and gentlemen, in a period of history in the making, when oppressed men throughout the world are clamoring to throw off the shackles of oppression, we here in America rely heavily upon our United States Congress to enact the necessary legislation that will make it possible for all citizens of America to share equally in America's wealth, according to his or her abilities.

Charles C. Diggs, Jr. (1923–1998)—A U.S. Congressman from Detroit, Diggs was first elected to the House in 1954 and served his district over twenty-five years. He helped to create and was the first chairman of the Congressional Black Caucus between 1969 and 1971. From 1973 to 1978, Diggs was chairman of the House District Committee. See Richard Pearson, "Charles Diggs Dies at 75; Congressman from Mich.," *Washington Post*, August 26, 1998, B6.

Hiram R. Revels (1822–1901)—A North Carolina–born minister, Revels became the first black U.S. senator in 1870 when he took over the seat vacated by Jefferson Davis ten years before. After serving the remainder of Davis's term, Revels returned to Mississippi and was named president of Alcorn College. See E.L. Thornbrough, *Black Reconstructionists: Great Lives Observed* (Englewood Cliffs, NJ: Prentice-Hall, 1972), 176–77.

Blanche Kelso Bruce (1841–1898)—During Reconstruction-era Mississippi, Bruce was a powerful politician in Beaufort, holding the offices of sheriff, tax collector and superintendent of education. In 1875, Bruce became a U.S. senator from Mississippi. President Benjamin Harrison appointed Bruce recorder of deeds for the District of Columbia in 1889. See Thornbrough (1972).

John R. Lynch (1847–1939)—Born a slave in Louisiana, Lynch became a justice of the peace in Natchez County. At age twenty-five he was elected to the state legislature and chosen as the speaker of the house. In 1889 President Benjamin Harrison appointed Lynch auditor of the U.S. Treasury for the Navy Department. See Thornbrough (1972).

Joseph H. Rainey (1832–1887)—Born a slave in South Carolina, Rainey acquired an education while working as a barber. During reconstruction, Rainey was elected to the state constitutional convention in 1868. In 1869 he became the state's first black U.S. congressman. He served in the House until 1876. http://www.famousamericans.net/josephrainey/.

19 Medgar W. Evers, Address

AUGUST 11, 1957
MT. HERON BAPTIST CHURCH
VICKSBURG, MISSISSIPPI

Christian friends, brothers and sisters, ladies and gentlemen. I consider it a blessing from almighty God to have this very spiritual pleasure to fellowship with you on this men's day program and to be able to acknowledge the very presence of God within me.

You know it was just above five years and eight months today that in this very same edifice that your Myrlie Louise Beasley and I were united in holy matrimony and to that union, today the Lord has blessed us with two fine youngsters, Darrell Kenyatta and Reena Denise Evers and to you I am eternally grateful.

All that I have said thus far leads me up to here. My topic for today is "Man's obligation to God and to man." *Obligation to God.* You know we are not as grateful and obliging to God as He would have us to be. We men often take our being too much for granted. We often feel that our responsibility and obligation to God ends when we make a liberal church contribution and attend services regularly. Granted, both are essential in our daily Christian lives but one equally important factor is often expressed in the "negative" by the following quotation: "Man's inhumanity to man makes countless thousands mourn." As I remember from my youth being taught the Golden Rule of "Do unto others as you would have them do unto you." That part of the Golden Rule is now in many instances being shelved as being obsolete or outdated and therefore no longer usable in this day and time which is possibly the saddest mistake we find ourselves making.

Man is, I would say, God's chosen creature on the face of the earth so much so until in the creation God said, "Let us make man in our image, after our likeness, and let them have dominion over the fish of the sea and the fowl of the air, and over the cattle, and over all the earth, and over every creeping thing that creepeth upon the earth." So God created man in his own image, in the image of God, created He Him: male and female, created He them.

If we note with care the word image which means likeness or an imitation of any person or thing one is immediately impressed with the fact that we are God's children who possess his likeness and who consequently should do His will. That is unquestionably the obligation man owes to God—do His will.

Now we come to the other part of our topic, "man's obligation to man." Certainly we cannot do the will of God without treating our fellow man as we would have him treat us. It is a biblical axiom that to say you love God and hate your fellow man is hypocrisy of possibly the greatest magnitude. So many of us fall into this category either consciously or unconsciously until it behooves each of us to check ourselves closely so as to avoid becoming a party to hate or misunderstanding.

While we must not hate our fellow man, black, white, yellow or what have you, we must nevertheless, stand firmly on those principles we know are right which brings us to the point of being reminded of the courage of Joshua and Caleb when after "400 years of bondage under the Egyptians and 40 years of freedom, there were many among the Israelites who wanted to go back into Egypt and slavery, because they were not willing to suffer for a cause and for a principle. So it is today many people are not willing to stand up for a cause and a principle. Many persons are willing to sacrifice their birthright, go back into slavery and maintain segregation, and take the easy way out, rather than to suffer a little and gain what is rightfully theirs. In this instance, we find history repeating itself.

We, as men, owe it to our fellow man and to our children to stand firm and stand out for those things that we are entitled to. I count it a blessing from God that I am able to withstand ridicule and abuse because I am willing to stand for my fellow man though many show no appreciation for the work that we are trying to do in their behalf. But let it not be said in the final analysis when history will only record these glorious moments and when your grandchildren will invariably ask: "Granddaddy, what role did you play in helping to make us free men and free women?" Did you actively participate in the struggle or was your support only a moral one? Certainly each person here, and man in particular, should be in a position to say "I was active in the struggle from all phases for your unrestrictive privileges as an American citizen."

Christian friends, we are in a righteous struggle. We are living in a great day, a momentous day, a glorious day, a day that will be forever inscribed in the annals of history and in the minds of men.

Now, my friends, I have one or two requests to make and I feel that these requests should be the paramount objective of each person here today. Number one: let us vow to treat our fellow man as we would like him to treat us. Two, let us be in a spirit of cooperativeness. For example, the Reverend Dr. Martin Luther King and others in Montgomery, Alabama, have to me set an example of cooperation that has been unexcelled in my lifetime and possibly yours.

Those Christian people in Montgomery have really demonstrated cooperation, and how effective it can be in a community. Certainly Reverend King and others demonstrating through actual practice that that they preach from the pulpit can be used in other forms of protest, such as registering and voting, which is my third request: that you select a committee in your community to teach the importance and use of the ballot, so that every person twenty-one years and above is provided with transportation to go down and register and also collect two dollars from everyone twenty-two through fifty-nine years and pay their poll tax.

My last request is that you support more earnestly the *National Association for the Advancement of Colored People,* an organization that has contributed possibly more than any other in our struggle for first class citizenship. Just think where we would have been today had it not been for the work of the *National Association for the Advancement of Colored People.* Many of the achievements of the organization have been forgotten or ignored. For example, the grandfather clause and the white primaries were declared unconstitutional through the legal maneuvering of the organization. Restrictive covenants, discrimination in public education, and the separate but equal doctrine have all been declared contrary to the U.S. Constitution and the American way of life. And even here in our state where sickness knows no color, veterans' hospitals have been integrated, and in Army, Navy, and Air installations the work of the NAACP has made the brotherhood of man a workable thing in Mississippi.

Furthermore, the average member of the organization is a member of some church, which strengthens our ties with the churches, almighty God and this great nation of ours.

As men living in as highly a diversified and complex society as ours, it is our duty and responsibility to our fellow men and our children to tackle the problems that lie ahead with faith and courage. Faith that is spoken of in the Bible, which in paraphrase says "Only possess the faith of a small mustard seed and you will be able to move mountains and then the courage to withstand the greatest onslaught the enemy can muster, and you are bound to succeed." No, it will not be easy, but neither does one find it altogether easy to be a Christian in this very sin sick world.

I am reminded here of a secular song, the lyrics of which are as follows: "Give me some men who are stout-hearted men, who will fight for the rights they adore. Start me with ten who are stout-hearted men, and I will soon give you ten thousand more. Oh, shoulder to shoulder, and bolder and bolder, they grow as they go to meet the foe. Then there is nothing in this world that can halt or mar a plan when we stick together man to man." There is no doubt in my mind that the lyrics to that song have a very appropriate meaning in this day and time.

Then it was Samuel Garth who said: "When honor is lost, it is a treat to die; death's but a sure retreat from infamy."

There is an urgent need for dedicated and courageous leadership. If we are to solve the problems ahead and make social justice a reality, this leadership must be four-fold in our various communities. Men and women in every possible community endeavor should busy themselves in an effort to work out our problem on a mutual respectful basis with our fellow men. This is no time for faint-hearted men, but rather a time when our true faith in God should emerge and take over our complete self. It is spoke of in one passage of the scripture, that man should not fear men who can only destroy the body but rather God, who can destroy both body and soul.

In closing, I am reminded of the writings of James Weldon Johnson, who wrote:

"God of our weary years, God of our silent tears, Thou who hast brought us this far on the way; Thou who hast by thy might, led us into the light, keep us forever in Thy path, we pray. Lest our feet stray from the places, our God, where we met Thee. Lest our hearts, drunk with the wine of the world, we forget Thee; shadowed beneath Thy hand, may we forever stand true to our God, true to our native land."

Samuel Garth (1661–1719)—A Neo-Classical poet and physician of Yorkshire, England. Garth attempted to establish a system of medical charity for the poor in the city. Upon the failure to implement his program, he wrote "The Dispensary," a satiric poem against medical traders' obsession with monetary interest, from which Medgar quotes here. The original reads, "When Honour's lost, 'tis a Relief to die; Death's but a sure Retreat from Infamy." See http://www.hn.psu.edu/Faculty/Kkemmerer/poets/garth/dispens5.html.

James Weldon Johnson (1871–1938)—A celebrated teacher, poet, songwriter, and civil rights activist. Johnson served as an American consul at Puerto Cabello, Venezuela, and later in Nicaragua. He anonymously published a novel, *The Autobiography of an Ex-Coloured Man* (1912). Appointed Executive Secretary of the NAACP in 1920, Johnson won praise as an effective organizer. He resigned from the position in 1930 due to the post's strenuous duties. Johnson was the author of *Black Manhattan* (1930), *Along This Way* (1933), and *Negro Americans, What Now?* (1934). See Robert E. Fleming, *James Weldon Johnson* (Boston: Twayne, 1987); and Lawrence J. Oliver and Kenneth M. Price, ed., *Critical Essays on James Weldon Johnson* (New York: G.K. Hall & Co., 1997).

20 Medgar Evers to Robert Carter, General Counsel, NAACP

September 4, 1957

Mr. Robert Carter
General Counsel
20 West 40th Street
New York 18, New York

Dear Bob:

On September 3 three men of good reputation, Negro, came into my office and said their plans were to ride the buses unsegregated here in Jackson. They also consulted with our local attorney and gave him a retainer to represent them legally if it becomes necessary.

No steps have been taken other than the above mentioned ones, pending an okay from the National Office. The attorney has been reluctant to proceed in any other field, except registration and voting, until he is otherwise instructed from the National Office, so if you deem the contemplated action advisable to pursue, please inform the attorney and myself of same *immediately* (by Monday, September 9).

Sincerely yours,

Medgar W. Evers
Field Secretary
MWE:mes
cc: Mr. Gloster B. Current

--- ∗

21 News Release

TUESDAY, OCTOBER 15, 1957
MISSISSIPPI STATE CONFERENCE OF N. A. A. C. P. BRANCHES
JACKSON, MISSISSIPPI

Negroes in Mississippi are being "hood winked" and "cow licked" into believing that everything is well with his condition here in the state. State and national officials are engaging in an extensive brainwashing campaign to induce the Mississippi Negro to remain silent and complacent about the rights he is now being denied. Evidence of these brainwashing techniques is found in the every day attempt on the part of some jurist or politician who praises the "so called harmonious race relations," that exist in the state, and at the same time deny Negroes, regardless to their educational qualification, the right to register and vote.

Any person with common sense (especially Negro), who has lived in Mississippi for any length of time, knows the fallacies that accompany such utterances.

--- ∗

22 "Integration Seen by '63, Mississippi N.A.A.C.P. Aide Finds Progress in State," United Press International

New York Times

NOVEMBER 10, 1957

JACKSON, Miss. (UPI)—Total racial integration will be accomplished in Mississippi by 1963, a state official of the National Association for the Advancement of Colored People said today.

Medgar Evers, N.A.A.C.P. field secretary for Mississippi, made the prediction as the association opened its annual state-wide convention.

Mr. Evers said the Mississippi branch might not seem to be making much progress "when you compare this state to some of the others." But, he said, "we are getting our feet on the ground, collecting information and making other preparations."

23 Annual Report, 1957, Mississippi State Office, N.A.A.C.P.

NOVEMBER 14, 1957

Total incoming mail	869
Total outgoing mail	2,474
Total branches visited	32
Total miles traveled	16,622

MEMBERSHIPS AND FUND-RAISING

Again, Mississippi has fallen short of its membership and financial quotas for the year of 1957, nevertheless, we are optimistic in our belief that another year may bring the desired results. The Miss N.A.A.C.P. Contest will be an annual affair and will be used as a direct means of procuring our Freedom Fund quota.

BRANCH ACTIVITY

There is an apparent decline in the activities of many of our branches, in fact we have lost some of them because of fear of economic reprisals, physical intimidations and the like. It is our design to absorb much of this loss from our smaller branches into our larger ones. We are still faced, especially in the smaller areas, with a degree of intimidation tactics which ultimately make our smaller branches somewhat inoperative.

REGISTRATION AND VOTING

Registration and voting have played a major part in the year's activities. A tour of the southern and northern N.A.A.C.P. Branches, setting up registration committees, was highly successful. The enactment of the recent civil rights legislation in Congress has given us a solid foundation upon which we can build a better Mississippi for the Negro as well as the whites.

Rev. W. D. Ridgeway, of Hattiesburg, appeared before the Senate Subcommittee on Constitutional Rights to testify in behalf of the Negroes who were denied the right to vote in Mississippi. His appearance, and others, aided Congress in passing the first civil rights bill since Reconstruction days.

With the support of the Federal Government we shall endeavor to get as many registered Negro voters in Mississippi as is possible, despite the fact that in many of our counties there are none. In cooperating with other organizations toward this objective we feel that this great endeavor can and will be one of our most effective weapons in combating segregation.

VIOLENCE

Violence and police brutality still have the upper hand in Mississippi, inasmuch as many of the victims are afraid to speak out because of threats upon their lives or fear of economic reprisals, intimidations, etc. We are proud of Mrs. Beatrice Young of Jackson, Mississippi, who had the courage to stand up and be counted as one of the few Negroes in Mississippi who could not and would not be intimidated. Her appearance before the Senate Subcommittee on Constitutional Rights once again spotlighted the State of Mississippi in the eyes of the world. Although the Federal Grand Jury, which convened in Jackson, June 3–June 13, hearing alleged cases involving police brutality in the Hinds County jail, wound up its session declaring a "NO TRUE BILL", we feel that Mrs. Young may have paved the way for stronger civil rights legislation in the future on police brutality and infringement of constitutional rights by officers of the law.

YOUTH COUNCILS

The organization, and in some instances reorganization, of several Youth Councils have brought a great deal of encouragement to the Field Secretary and others dedicated to the cause, for we realize fully that the success of this great organization lies with the men and women of tomorrow. In observing their activities and the cooperation with which they wholeheartedly support the program, it is our belief that the N.A.A.C.P. in Mississippi has a wonderful opportunity of becoming one of the best. A special commendation is extended to Dr. B. E. Murph, president of the Laurel N.A.A.C.P. Branch, who has, in a short time, organized one of the finest Youth Councils in Mississippi. It is our hope that his excellent leadership and success with the youth will inspire the hearts of others, so that in the ensuing year we will see the dawn of a bright tomorrow as a result of the birth and growth of more Youth Councils in Mississippi.

ANNUAL STATE CONFERENCE

November 8–10, 1957, the 12th Annual Mississippi State Conference of N.A.A.C.P. Branches was held in Jackson, Mississippi. The three day conference dealt with registration and voting, desegregation, branch administration and the organization of a State Conference of Youth Councils.

The guest speakers were: Mr. Gloster B. Current, Director of Branches, keynote address; Mrs. Ruby Hurley, Southeast Regional Secretary, Freedom Fund Dinner; and Mr. Clarence Mitchell, Director, Washington Bureau N.A.A.C.P., Sunday's Mass Meeting.

Inasmuch as our attendance and financial contributions fell short of last year's we sincerely believe that the success of the workshops and wholehearted support of the youth in the activities of the conference, contributed greatly in making the 12th Annual Mississippi State Conference one of the best we have ever had. With this thought always in mind we shall look forward to the next annual conference with renewed faith and the hope that we can in some way increase our memberships and financial contributions.

MEETINGS, CONFERENCES (OUT OF STATE)

The following meetings and/or conferences were attended by the Field Secretary during the year of 1957:

Annual Staff Meeting
January 6–11
National Office, New York

Southeast Regional Conference
February 28–March 3
Atlanta, Georgia

48th Annual N.A.A.C.P. Convention
June 23–30
Detroit, Michigan

Southeast Regional Staff Conference
August 30–31
Atlanta, Georgia

Other
Prayer Pilgrimage
May 17, 1957
Washington, D. C.

FUTURE OUTLOOK

The year of 1958 looms ahead with a far brighter outlook than ever before. The passage of the recent civil rights legislation, in getting more registered Negro voters in Mississippi, and the fine support of the Youth Councils, shall be used as a stepping stone toward our goal of first-class citizenship.

"We shall face each dawn and night,

With faith and courage true;
And as our goal of '63 grows near,

Strive to see our struggle through."

Respectfully submitted,

Medgar W. Evers
Field Secretary
MWE:mes

Clarence Mitchell, Jr. (1911–1984)—A lawyer and lobbyist, Mitchell first became the secretary of labor for the NAACP in 1946, and was the director of the Washington, D.C., NAACP office from 1950 to 1978. He was behind many civil rights–related pieces of legislation and executive orders during the period, and was often called the "101st Senator." See Denton L. Watson, *Lion in the Lobby: Clarence Mitchell, Jr.'s Struggle for the Passage of Civil Rights Laws* (New York: William Morrow, 1990).

✳

CHAPTER III

WHY I LIVE

IN

MISSISSIPPI

Documents 24–34
(January 24, 1958–March 23, 1959)

THE LYNCHING

His Spirit in smoke ascended to high heaven.
His father, by the cruelest way of pain,
Had bidden him to his bosom once again;
The awful sin remained still unforgiven,
All night a bright and solitary star
(Perchance the one that ever guided him,
Yet gave him up at last to Fate's wild whim)
Hung pitifully o'er the swinging chat.
Day dawned, and soon the mixed crowds came to view
The ghastly body swaying in the sun.
The women thronged to look, but never a one
Showed sorrow in her eyes of steely blue.
And little lads, lynchers that were to be,
Danced round the dreadful thing in fiendish glee.

Claude McKay, "The Lynching," Cambridge
Magazine, 10 (Summer 1920), 56; republished in
The Selected Poems of Claude McKay (New York:
Bookman Associates, 1953), 8.

BY THE LATE 1950s, the Black Freedom Movement throughout the South and, to a lesser extent, across the entire country had reached a stalemate. The Eisenhower administration was at best lukewarm toward civil rights. At the NAACP's forty-eighth annual convention in Detroit in June 1957, the Association's labor secretary, Herbert Hill, noted that Eisenhower's Committee on Government Contracts had routinely failed to enforce anti-discrimination provisions. On August 28, 1958, at a press conference, President Eisenhower declared that school desegregation must proceed at a "slower pace," generating praise from Southern segregationists.[1] The failure of the Eisenhower administration to vigorously support desegregation reinforced the growth of massive resistance by Southern governors and legislatures. For example, in September 1958, when the Supreme Court ordered the implementation of a gradual desegregation plan in Little Rock, Arkansas's public school system, state governor Orval Faubus closed all four of the city's high schools. In 1957 the Tennessee legislature adopted a segregationist "manifesto" designed to block school-integration measures. By late 1958, in six Southern states governors had been granted the power to shut down all public schools in their states. Eight states had passed legislation creating provisions for substituting state funding for all-white, private schools for desegregated public schools.[2]

Nearly everywhere the movement seemed to be on the defensive. On January 7, 1958, Wilkins announced to reporters that the NAACP ended 1957 with a deficit of over $52,000 because of court costs incurred in Southern desegregation efforts. Total NAACP membership nationwide, which stood at 350,000 in 1956, had fallen off to 302,400 by the end of 1957. The states recording the most serious membership losses were Mississippi, Georgia, Florida, South Carolina, and

Tennessee.[3] As a result of their own organization's erosion in the region, Wilkins, Current, and other national NAACP officials opposed cooperation with King's SCLC. Medgar Evers was heavily pressured by the national office not to offer assistance or support to the SCLC's organizing efforts in his own state. Medgar's response, however, was a delicate balance between covert cooperation and public distance. He disagreed with the gradualistic civil-rights strategy of the NAACP, but was not in a political or personal position to break with the NAACP. Consequently he had to carry out certain policies with which he disagreed, but he also used his extensive personal contacts and knowledge about the state to help the SCLC quietly [see Document 24].

Most of Evers's time was still overwhelmed by his extensive responsibilities as the NAACP Field Secretary in Mississippi. The largest and most successful mass public event he coordinated during 1958 occurred on February 16, when Brooklyn Dodgers baseball star Jackie Robinson came to Jackson after intensive efforts to bring him there to promote the NAACP. An enthusiastic crowd of 4,000 was in attendance to see Robinson. The Robinson event encouraged many local African Americans whose NAACP memberships had lapsed to consider rejoining the Association, or at least show support by attending its public meetings and rallies. This probably explains the surprisingly large turnout of 1,500 to 2,000 on March 30, 1958, at an NAACP-sponsored statewide meeting to discuss civil-rights issues [see Documents 25 and 26]. On June 11, Medgar participated in and spoke at a mass meeting denouncing police brutality and misconduct in Hattiesburg. On October 16, Evers spoke out on the closing of Little Rock's public schools in a talk at Campbell College. The next month, on November 28, Evers addressed the members of the Stringer Grand Lodge, urging blacks to pay their poll-tax fees, to register and demand the right to vote in local elections. He urged his audience to file formal complaints with the U.S. Commission on Civil Rights, a federal advisory body established by the Eisenhower administration in 1957.

Evers had both policy and personal differences with the Mississippi NAACP president C. R. Darden of Meridian, and he increasingly relied on his own network of political allies within the Association. One of his closest and most effective associates was civil-rights activist Aaron Henry of Clarksdale. In 1954, Henry was elected NAACP state secretary. In 1955, he was elevated to state vice president. By the late 1950s, Henry occasionally traveled with Evers to attend national conferences and important meetings. With the invaluable help of Henry, Amzie Moore, and other local stalwarts, the decline in state NAACP membership was reversed. Statewide African American voter registration, which had declined to only 8,000 in 1955, grew to 15,000 by 1959.[4]

The modest revitalization of the NAACP in the Deep South did not make Evers's job any less difficult. As the documents in Chapter three illustrate, Evers continued to live under enormous pressure, spending days on the road, traveling frequently in laborer's clothing to hide his identity. Evers seriously contemplated resigning as field secretary in early 1958, and requested that the national office allow him to enroll in law school, beginning in September, 1959 [see Document 33]. On March 11, 1958, while returning from an NAACP Southeastern Regional meeting in Greensboro, North Carolina, he was attacked by a white passenger and then harassed by local police when he refused to relocate to the rear of an interstate bus returning to Jackson [see Document 26]. This confrontation, and Medgar's determination not to buckle under to threats and physical violence, had a profound affect on him and his subsequent public career. Evers reported to the NAACP's state members that despite efforts to locate him, "this passenger remained seated on the very front seat of the bus where he rode, even after having been attacked, ninety-three (93) miles to Jackson without moving."[5]

Another significant turning point in Evers's public career was his address to the Milwaukee, Wisconsin, NAACP branch, on May 18, 1958 [see Document 28]. Although located in the north, Milwaukee was in the late 1950s a largely segregated city, especially in terms of its residential patterns. In 1960, only 22 blacks served on the police force of 1,869; in Milwaukee's fire department, there were five African Americans out of 1,061 firemen. In 1955 only 45 black teachers were employed in the city's public schools.[6] Evers's talk focused primarily on the political situation in Mississippi, but he also spoke about civil rights in a larger, national context. He criticized Eisenhower's public statement urging blacks to be "'forbearing in . . . efforts for first-class citizenship.' . . . I say to you, who could be more forbearing than a people whose homes, churches and businesses have been bombed, and individuals shot down in cold blood with nothing having ever been done about it." The challenge, Evers explained, was whether "our Federal Government would one day intervene, to insure that the principles upon which this great nation of ours was founded would be applied to all alike."[7] The quiet, unassuming local leader from Jackson was slowly evolving into a national figure.

The political metamorphosis of Medgar Wiley Evers from local to national leadership took another critical step forward with the publication of "Why I Live in Mississippi" in the November 19, 1958, issue of *Ebony* magazine [see Document 31]. Evers was profiled as "Mississippi's chief NAACP man," a dedicated organizer who had logged 78,000 miles on his Oldsmobile during the previous two years working in dozens of local communities, a man "constantly on call." The story highlighted Evers's bus confrontation to make the point that this civil-rights activist possessed the quiet courage not to fight back. "While the bus incident was just a ripple on the tide of anti-Negro incidents in the state," writer Francis H. Mitchell observed, "it convinced many of the uncommitted that Evers was lacking neither in personal bravery nor good judgment."[8]

24 Medgar Evers to Ruby Hurley, NAACP Southeastern Regional Secretary

January 24, 1958

Mrs. Ruby Hurley
859–1/2 Hunter Street, N.W., Room 107
Atlanta 14, Georgia

Dear Mrs. Hurley:

Attempts are being made by Rev. Martin L. King and the Southern Christian Leadership Conference to establish a movement here in Jackson. Their contacts, thus far, have been N.A.A.C.P. officials who have in turn come to our office for advice. We have naturally discouraged, "tactfully," any such movement here in Jackson. It will be our design through the N.A.A.C.P. and the Progressive Voters League, of which our leaders are in key positions, to control the present state of affairs.

There was an apparent move to cut across our "Jackie Robinson Day Program" with a King meeting here in Jackson on February 12. However, the person who was contacted to arrange such a meeting came immediately to our office for advice. We immediately halted those plans.

I shall await comments from you. In the meantime we are going to hold fast.

Sincerely yours,

Medgar W. Evers
Field Secretary
MWE:mes
cc: Gloster Current
Roy Wilkins

Jackie Roosevelt Robinson (1919–1972)—Best known for breaking the barrier of racial segregation in Major League Baseball when he became a Brooklyn Dodger in 1947, Robinson actively endorsed the movement by working with NAACP. He received NAACP's Spingarn Medal in 1956, was a director of the board, and chaired Freedom Fund Drive campaign in 1957. Locally, he supported Republican Governor Nelson Rockefeller in his unsuccessful attempt to win his party's presidential nomination, and his 1966 gubernatorial race. See Arnold Rampersad, *Jackie Robinson: A Biography* (New York: Knopf, 1997); and David Falkner, *Great Time Coming: The Life of Jackie Robinson, from Baseball to Birmingham* (New York: Simon & Schuster, 1995).

25 Medgar Evers to Roy Wilkins

April 1, 1958

Mr. Roy Wilkins
Executive Secretary
20 West 40ᵗʰ Street
New York 18, New York
Dear Mr. Wilkins:

On Sunday, March 30, as a follow-up to the filing of our first civil rights suit in Mississippi in the field of registration and voting, we had a statewide mass meeting, at which time Mr. Clarence Mitchell, Director, Washington Bureau, delivered one of his most eloquent and persuasive addresses. We had in attendance at this meeting between 1500–2000 persons from across the State of Mississippi— North, South, East and West. Men and women with determination in their eyes, in their hearts, that they were ready for a better day in Mississippi and ready to take whatever action necessary to bring about that better day.

The comments we have heard about the meeting have been to the effect it probably has been the most far-reaching and significant meeting that we have had in recent years. Certainly the filing of the suit in Jefferson Davis County would lead support to such a contention.

The meeting, sponsored by the Mississippi State Conference of N.A.A.C.P. Branches, had as its participants members of the Regional Council of Negro Leadership, Ministerial Improvement Association of Mississippi and the Progressive Voters League. Of course there were many other small groups, such as, social clubs and local civic clubs that participated.

As a follow-up to this meeting, registration and voting campaigns have been planned for Jackson and Meridian, Mississippi. Mr. Brooks, our director of registration and voting, is scheduled to be in Jackson on April 7 and in Meridian on April 8, for the specific purpose of helping us to adequately formulate our plans for this registration campaign.

It is my opinion that with the enthusiasm as high as it is, a properly well organized campaign in the cities mentioned earlier will prove quite profitable in our efforts to increase the number of Negro voters in Mississippi.

Sincerely yours,

Medgar W. Evers
Field Secretary
MWE:mes
cc: Gloster B. Current
Ruby Hurley

✳

26 Monthly Report: "Registration and Voting," "Fund-Raising," and "Memberships"

April 11, 1958
News and Action
National Association for the Advancement of Colored People
Mississippi State Office
N.A.A.C.P., 1072 West Lynch Street
Jackson, Mississippi
Phone: 3–6906
Medgar W. Evers
Field Secretary

REGISTRATION AND VOTING

The month of March brought in a number of events in our struggle for first-class citizenship. For the first time in the history of the State of Mississippi a suit was filed in Federal Court by a Negro minister, Rev. H. D. Darby, in an effort to declare the unconstitutionality of the rigid voting restrictions that are applied against Negro Mississippians when they attempt to exercise their constitutional rights as Americans.

Rev. Darby was among some 1200 Negro citizens of Jeff-Davis County who, through willful and wanton prejudice, were disqualified as registered voters, largely through the efforts of the White Citizens Council of Jeff-Davis County.

Rev. Darby, and others similarly situated, have made numerous attempts to register since their names were stricken from the poll books in 1956, but in no instances were they permitted to re-register. The only alternative left to Rev. Darby and others was to seek remedy in the courts. With the assistance of the N.A.A.C.P. Legal Department the first civil rights suit was filed.

MITCHELL SPEAKS

As a follow-up to the filing of the petition in Federal Court, a statewide mass meeting was called in Jackson, Sunday, March 30, at which time Clarence Mitchell, Director of the Washington Bureau, gave a very stirring and informative address. In attendance were some 1500–2000 persons, and representatives from three other organizations—The Regional Council of Negro Leadership, Mississippi Progressive Voters League and the Ministerial Improvement Association of Mississippi. The meeting proved to be one of the most successful we have had in the state.

We want to thank each of you for contributing to the success of this meeting and may we *urge* you to go to your circuit clerk and attempt to register.

FUND-RAISING

As you know our state budget for 1958 is $17,825.00 and in order that we can function to our capacity to the extent that we can make democracy work here in Mississippi, it will be necessary that we receive these funds. Therefore, use every possible avenue to bring in your branch quota. Let the people know that we are not taking their money as the White Citizens Council plan to do and fight them with it, but the money that is given to the N.A.A.C.P. will be used in their behalf. We are moving now, let's all join this freedom train and arrive at our destination together.

Remember the Mother of the Year Contest, whereby your branch can raise most of its funds, and also entitle the winner to a free trip to our National Convention in Cleveland, Ohio. Begin work on this program immediately. It should prove most profitable to you. If more patron lists are needed request them from this office.

MEMBERSHIPS

Our membership quota this year should easily be reached, but only if we get out and work. The Laurel Branch N.A.A.C.P. did an exceptional job with their membership last year, when more than 300 members were enrolled. However, Jackson has indicated that the few members Laurel got last year will be but a smithering to what Jackson will get in 1958. Of course, for my money, there are other branches that bear watching—Gulfport, Columbus, Clarksdale,

Vicksburg, Cleveland, Florence, Meridian, McComb, and yes, even Amite County. So look out Laurel and Jackson!!!!

MAY 17TH CELEBRATION

Each branch is expected to celebrate the May 17, 1954 Decision of the U.S. Supreme Court, either on the seventeenth, or a day before or after. Let us hear from you in this regard.

YOUTH COUNCILS

Each branch is hereby requested to organize a Youth Council in order that your leadership will not die, but will continue to grow and be of benefit to your county and state.

INTEGRATION

The Field Secretary, Medgar W. Evers, was on his return trip from the Southeast Regional Meeting in Greensboro, North Carolina, March 11, when he was attacked by a white man, because he, Mr. Evers, refused to move from the front of the bus to the rear. The bus was en route from Meridian to Dallas, Texas via Jackson, Mississippi. Despite attempts of the Police Department of Meridian, Mississippi to persuade him to take the "customary seating pattern," (rear seat), this passenger remained seated on the very front seat of the bus where he rode, even after having been attacked, ninety-three (93) miles to Jackson without moving. Mr. Evers indicated that he was not trying to stir up trouble, but since he had bought a ticket and paid the same fare as the others paid he felt he should ride where he chose, and that he did.

*

27 (1) Medgar Evers to Johnnie M. Brooks

May 15, 1958

Mr. Johnnie M. Brooks
Director, Registration and Voting
404–1/2 North Second Street
Richmond, Virginia

Dear Mr. Brooks:

On last night, May 14, I attended the third successful meeting of the "Crusade for Voters" in Meridian, Mississippi. It is amazing how the enthusiasm that was generated in the first two meetings has continued. It is definitely an encouraging sign. At last night's meeting there were represented persons from six of the seven precincts in Meridian, Mississippi, also representatives from two of the county supervisory districts. At this meeting we set up temporary precinct machinery and indications are that within the next two weeks the precinct organizations will be a reality.

The list of qualified Negro voters is in the process of being secured, also maps setting forth the boundaries of the various precincts. I do feel personally that in Meridian we are getting off to a very good start.

Tonight is Jackson's night. I shall report to you on the progress later.

We had at last night's meeting approximately forty persons, more or less.

Sincerely yours,

Medgar W. Evers
Field Secretary
MWE:mes
cc: Wilkins, Current, Hurley

(2) Evers to Brooks

May 23, 1958

Mr. Johnnie M. Brooks
Director, Registration and Voting
404–1/2 North Second Street
Richmond, Virginia

Dear John:

Our meeting in Jackson on May 14 was rather successful, in that although we did not have as large attendance that we had in Meridian there were a number of ministers who were present and very enthusiastic about our program, and who pledged complete and wholehearted support in seeing that the job is done.

We were able to split up into approximately seven different precincts where temporary chairmen were selected who are to return to us at our next meeting with more people from their various precincts, and with a nucleus of a working organization in their respective precincts.

Rev. G. R. Haughton, who is acting vice-chairman of the group, was elected chairman and Mr. Carsie Hall, who was acting chairman, was elected vice-chairman.

Enclosed is a reproduction of your "How to Get A Precinct Club Organized" and the boundaries for ten of Jackson's densely populated Negro precincts. Our plans are to have our next meeting in Jackson on June 5 at which time we hope to have the boundaries of all of the precincts.

Meridian has already secured the names of all of their Negro registered voters. However, Mr. Jones indicated that he had not yet been successful in getting the precinct boundaries, so that we could do for Meridian what we are now doing for Jackson.

Sincerely yours,

Medgar W. Evers
Field Secretary
MWE:mes, cc: Wilkins, Current, Hurley

John Mitchell Brooks (1917–1978)—Brooks was raised first in Pennsylvania, then moved to Richmond, Virginia during the 1930s. He served in the US army during the Second World War and received a Bronze Medal for bravery. Upon returning from the war, Brooks began his business career by establishing restaurants. In 1957, he became involved with the NAACP's voter registration campaign, and a year later was appointed the Director of the NAACP national voter registration and education program. It was in this capacity that Brooks co-founded the Crusade for Voters. See "Virginia Black History Archive, John Mitchell Brooks NAACP Files Collection" http://www.library. vcu.edu/jbc/speccoll/vbha/brooks.html

Carsie Hall—Hall, a young federal railway postal worker studying for a career in law, led the Jackson branch of the NAACP in the late 1950s, along with John Dixon and Jack Young. Hall eventually joined the NAACP Legal Defense Fund. See Dittmer, 20, 30, 229.

Rev. G. R. Haughton—Haughton was the pastor of the Pearl Street AME Church in Jackson and was the Church Work Chairman of the State NAACP. In 1963 he was one of the delegates to negotiate with Jackson Mayor Allen Thompson to push for the desegregation of public facilities. After Medgar's murder, Haughton developed a rift with Charles Evers over the course of the movement, and he was subsequently relieved from the church and moved to New Orleans. See Dittmer, 168; Also the online State Sovereignty Commission Files, # 9–31–3–52–1–1–1. http://mdah.state. ms.us/arlib/contents/er/

*

28 Medgar Evers Address, Celebration of the *Brown* Decision's Fourth Anniversary

MAY 18, 1958
MILWAUKEE, WISCONSIN BRANCH OF NAACP,
MASONIC HALL, MILWAUKEE, WISCONSIN

Distinguished platform guests, members of the Milwaukee Branch N.A.A.C.P., Fighters for Freedom, Ladies and Gentlemen: I bring you greetings from the National Office, the Mississippi State Conference of N.A.A.C.P. Branches, its president, Mr. C.R. Darden, and fellow Mississippians, who share with you the aspirations of freedom, and the dignity and worth of individual Americans. I was pleased above and beyond expression to be extended an invitation to speak to you on this very auspicious and historic occasion. For certainly the event we commemorate here today will mean a bright future for our youth of today and tomorrow, and will make for a stronger and more progressive America.

I come from a section of these United States called the Deep South, particularly Mississippi—better known as the Magnolia State, or frequently referred to as the "territory of Mississippi," or "the last state in the Union." However, be that as it may, Mississippi's reputation of being the most backward state in the twentieth century U.S.A. ranks uppermost in the minds of people, even those in the State of Arkansas.

Being a native Mississippian, and having lived there all of my life, except for the two and one half years when I proudly served my country in World War II, with the U.S. Army, I have been pleasant and delightful, but gruesome and unchanging. However, today, it is not my desire to bore you with my experiences, but rather to relate to many of you the multitude of complexities which confront, harass, and keep the Mississippi Negro in a state of second-class citizenship in this twentieth century.

Doubtless, many of you present either come from Mississippi or have relatives who live there. To you I will merely be repeating some of your experiences, or some of the experiences of your relatives. But for others of you, some of the things which will be mentioned here will sound unbelievable in the twentieth century U.S.A., but I assure you that I shall not unjustly censure the state of my birth.

Many of the cries that are now heard echoing throughout the United States by white southerners, for more time to equalize schools, were never heard before the 1954 Supreme Court Decision declaring segregation unconstitutional. There was hardly a whisper to give Negroes adequate schools, not to mention equal. There is still in operative existence, *now, today*, less than twenty-five miles from Jackson, the state capitol of Mississippi, a two room school, with pot-bellied stoves, housing some forty-five students to the room, with most of the window panes out, and the responsibility of securing wood for fuel heat left to the students and teachers. There are many other such schools throughout the state. Doubtless in each county the number could be doubled, certainly in most of them.

Mississippi started its ambitious equalization program after May 17, 1954 in an effort to "get around the Supreme Court Decision." However, the $120,000,000 program is too little, and it has come too late. Negroes in Mississippi want for their children the quality of education that will help make them top scientists, top diplomats, and top engineers of tomorrow, and it cannot be done under the so-called "separate but equal" doctrine.

Less than three weeks ago one of the Negro high schools in Jackson, Mississippi could have been the scene of one of the nation's most tragic incidents had the incident occurred eight hours earlier or eight hours later. The ceiling of a room that houses some thirty-five students and a teacher fell to the floor, amid the seats where the children sat eight hours earlier. Now you say, that could have happened here. That is true, but when you are aware of the fact that this mad rush to try and offset the Supreme Court's Decision is bringing on inferior material and inferior construction, there is a different picture altogether.

In many areas of Mississippi today one may ride down our beautiful highways and marvel at some of the school buildings being constructed, but as you get nearer the deception becomes clearer. Then upon entering, the almost complete emptiness of the school's facilities will dawn on you that you have had a mirage.

We are not discussing fantasy here. We are discussing facts, as they exist, probably not only in Mississippi but in other parts of the South where the people are being overloaded with taxes in an effort to carry out a scheme that is as archaic as the horse and buggy age, and as detrimental to democracy as the atheistic ideology of Communism.

Ladies and gentlemen, truly the May 17, 1954 Decision of the Supreme Court could not have come to America and Americans at a more opportune time, for just three years later the challenge of the

Russian Sputnik has made it incumbent upon every American, regardless of race, creed, or color, to meet this challenge head on, which can only be done through access to a quality education for all.

We come now to a phase of our current struggle, where in 1955 some five petitions to separate boards of education, in five cities and counties in Mississippi, were filed, and brought only the wrath of the Nazi-like activities of the White Citizens Council; calling on each one of the petitioners; bringing with them economic pressure, and in many instances, violence. I am reminded here of one town that stands out most vividly in my mind. That town is Yazoo City, Mississippi, some forty-five miles northwest of Jackson, and on the edge of the Mississippi Delta. It was there that fifty-three Negroes petitioned that the city integrate its school, and the next day after the petition was presented, the names and addresses of every person who had signed the petition were published in the local weekly paper as a public service of the Citizens Council. One by one the Negroes began receiving obnoxious and threatening telephone calls. Many were visited personally by members of the Council; others returned to their jobs only to find that they were no longer employed; while merchants found it increasingly difficult to get wholesale produce, and later discovered that the Council had organized a boycott against their business which later folded because of the pressure. This type of activity began to spread throughout Mississippi, and especially where the petitions were filed. Might I pass on from this phase of our struggle by saying that we shall not cease in our efforts in Mississippi until every child shall have the same opportunity, at the same time, for the quality education that the other child has.

Ladies and gentlemen, as the late General George S. Patton often remarked, "War is hell." I would like to paraphrase and say, "Psychological, economical, and physical war is hell." But I am reminded here of the words of an early American, Tom Paine, who wrote, "These are the times that try men's souls; the summer soldier, and sunshine patriot in the time of crisis will shrink from the service of his country, but those who stand it now deserve the love and admiration of men and women alike." You know, it is a wonderful and thrilling time to be alive, for God's manifestation to man of his omnipotence is truly a wonder to behold.

Now the political situation in Mississippi has been a corrupt politician paradise or utopia, which I will explain after I shall have given a few statistics. First of all, Mississippi has a population, according to the last U.S. census, of 2,178,914, of which 986,707 are Negroes and 1,188,429 are whites. There are approximately 400,000 voters in Mississippi, and of that total some 22,000 or less are Negroes. There are 13 counties in Mississippi where there are no Negro registered voters at all. Included in this number are 5 counties where Negroes constitute a population ratio of 2–1 over their white brother; also included in this number are persons of the Negro group with A.B., B.S., M.A. degrees who are teaching government, civics, and courses necessary to the development of the total individual, but even they are denied the right to vote. There are 12 more counties with less than 10 registered voters; 29 counties with less than 100 Negro voters; 16 counties with less than 500 voters; 5 counties with more than 500, but less than 1000 voters; and 7 counties with more than 1000 but less than 5000 voters.

I am reminded here of one of the Negro schools in the Mississippi Delta where the superintendent called in the instructor in social science and told him to skip over the chapter in government which dealt with voting. You wonder to yourself why there are so few Negroes registered in Mississippi. Well, one subtle reason was given as an example—that of the school superintendent in one of the small Mississippi Delta communities, with his instructions as to what chapters to teach. Then there are cases where economic pressure is brought on the would-be voter, and where that does not seem to be a deterrent, often there is sporadic violence to intimidate; as in the case of the late Rev. George W. Lee of Belzoni, Mississippi, who was shot-gunned to death, gangland style, for not removing his name from the registration book. Then there was the Rev. Gus Courts who was ambushed as he made change in his small grocery store in Belzoni, Mississippi. These, and many other similar incidents, are responsible for the small number of registered voters in my state, yes, and even apathy in some areas where the resistance to voting is not as severe is also a reason.

In 1955 there was enacted into law an amendment to the Mississippi Constitution, making it mandatory that a prospective elector (voter) answer twenty-one questions and interpret to the satisfaction of the circuit clerk, who happens to be the registrar, a section of the Mississippi Constitution. The purpose, as the sponsors pointed out, was to cut down on the increasing Negro vote. In one county where there were some 1,300 registered Negro voters the slate was wiped clean and less than 100 Negroes in this county have been able to re-register. These are many of the obstacles that we face in our struggle for first-class citizenship, but we shall not become discouraged.

Year after year, campaign after campaign, politicians have exploited the Negro issue to get into office, and after getting in they have on the state levels enacted, and proposed to enact, punitive legislation that has for lo these many years helped to keep the Negro a second-class citizen in this great country, and in the State of Mississippi. As Mr. Albert Powell, president of the Mississippi Progressive Voters League, says, "The politician that hollers nigger, nigger the loudest is usually the one elected." While that has been true in the past, many decent white citizens, and there is a number which is growing daily in Mississippi, that frown on the demagoguery that has brought into office mediocre politicians that have brought nothing but ridicule and sympathy for our state.

Indicative of the mediocrity of many of the politicians elected is the spectacle of our more recent 1958 legislature, which on many occasions, with little or no debate, passed far-reaching bills which, if signed into law, would gravely hinder the economic progress of our state. One such bill would give the Attorney-General unlimited power in dealing with foreign and domestic corporations. Of course the sponsors pointed out specifically that it was aimed directly at the N.A.A.C.P. but it was necessary to include all corporations in order to show *no* discrimination.

One legislator, I believe, from Madison County, introduced a bill to separate Negro and white blood in the blood bank, because, as he related, all Negroes suffered with a disease called sickle cell anemia, which whites didn't have, and for that reason it should be separated. Possibly what this legislator was not aware of is the fact that before any blood is received in the bank the donor has to be accepted by a blood test.

These are just two examples of how the 1958 Mississippi legislature spent about three-quarters of its time and taxpayers' money on frivolity and efforts to patch up a way of life that is as obsolete in this space age as conventional propeller-driven combat airplanes.

But aside from all that has been said, the President of the United States, the respected man that he is, in a recent address before the National Newspaper Publishers' Association meeting in Washington, D.C., asked Negroes to be "forbearing in our efforts for first-class citizenship" in the United States, the land of our birth. I say to you, who could be more forbearing than a people whose homes, churches, and businesses have been bombed, and individuals shot down in cold blood with nothing having ever been done about it. In spite of this the Negro has remained calm and confident that our Federal Government would one day intervene, to insure that the principles upon which this great nation of ours was founded would be applied to all alike.

The President's plea for forbearance is an invitation to some Southerners to be more contemptuous of the already existing Federal laws and the Supreme Court of these United States. Certainly the Negro has been and is forbearing, but it would seem to me that the President could have been more stern with the terrorists who have roamed the Southland at will and terrorized law-abiding citizens, both white and Negro, and have caused the prestige of the United States foreign policy to possibly be at its lowest ebb in the history of our country.

For two and one half years I endangered my life as many other Negro Americans, on the far-away battlefields, to safeguard America and Democracy, only to return to our native country and state and be denied the basic things for which we fought. Now if that is not forbearance, I do not know what it is. Even while serving Uncle Sam in Europe I would read in the Stars and Stripes, the U.S. Army publication, of the horror that my people were experiencing in the Southland, while we faced the merciless onslaught of the German Air Force and their eighty-eight field guns. However, I have been told that "resistance to tyranny is obedience to God," and for that reason if for no other we shall not cease to press forward, relentlessly, until every vestige of segregation and discrimination in America becomes annihilated.

I shall close, ladies and gentlemen, by paraphrasing the Gettysburg Address: "The world will little note nor long remember what we say here, but it can never forget what we do here. It is for us the living, rather to be dedicated here to the unfinished work which they who fought here have thus far so nobly advanced. It is rather for us to be here dedicated to the great task remaining before us—that from this Supreme Court decision we take increased devotion to that cause for which it was rendered, and we here highly resolve that this decision shall not have been rendered in vain, that this nation under God shall have a new birth of freedom and that the government of the people, by the people, for the people, shall not perish from the earth."

*

29 Medgar Evers to Gloster B. Current, Director of Branches, NAACP

September 8, 1958
National Association for the
Advancement of Colored People
20 West 40TH Street, New York 18, N. Y.
Longacre 3–6890
Please reply direct to:
Medgar Evers
Mississippi State Office
Masonic Temple Building
1072 Lynch Street Rm. 7
Jackson, Mississippi
Telephone Jackson 3–6906

Mr. Gloster B. Current
Director of Branches
20 West 40th Street
New York 18, New York
RE: Special Report—Amos Brown Case

Dear Mr. Current:

Amos Brown, seventeen year old president of the West Jackson Youth Council and president of the Southeast Region of Youth Councils, has thus far been prevented from attending classes, based on an interview made of him while attending our National Convention in Cleveland, which appeared in the Plain Dealer, Cleveland, Wednesday, July 9, 1958, page 7, column 1, under the title "Negro Youth Resists Elders' Brainwashing."

The article referred to is alleged to have been sent to the Superintendent of Schools, a Mr. Kirby Walker, from someone who gave their address as The Statler Hotel, Cleveland, Ohio.

After receiving the letter, the superintendent, in a conference with Mrs. Brown, the mother of Amos, suggested to her that she teach her son to "obey his elders." Mrs. Brown was later called by the principal, Luther Marshall, and was told to bring Amos to the school for a conference as soon as he returned from his trip (Cleveland and Detroit). Amos returned Tuesday night, September 2. The next day, Wednesday, he and his mother went to the school for this conference with the principal, Marshall, who is said to have been very nasty, and ignored them for an hour and a half while they sat waiting. He then began to question Amos in the presence of his mother and a tape recorder as to why he made the statements that were made when he was in Cleveland. After their lengthy conversation he asked Amos to leave the room, whereby he began talking with Mrs. Brown. He told Mrs. Brown that he would rather Amos transfer to another school because of the influence that he would have on the other children, and that he (Amos) did not respect the administration.

Marshall then told Mrs. Brown that he did not want Amos to be caught on the campus, otherwise he would have him put in jail. Amos, nevertheless, returned the next day and attempted to register. After filling out the application for registration Marshall did not say anything to them at that particular time, but after they had gone home he called Mrs. Brown and told her that Amos would not be permitted to register despite his having filled out an application.

Monday morning the Rev. G. R. Haughton, Rev. G. W. Williams, Miss Mary Cox, Mr. Samuel Bailey, Mrs. C. D. Brown, and the Field Secretary, Medgar W. Evers, went again to see the principal about Amos's admission. The principal refused to talk to us, alleging that it was a parent-administration problem. From Hill High School on Dalton we proceeded to the office of the Supervisor of Negro Schools, James Gooden (Negro) on South Roach Street, where we spent approximately two hours waiting and conferring with the supervisor, who in turn called in Mr. Marshall to participate in the conference. Our discussion there was fruitless.

The principal and supervisor stated that if Amos would change his attitude he might be permitted to reenter the school. At this point the Field Secretary asked what did they mean by change his attitude. Marshall quoted his "pet" statement, it is a parent-administration problem and he would not deal with us any further.

Presently, Amos is not in school. Thus far we have not issued a public statement to the press. The students, however, are very much concerned about the issue.

Sincerely yours,

Medgar W. Evers

Field Secretary
MWE:mes
cc: Mr. Roy Wilkins
Mr. Robert Carter
Mrs. Ruby Hurley
Mr. C. R. Darden

Amos Brown—One of the key student activists of the Mississippi freedom movement, Brown later moved to San Francisco and became a Baptist minister. Brown was a leading supporter of Jesse Jackson's presidential campaigns in the 1980s. In 1996, Brown became a San Francisco City Supervisor. See Clarence Johnson, "The New SF Supervisors; To Amos Brown, This Job is Fulfillment of Destiny," *San Francisco Chronicle*, May 28, 1996, A1; and Max Millard, "The Long Political Road of Reverend Amos Brown," *Sun Reporter*, May 23, 1996, Volume 52, Issue 21, pg. 1.

✳

30 Monthly Report, "Intimidation"

SEPTEMBER 23, 1958

INTIMIDATION

There appears to be a well-planned program to intimidate members of our youth movement in Mississippi. Two cases in point are: The Amos Brown story, which was reported earlier in two separate special reports, and the case of the Jones County Grand Jury investigating the activities of some members of our youth group in Laurel, Mississippi September 18, 1958. In this investigation the Grand Jury subpoenaed six members of our Laurel Youth Council, who were taken out of school at 1 p.m. and were not released until after 5 p.m. the same day. As a result of these two incidents, the Mississippi State Conference of N.A.A.C.P. Branches issued the following news release:

"The most sinister action to date was taken by the Grand Jury in Laurel, Mississippi, September 18, 1958, when this Nazi-like group, without any just cause, subpoenaed six members of the Laurel, Mississippi Youth Council of N.A.A.C.P., and interrogated them as if they were dangerous criminals.

We deplore and condemn these bigoted actions, also those responsible for this heinous crime against these young people.

We further condemn the actions of those responsible for the harassment and intimidation of young Amos Brown on his attempt to enroll at the Jim Hill High School for Negroes, allegedly because of the factual statements he made concerning the inferior school facilities for Negroes in Jackson, Mississippi.

These acts of intimidation against Negro students in our state point up the need for Negro citizens to press for immediate integration into the public schools of this state, or otherwise face the continued indignities and harassment meted out to our young people."

One interesting thing about these acts of intimidation, instead of frightening the youth they became more determined in their efforts than ever before. We have even been approached by some who are ready to start the integration battle for the public schools.

———————————————————————————————————— *

 31 "Why I Live in Mississippi," Medgar Evers (as told to Francis H. Mitchell)
Ebony

NOVEMBER 1958

The white boy stood by the highway on the outskirts of Jackson, thumb uplifted in the traditional plea of the hitchhiker. "Look at him," the Negro said, unconsciously bearing down on the accelerator, "he's free. They've taught him that he owns the world. That's what I want for my kids—freedom—right here in Mississippi. And as long as God gives me strength to work and try to make things real for my children, I'm going to work for it—even if it means making the ultimate sacrifice."

The kid by the highway was a cipher, a nobody in the broad scheme of things. The Negro in the Oldsmobile was Medgar Evers, field secretary of the Mississippi Conference of NAACP Branches—a man who swears he "loves" the land that produced a Bilbo and exterminated an Emmett Till. Says Evers, "this is home. Mississippi is a part of the United States. And whether the whites like it or not, I don't plan to live here as a parasite. The things that I don't like I will try to change. And in the long run, I hope to make a positive contribution to the overall productivity of the South."

Evers had not always planned to be a productive member of Mississippi's society. In fact, during the army days, he read extensively of

Jomo Kenyatta's Mau Mau reign of terror in Africa, and dreamed of arming his own band of blackshirts and extracting an "eye for an eye" from whites who mistreated their black brothers. "I admired the man," he admitted, "he was intelligent, and he didn't believe in compromise. And while I never cared for brutality, I realized that just as the Africans followed Kenyatta, Negroes might have successfully followed someone like him. It didn't take much reading of the Bible, though, to convince me that two wrongs would not make the situation any different, and that I couldn't hate the white man and at the same time hope to convert him."

Like many a Mississippi Negro, Evers has known for some time where he stood in the social and economic scale. As a kid in Decatur, Miss. ("my parents were poor, but not destitute"), he had grown up with a white playmate; "a kid next door who practically lived at my house," and who introduced him to the world of color. "In the long, hot summers," Evers recalled, "we would do all the things that kids do—play hide and seek, talk about our big plans for growing up, swap the little personal treasures that boys grow friendly over, and argue over his double-barreled stopper gun. Then, one day my friend stopped coming by. In a little while, he began to get nasty. Finally, out in the street with a group of his friends, he called me 'nigger.' The split had come. The lines were drawn, black on one side and white on the other. I guess at that moment I realized my status in Mississippi. I have lived with it ever since."

"Living with it" has not always meant working with the NAACP. Until he was 21, Evers had never heard of the National Association for the Advancement of Colored People. Returning from European service with a port battalion (and with a little Kenyatta still in his blood), Evers talked five friends into going with him to register and vote at the little county courthouse in his hometown of Decatur, Miss. It was 1946, and though he had not finished high school, he had seen part of the world—Normandy 26 days after D-Day, Le Havre, Liege, Antwerp, Cherbourg—and coming back to Mississippi he had made up his mind. He had not finished high school but he would vote. He was a black man, but he would vote. So in the steamy little sawmill town ("where there were 900 white voters and no Negroes even registered") he went with his brother, Charles, and four others to register at the clerk's office.

"I never found until later," he said, "that they visited my parents nightly after that. First, it was the whites, and then their Negro message bearers. And the word was always the same: 'tell your sons to take their names off the books. Don't show up at the courthouse voting day.' Then, the night before the election, Bilbo came to town and harangued the crowd in the square. 'The best way to keep a nigger from the polls on election day,' he told them, 'is to visit him the night before.' And they visited us. My brother came from Alcorn college to vote that next day. I laid off from work. The six of us gathered at my house and we walked to the polls. I'll never forget it. Not a Negro was on the streets, and when we got to the courthouse, the clerk said he wanted to talk with us. When we got into his office, some 15 or 20 armed white men surged in behind us, men I had grown up with, had played with. We split up and went home. Around town, Negroes said we had been whipped, beaten up and run out of town. Well, in a way we were whipped, I guess, but I made up my mind then that it would not be like that again—at least not for me."

Six years later, out of Alcorn college where he was a track star, first-string halfback for four years, president of his junior class, vice-president of the student forum, and editor of the Alcorn Herald, Evers was still no closer to "making things right" than he had been with his dream of an American "Mau Mau" band, roaming the delta in search of blood. In his senior year he married Myrlie Beasley, a promising 18-year-old music student. In 1952, he began working with the Magnolia Mutual Life Insurance Company and a subtle change in his thinking took place.

"You know," he confided, "any man with an ounce of pride who works in the delta soon wants to do something. You discover that the education the Negro gets is designed to keep him subservient. The poor black man is exploited by whites and by educated Negroes, too." Out of this conviction, he voluntarily reorganized a dead

NAACP branch in Mound Bayou, and set up a branch in Cleveland, Miss., which eventually grew to 500 members. He haunted the organization's state meetings and himself held "old-fashioned" sessions at the Cleveland branch, "trying," he said, "to arouse Negroes to their responsibilities and urging them to register and vote." His first child was born and he named him Darrell Kenyatta Evers.

In early February, 1954, Evers applied for admission to the University of Mississippi law school. "A number of white people complimented me on the move and there were no reprisals." While his application was pending, the Supreme Court ruled on public education, and the White Citizens Councils sprang up. He was interviewed by the then Attorney General James P. Coleman (now governor), and state school officials.

"They asked me was I sincere. I told them, yes. They asked me was I prompted by the NAACP, and I told them, no. They asked me where I would stay, and I answered 'on the campus, sir. I'm very hygienic, I bathe every day, and I assure you this brown won't rub off.' Coleman said he would let me know. I wanted to know then. He said I would hear 'in time,' and the day after registration, they sent me a letter, saying my application had been denied because I didn't have two recommendations from people in the community."

In December of that year, in the 13th anniversary month of Pearl Harbor, Evers joined the staff of the NAACP. By 1955, he was the youngest man on a nine-man "death list." The list was reduced to eight when Rev. George T. Lee was shotgunned in Belzoni, Miss., after refusing to take his name off a voter registration list. Said Evers then, "you don't have time to be afraid."

Many things went into Evers' decision to join the NAACP staff, the effects on his wife and child, the fruitlessness of trying to work as an insurance man full-time while giving more time (in his off hours) to NAACP work . . . and the night his dad died.

"I was in the basement of the hospital at Union, Mississippi (that's where Negro patients stayed), at my dad's bedside. He had had a hemorrhage and was sinking fast. I heard a rising murmur of voices . . . a rushing of feet, and there was an ugly crowd outside the building.

A nurse called me upstairs and asked me to help. There was a Negro, with his leg bandaged. He had been in a fracas with a policeman, someone had shot him in the leg. The whites were like madmen, muttering among themselves about the 'nigger,' peeping in the windows to see if they could spot him. My dad died a short time later, and outside, those whites were demonstrating like animals. I've never forgotten that either. A Negro cannot live here or die here in peace as long as things remain as they are."

Since 1954, the tall (5 ft., 11 in.) stockily built Mississippian has roamed his state cajoling the frightened, counseling the troubled, smiling and shaking hands with some Negroes who view him as a Messiah for their troubled times, and with others who see him as an eager leper who would infect them with the same disease that makes him the object of the white man's hatred.

In Laurel, he smiles with satisfaction at the Youth Chorus, whose members were forced to quit their high school choirs because their spare-time singing was for the NAACP. And in Jackson, where hundreds of Negro teachers draw good salaries, he curses his inability to attract more of them to the NAACP. In Vicksburg, his wife's native home, he drives visitors through the streets to show them Negroes and whites living side-by-side, and points them out as an example of what can happen if people are not reminded of their differences. At the same moment he bitterly assails their situation as an example of the "lethargy" which afflicts Negroes who cherish their "good relations" with the white man more than they do their own freedom.

Outside Vicksburg, in the national park which entombs hundreds of Civil War dead—from Mississippi, Illinois, both sides of the struggle—Evers strolls with other sightseers over the bones of the dead, is drawn to "our spot," where he and his wife courted, politely answers the question of a white man whose ten gallon hat and deep drawl identify him as one of the "enemy."

"You know," he said later, "it may sound funny, but I love the South. I don't choose to live anywhere else. There's land here, where a man can raise cattle, and I'm going to do that some day. There are lakes where a man can sink a hook and fight the bass (he has a four-pounder mounted on his wall). There is room here for my children to play and grow, and become good citizens—if the white man will let them."

By "let them," Evers does not mean a condition made possible by the white man's will, alone. Like the horseflies that buzz violently into his car as he roars down his road to destiny, he means to string the whites into making Mississippi right. "At the moment," he explains, "we don't have any suits pending. But we are doing our best to embarrass the whites to death. For a long time, they literally got away with murder. Now, when a Negro is mistreated, we try to tell the world about it."

For Mississippi's chief NAACP man, this means long hours on the road (his Olds logged 78,000 miles in the past two years), chasing down stories of brutality and civil rights abuses, and long sessions in the office examining and weighing valid and invalid complaints.

At home and at the office, Evers is constantly on call—sometimes answers the phone to receive a threat: "meet us out by the old car junkyard, we want to have a talk with you," or to hear a problem: "shall I sign the petition that some Negroes are circulating in favor of a new segregated park and playground?" To the youngsters, Evers, at 32, is still young enough to be a companion. He remembers a phenomenal number of them by name, indulges in their horseplay, treats them like members of a young scout troop bent on no more serious business than learning to tie knots and reciting "on my honor I will do my best to do my duty. . . ." Their business, however, is inherently more serious. For out of the youth organization's ranks are coming "and must continue to come," he says, "the leaders in the future fight." The youth, he declares, "have a definite responsibility to help, because much of what we are struggling for now will benefit them directly 10 years from now—will open up opportunities that were not open when I came along." In some areas, he readily admits, there are weaknesses in the youth program. But in others, "where leadership among the adults has given them the right guidance and stimulation," he says, "the young people are responding beautifully."

How some kids respond is best typified by a young boy, who seeing Evers in a Jackson restaurant, proudly reached into his wallet and pulled out an NAACP membership card. "There it is, Mr. Evers," he exclaimed with a broad grin, "my card finally came." "Aw shucks," countered another youngster, lounging on a stool at the counter, "that's nothing. I've been an NAACP member for a long time."

"That's what I mean about this race business," Evers confessed when he had left the restaurant, "at their ages most white boys don't have to be concerned with anything more serious than where to play tomorrow, or some childhood foolishness like the secret signs and passwords of their television heroes. But a Negro kid . . . well . . ." and his voice trailed off as he crossed the street to his office.

In March, Evers put his personal philosophy to the acid test and proved to himself that he was no longer the firebrand who was once willing to do violence. Boarding a Trailways bus in Meridian, Miss., he took a seat near the front and refused to move at the demand of the driver. After a 20-minute conference between the driver and officers, he was removed and taken to the police station for questioning. Returning to the bus, he took a front seat and the bus pulled away. Four blocks from the station, a cabbie flagged the bus to a halt, rushed in and slugged Evers in the face before being ordered outside. Says Evers of his refusal to fight back: "You can't let your emotions run away with you. If I had retaliated, it would have helped defeat the cause for which I am struggling.

"Violence, certainly, is not the way. Returning physical harm for physical harm will not solve the problem. And one of our strongest appeals to the conscience of southern whites is that the NAACP has never been linked to violence. Not even the southern bigot has much ground to stand on when he tries to rabble rouse about our winning court decisions. But give him a little Negro violence to point to, and he will have a good selling point for stirring up race hatred." While the bus incident was just a ripple on the tide of anti-Negro incidents in the state, it convinced many of the uncommitted that Evers was lacking neither in personal bravery nor good judgment.

His principal "people" are the "little men" who, hired by whites at daily labor tasks, have more to lose than their professional brethren who have irked him by shunning the fight. With a tinge of bitterness he declares, "As much good as the NAACP has done to make opportunities greater for teachers who once made $20 a month and are making up to $5,000 a year now, we don't get their cooperation. The professionals are the same way. Only in isolated cases do they go all out to help us. Some ministers are in almost the same category—in that class of people who won't be hurt by belonging to the organization, but who won't give us 50 cents for fear of losing face with the white man. Our biggest support is with the rank and file of people and their ranks are growing all the time." Because whites are interested in the NAACP's numbers in Mississippi, Evers will not give any figures. But he does admit "One of our chapters has more than 400 members, and we have more than 20 chapters in the state."

Increasing the organization's ranks is a job he tackles in a manner which is frequently embarrassing to non-voters and non-NAACP members. On introduction, Evers may make "small talk" but before long, he inevitably swings into question and answer. "Are you a registered voter, sir? Would you mind saying why you haven't registered? Do you feel you should take advantage of the ballot (in areas where there is no voting difficulty)?" Given "no" answers, Evers will patiently explain the power of the vote. Then, switching his theme, he will ask bluntly, "Are you an NAACP member . . . familiar with the work of the organization . . . like to know more about it?" His personal contact is a sometimes slow process, but it gets results.

In the relative quiet of his home (as quiet as Darrell Kenyatta, 5, and Reena Denise, 4, will let it be) Evers thinks most times about his problems, then abruptly focuses his attention on fishing. He tries to work a six-day week—keeping Saturdays free for fly and flat casting on the lakes near Jackson. "On the banks, or in a boat," he says philosophically, "you can forget everything except the fish. You concentrate on the fish being there and you can shed your worries . . . until you start home again."

Leaving the woods, and driving past the site of a new lake outside Jackson, he stopped the car and bounded out to tramp along the muddy rim and calculate the depth of the still unfinished project. "I'll sure be able to sink a hook deep there," he bragged. "Yeah," answered his neighbor and fishing partner for the day, "but you know that's the white part of the lake." Evers thought for a minute, then sloughed through the red clay back toward the car. His brow furrowed in concentration for a moment, and he was the NAACP man again. "I don't have any bitterness toward the white man," he said, as if to convince himself of the truth of it. "There are some of his ways that I don't care for, and as long as God gives me strength to work and change them, I'm going to do it."

On the wall of his living room hangs a plaque that seems to sum up his relationship with this God and the white man at the same moment. The lines are from something written by Abraham Lincoln, at a time and place that matter little to Evers except that they speak to him in his own time of trouble. They read: "I have been driven many times to my knees by the overwhelming conviction that I had nowhere else to go. . . . My own wisdom, and that of all about me seemed insufficient for that day."

This same "overwhelming conviction" which sent Lincoln to his knees has sometimes sent Evers to his Bible, his prayer, his God, and his knees, and has brought him back, each time, with renewed vigor to the battle he knows he was made for. "I'll be damned," he says viciously, and in a rare burst of profanity, "if I'm going to let the white man lick me. There's something out here that I've got to do for my kids, and I'm not going to stop until I've done it."

My parents were poor, but not destitute. I grew up with a white playmate, a kid next door who practically lived at my house. In the long, hot summers we would do all the things that kids do—play hide and seek, talk about our big plans for growing up, swap the little personal treasures that boys grow friendly over, and argue over his double-barreled stopper gun. Then, one day, my friend stopped coming by. In a little while, he began to get nasty. Finally, out in the street with a group of his friends, he called me "nigger." The split had come. The lines were drawn, black on one side and white on the other. I guess at that moment I realized my status in Mississippi. I have lived with it ever since. . . . But this is home. Mississippi is a part of the United States. And whether the whites like it or not, I don't plan to live here as a parasite. The things that I don't like I will try to change. And in the long run, I hope to make a positive contribution to the overall productivity of the South.

In Decatur [Mississippi] where there were 900 white voters and no Negroes even registered, I went with [my brother] Charles, and four others [in 1946] to register at the clerk's office. I never found out until later that they visited my parents nightly after that. First, it was the whites and then their Negro message bearers. And the word was always the same: "Tell your sons to take their names off the books. Don't show up at the courthouse voting day." Then, the night before the election, Bilbo came to town and harangued the crowd in the square. "The best way to keep a nigger from the polls on election day," he told them, "is to visit him the night before." And they visited us. My brother came from Alcorn College to vote the next day. I laid off from work. The six of us gathered at my house and we walked to the polls. I'll never forget it. Not a Negro was on the streets, and when we got to the courthouse, the clerk said he wanted to talk with us. When we got into his office, some fifteen or twenty armed white men surged in behind us, men I had grown up with, had played with. We split up and went home. Around town Negroes said we had been whipped, beaten up and run out of town. Well, in a way we were whipped, I guess, but I made up my mind then that it would not be like that again—at least not for me.

It may sound funny, but I love the South. I don't choose to live anywhere else. There's land here, where a man can raise cattle, and

I'm going to do that some day. There are lakes where a man can sink a hook and fight the bass. There is room here for my children to play and grow, and become good citizens—if the white man will let them. . . . The youth have a definite responsibility to help, because much of what we are struggling for now will benefit them directly ten years from now—will open up opportunities that were not open when I came along. . . . Violence, certainly, is not the way. Returning physical harm for physical harm will not solve the problem. And one of our strongest appeals to the conscience of southern whites is that the NAACP has never been linked to violence.

Jomo Kenyatta (1889–1978)—A Pan-African independence leader, Kenyatta was a leader of Kenyan African Union party that campaigned for independence after the Second World War. In 1952, Kenyatta was arrested and tried for the charge of managing the Mau Mau uprising, and sentenced to seven years of imprisonment and hard labor. Two years after his release, he became Kenya's prime minister, and then the president of the newly independent republic. As a political intellectual, his best-known work is 1938 *Facing Mount Kenya* (New York: AMS Press, 1978), an anthropological defense of Kikuyu culture. See A. B. Assensoh, *African Political Leadership: Jomo Kenyatta, Kwame Nkrumah, and Julius K. Nyerere* (Malabar, Fla. : Krieger Pub. Co., 1998); and Jeremy-Murray Brown, *Kenyatta* (London: Allen & Unwin, 1979); http://www.africawithin.com/kenyatta/kenyatta_bio.htm

Mau Mau—The roots of Mau Mau movement in Kenya can be found during the 1940s, as land shortage afflicted members of the Gikuyu, Embu, Meru and Kamba communities, who became convinced that nothing short of armed struggle against British colonialism would restore their rights to the lost land. After the harassment and internment of political leaders and the banning of opposition parties in 1952, the Mau Mau insurrection began. Kenyatta's complicity in the movement was marginal at best, however, since he was mostly abroad or in jail for the period of the Mau Mau uprising. See E.S. Atieno Odhiambo, John Lonsdale, eds., *Mau Mau & Nationhood: Arms, Authority & Narration* (Athens: Ohio University Press, 2003); David Throup, *Economic & social origins of Mau Mau 1945–53* (Athens: Ohio University Press, 1988). http://www.africawithin.com/tour/kenya/mau_mau.htm

---

*

32 Annual Report, 1958

JANUARY 1959

REGISTRATION AND VOTING

Great emphasis has been placed on registration and voting in 1958. Probably one of the most concerted efforts among Negroes to get registered voters took place in 1958.

Our November 16–17, 1957 Conference, in Atlanta, dealt with an intensified effort to get Negroes to pay their poll taxes and become registered voters. January is the month in which poll taxes are to be paid, and in most of the larger cities of the state we encouraged, by telephone and handbills, payment of poll taxes by Negro citizens. While we have not been able to determine exactly how many persons paid their poll tax, we are positive that in some of the larger cities the program was quite successful.

Mississippi has a law whereby you may register at any time during the year, and we have taken advantage of that situation by encouraging Negroes to constantly register throughout the year. However, because of a rather stringent qualification law, we have found it difficult in some areas and possibly in others to get our people registered. Because of the stringent laws, however, it was in March of this year that the first suit was filed in Federal District Court by the Rev. H. D. Darby of Prentiss, Mississippi, in an effort to have declared unconstitutional the rigid qualification status.

During the public hearing of this voting case, in the courtroom of the Federal Building in Jackson, Negroes throughout Mississippi sat in rapt attention as the proceedings were carried on. Mrs. Constance Baker Motley of New York City and Mr. R. Jess Brown of Jackson, Mississippi were the attorneys for the plaintiff. The subsequent decision of the three-judge District Court, presided over by Federal Judge, Ben Cameron of the U.S. 5th Appeals Court of New Orleans, rendered a negative decision, which left Mississippi's stringent law still intact. The attorneys for the plaintiff and the Legal Defense and Educational Fund of the N.A.A.C.P. declined an appeal to the Supreme Court and, instead, indicated that the case would be turned over to the Civil Rights Commission.

Mr. John Brooks, National Director of Registration and Voting, visited our state April 16th and 17th, and with the assistance of the President of the Mississippi State Conference of N.A.A.C.P. Branches, Mr. C. R. Darden, and yours truly, began coordinated movements in the cities of Jackson and Meridian, to increase the voting strength among Negroes in these two areas. Our coordinated movements have met with stiffened resistance of already organized suffrage groups, who do not want to lose their identity and little prestige engendered in the community. Despite the assurance that they would not lose their identity, it is difficult to overcome their doubts. However, we have been able to organize many of the precincts in the two cities mentioned. These precincts are working with ever increasing know-how to get more registered voters.

Plans are underway in both cities to double the number of voters in 1960. There were 1,500 registered voters in Meridian, and 5,000 in Jackson, in 1958. Coordinated programs have been set up in Vicksburg and Laurel, with efforts having been made to set up coordinated movements in Clarksdale and Greenville.

There are increasing signs that some of the county officials, who have hitherto refused to permit Negroes to register, are beginning to change their tactics in the face of the civil rights bill that was enacted by Congress in 1957. One particular county is that of Walthall. Previous to 1957 Negroes were not registered, nor allowed to register. However, since 1957, members of our Walthall County Branch reported that many of them have been permitted to register. It is not known to what extent this policy will be extended, because so few people are willing to make an attempt to register. The Field Secretary, nonetheless, has urged each member of the branch, of voting age, to register, and to encourage other similar persons in the community to do likewise.

There are counties, however, where we still do not have a single Negro voter. This, of course, is due to the lack of pressing for the right to vote. Conversely, there is one county in particular where Negroes have exerted every possible effort to get themselves registered, but the circuit clerk refuses to do so. It was in this county (Forrest) that the Civil Rights Commission conducted an investigation into the denial by the circuit clerk to disfranchise the Negro citizens. Some twenty-four witnesses from three counties were questioned.

Our State Conference was highlighted with a workshop on registration and voting, which revealed some Negroes who had been previously registered were "purged" after a re-registration was called. These same individuals plan to submit an affidavit to the Civil Rights Commission and the Department of Justice.

DESEGREGATION

The word desegregation in Mississippi has been "mythical" in the true sense of the word. There has been no desegregation in any phase of community life anywhere in Mississippi, particularly in education and transportation. However, on March 11th the Field Secretary desegregated the Trailway bus between Meridian and Jackson for one night, and only then after having been struck in the face by a taxi driver, and interrogated at length by the Meridian Police Department. Despite these obstacles, the Field Secretary boarded the bus in Meridian and rode to Jackson, for some ninety-four miles, desegregated.

Constance Baker Motley (b. 1921)—A prominent New York–based civil-rights lawyer, Motley is known as the writer of the brief of the *Brown v. Board of Education* case, and argued before the Supreme Court for the rights of James Meredith, who was attempting to enroll at the all-white University of Mississippi. She became the first African American woman to be appointed to the federal bench in 1966, and became the senior judge for the Southern District of New York in 1986. See Motley, *Equal Justice—Under Law: An Autobiography* (New York: Farrar, Straus and Giroux, 1998).

R. Jess Brown (1912–1989)—One of the few African American attorneys in Mississippi during the 1940s and 1950s, Brown took on the cases on behalf of Evers, Clyde Kennard, and Mack Parker, who was accused of raping a white woman and later was lynched. For those activities he was threatened on numerous occasions but kept defending the rights of black citizens. See Howard Smead, *Blood Justice: The Lynching of Mack Charles Parker* (Oxford University Press, 1988), 18–19, 34; and "One of America's Greatest Treasures," http://thomas.loc.gov/cgi-bin/query/z?r105:E27FE7–248.

*

33 (1) Medgar Evers to Gloster B. Current

February 24, 1959
National Association for the
Advancement of Colored People
20 West 40th Street, New York 18, New York
Longacre 3–6890
Please direct reply to:
Medgar Evers
Mississippi State Office
Masonic Temple Building
1072 Lynch Street Rm. 7
Jackson, Mississippi
Telephone Jackson 3–6906

Mr. Gloster B. Current
Director of Branches
20 West 40th Street
New York 18, New York

Dear Mr. Current:

While in New York in January, I discussed with you my interest in attending law school, and that I would like to begin such study in September of 1959. During the course of our conversation, you suggested several schools to which I might seek application, among those mentioned were the University of Arkansas, Loyola University, New Orleans, Louisiana, and St. Louis University. As I recall, the reason we thought of these nearby universities was, I could, while obtaining my degree in law, continue to work with the N.A.A.C.P. here in the state. That is highly desirable.

I feel that since I have an application already on file with the University of Mississippi Law School (since January, 1954 and before employment with the NAACP), I would like to pursue that application to the fullest extent, realizing, however, that it might not be possible for me to enter in September. Nevertheless, an attempt would be made to open the university to Negroes.

This move would certainly gain for us more financial and moral support from such professionals, as teachers, who desire to go to the University of Mississippi, or some other state school, rather than leave the state. Any sacrifice of me would not be too great.

The record of my application to the university should be familiar to Mr. Carter.

Please give this your very serious consideration, and let me hear from you immediately in this regard.

Sincerely yours,

Medgar W. Evers
Field Secretary
MWE:mes
cc: Mr. Roy Wilkins

(2) Current to Evers

PERSONAL & CONFIDENTIAL

March 24, 1959

Mr. Medgar W. Evers
1072 Lynch Street, R. 7
Jackson, Mississippi

Dear Medgar:

Sometime ago we talked about the possibility of your attending law school.

I discussed this matter with Robert Carter and his comments are being sent you for your information.

It would appear that a combination study-work program is out of the question. Therefore, you may want to think this matter very carefully as to possible alternatives.

Sincerely yours,

Gloster B. Current
Director of Branches
GBC/pt
encl.

Robert L. Carter (b. 1917)—The general counsel of the NAACP and later a federal district judge, Carter was in the team of lawyers that ultimately won the *Brown* decision in 1954. He was involved in many other important cases for the NAACP Legal Defense Fund. After resigning from the NAACP in 1968, he taught at several prominent law schools and was appointed to the United States District Court for the Southern District of New York in 1972. See "Robert L. Carter," http://www.jtbf.org/article_iii_judges/carter_r.htm.

34 Monthly Report: "Registration and Voting" and "Mississippi Teachers Association"

MARCH 23, 1959

REGISTRATION AND VOTING

The Field Secretary visited the Claiborne County Branch at Port Gibson, February 24, after complaints were made by branch members that they were being denied the right to register in order to vote. In a meeting, which lasted about seven hours, some twenty persons were in attendance, five of whom gave us affidavits that were forwarded to the Department of Justice and the Civil Rights Commission, with copies going to Mr. Clarence Mitchell, Director, Washington Bureau N.A.A.C.P. Claiborne County is a southwestern Mississippi river county, with a Negro population of two and one half to one ratio over the white population, and with less than a hundred Negroes registered to vote.

Our branch, under the leadership of Mr. Earnest Jones and Mr. D. A. Newman, have started a campaign to get more Negroes registered to vote, and are attempting to clear away all the obstacles that have been erected to prevent their registration.

Carroll County, with a Negro ratio of one and one half to one over the white residents of the county was, until recently, listed as not having had any Negro voters whatsoever. However, according to contact made in the county just recently, Friday, February 27, there are two Negroes registered. It is generally felt that, since the Goldsby decision, there have been efforts on the part of some of the whites to get a "few" Negroes registered in order to get a reversal of the decision rendered in Goldsby's favor.

Fear, being as prevalent throughout the county as it is, it is increasingly difficult to talk with Negroes about registering to vote, not to mention urging that they go down and try to register themselves.

Contact has been made in Jefferson County, where no Negroes are registered, with a young collegian (Alcorn), who will be twenty-one in May, and who promises to go down as soon as he is eligible and register, which will be a break in the ice in that county.

Amite County is another county that has no Negro voters, and my recent visit to that county, with members of our branch there, indicated that we will get some registration attempts in early April, and if denied will proceed to ask for a federal investigation into the discriminatory practices of denying Negroes the right to register and vote.

In cities where we have set up our coordinated voting program, we are proceeding with a steady increase in registration—nothing spectacular, but steady.

[...]

MISSISSIPPI TEACHERS ASSOCIATION

The Director of Registration and Voting, Mr. Johnnie M. Brooks, was on hand for the 53rd Annual Mississippi Teachers Association Meeting, in Jackson, March 19–20, and was scheduled to speak the night of the nineteenth. However, thirty minutes prior to his appearance as platform guest, he was told by one of the officials that it would be better if he would not appear, which was not intended as a threat, but rather to satisfy some of the Uncle Toms who did not approve of Mr. Brooks' appearance on the program.

Even though Mr. Brooks did not appear on the program on the nineteenth, the closing program Friday night witnessed an address by Mr. W. M. Bell, Registrar of Texas Southern University, who urged that all Negro teachers register and vote. The president of the M.T.A., himself, urged that all teachers register and qualify to become first-class citizens of their respective communities.

"The Goldsby Decision" (1959)—The case involved the conviction of a black man, Robert Goldsby, charged with raping and killing a white woman. Goldsby was granted a second trial, in which he was convicted to die. After several appeals for a stay, he was executed in 1961. In conjunction with the case, U.S. Fifth Circuit Court struck down a Mississippi law that required that members of the jury be selected from a registered voters list, which included few African Americans. The Court held that Mississippi's jury-selection practices constituted a pattern of "systematic exclusion" and hence were unconstitutional. See 263 F.2d 71; 1959 U.S. App. LEXIS 4557. "Vaiden, Mississippi: The Case of Robert Lee Goldsby," http://www.vaiden.net/goldsby.html.

CHAPTER IV

OUR NEED FOR

POLITICAL

PARTICIPATION

Documents 35–44

(May 21, 1959–March 22, 1960)

"I remember realizing that with what we were doing, trying to abolish segregation, we were coming up against governors of seven states, judges, politicians, businessmen, and I remember thinking, 'I'm only 22 years old. What do I know? What am I doing?' I felt very vulnerable. So when we heard that other cities had demonstrations, it really helped, because there were more of us. And I think we started feeling the power of an idea whose time had come. The movement had a way of reaching inside me and bringing out things that I never knew were there. Like courage, and love for people. It was a real experience to be seeing a group of people who would put their bodies between you and danger. And to love people that you work with enough that you would put your body between them and danger."

Diane Nash, first chairman of the Nashville Student Movement, and activist in the 1960 sit-ins in Nashville, Tennessee

Juan Williams, Eyes on the Prize: America's Civil Rights Years, 1954–1965 *(New York: Penguin, 1987), pp. 130–131.*

O NE OF THE most notorious racial atrocities during the civil-rights era in the South was the case of Mack Charles Parker, of Poplarville, Mississippi. Parker, a twenty-three-year-old African American truck driver, had been unjustly arrested for the rape of a local white woman. Although the victim would later insist that she had told the police at the line-up that she "wasn't positive, but it looked like" the man who had raped her, Parker was jailed and held for trial. On the evening of April 24, 1959, a lynch mob numbering twenty or more white men went into the sheriff's office, removed Parker from police custody, and carried him off in a convoy of automobiles. Parker was brutally beaten, mutilated, and his corpse was discovered in the Pearl River nine days later. Evers hired a photographer to take photos of Parker's body, which he described as being in a "gruesome state."[1] The FBI investigated the Parker case, and although the individuals who were directly involved in murdering Parker were widely known, no one was prosecuted or arrested for the crime.[2]

The Parker lynching and the FBI's involvement brought the case to national attention, and Evers was central to the controversy. A two-week speaking tour for Evers and Parker's mother was planned for the west coast [see Document 36]. Wilkins flew to Jackson to speak on May 17, 1959, at a major NAACP event celebrating the fifth anniversary of the *Brown* decision. Over 2,500 people attended the Wilkins rally. Although the Parker case elevated Evers into national prominence, the brutal experience and others like it took a toll on Medgar. "If the years were stamped with the names of the murdered, the months were inked with those of the beaten and maimed," Myrlie recalled. "Affidavits testifying to the routine cruelty of white Mississippians toward Negroes piled up in Medgar's files. Each represented an hour, a day, a week of Medgar's life in a surrealist version of Hell."[3]

The pressures on the Evers family were unrelenting, and Medgar at times simply "shut down," refusing to communicate frankly with Myrlie. Undoubtedly part of his motivation was to shield his wife and children from the most horrific aspects of his job. "I continually bugged him by saying, 'What's wrong? . . . Tell me what's wrong,'" Myrlie now states. She decided to retaliate by becoming "unavailable to him." For the first time in their marriage, she did not drive her husband to the airport for the long California trip. Medgar was puzzled and perhaps worried. "It's the first time we broke a rule, to never leave each other angry," remembers Myrlie. After arriving in California, Medgar wrote a quick letter back to his wife, stating that he would soon telephone home, "'to check on my children.' Not me," adds Myrlie. When Medgar returned to Jackson, he encountered a changed woman. "I don't know what's going on with you," she complained to her husband. "I'm not going to worry about it. I'm going to be the strong woman that you said you wanted me to be. Now, deal with it."[4]

This was still more than a decade before the "feminist revolution," and it is unlikely that Medgar was fully prepared to cope with what Myrlie was expressing. He managed nevertheless to understand how important it would be "to get me ready for his demise," Myrlie explains. Medgar apologized, and finally said: "This is why I did that. Because I was fearful for you." Medgar was no longer fearful of his own death. He normally carried a rifle with him in his automobile, and was a skilled hunter and gamesman. What he could never accept, however, was the terrible possibility "that we could be killed. And he wanted to protect us," Myrlie states. "He didn't know whether someone else would come in . . . and try to assume his role."[5]

During his California tour, Medgar gave a public speech hosted by the Los Angeles branch of the NAACP, on May 31, 1959 [see Document 36]. The address represents one of the most important expressions of Evers's political beliefs and evolving protest ideology. Evers recounts in grim detail the racist atrocities in Mississippi, from Reverend Lee's murder to the death of Parker. Medgar cautioned his audience that while "the white man is responsible, to a great degree, for this one-sided situation," African Americans contributed to their own oppression. In several Mississippi cities where "Negroes are permitted to register and vote without molestation," tens of thousands refused to do so either out of fear or apathy. Middle-class blacks, especially those who personally "profit . . . from human misery." Whites in Mississippi had elevated these "Uncle Toms" into prominent positions "as leaders of the Negro community, in an effort to stamp out any semblance of fight for justice and equality by the more militant Negro people." In an analysis reminiscent of Malcolm X, Evers criticized conservative black educators who suppressed the political activism of young African Americans. "We encounter [oppression] a great deal from some of our people, some of our people who are on the way up there, those people who feel that they have too much to lose than to get into this fight so that we can all become free men and women."[6] Evers highlighted the growing class divisions within the black community, and the real contradictions between those who favored democratic reforms versus those privileged black elites who benefited from racial segregation.

Medgar continued to concentrate on his difficult job of investigating crimes and encouraging blacks to register to vote. On October 25, 1959, he delivered a speech at Campbell College on "Our Need for Political Participation" [see Document 39]; the following day he drove to New Orleans to participate in an NAACP rally; on November 29, he delivered a lecture before the Central Methodist Church in Jackson, arguing that it was a Christian duty to create a "clean and honest government" in Mississippi. Increasingly Medgar relied on the contributions and support of working-class and the poorest African Americans to build the NAACP. "Medgar called them 'the salt of the earth'," Myrlie now recalls. "Women who worked in homes of white folks, who nursed their babies. Yes, the working class. Those were the ones that he could count on." Myrlie remembered one poor working woman who came into Evers's Jackson headquarters one late weekend evening, "sweaty, smelling slightly, who would walk into the office. 'Mr. Evers? I'm here, just like I said.' And she would open up her blouse and put her hand in and pull out this soggy handkerchief, filled with perspiration, and untie it. And take a dollar or two and say, 'This is for the cause. It's all I can do this week, but I'll be back next week. Mr. Evers, if you need me to do something, make some phone calls, make an announcement at my church, I'll be there.'"[7]

As the documents in this chapter illustrate, the political and personal differences between C. R. Darden and Evers finally erupted into open conflict in February–March, 1960 [see Document 43]. To Myrlie, her husband's conflict with Darden was motivated by one simple fact: "He wanted Medgar's job. . . . He had done everything that he possibly could to discredit Medgar. People knew what he was saying were lies and what not." Medgar responded by mobilizing allies like Aaron Henry, and recruiting into NAACP membership hundreds of African American World War II veterans who were part of the Jackson American Legion. Darden was politically more conservative than both Evers and Henry, and he believed that nonviolent, "sit-in" demonstrations could not be an effective protest tactic in Mississippi, due to its repressive environment. Evers, however, correctly recognized that a new phase of the Black Freedom Movement had begun on February 1, 1960, when black students in North Carolina started the sit-in movement [see Document 44]. Henry replaced Darden as the head of the NAACP branches in Mississippi, and Evers's personal authority was backed by Wilkins and the national office.

35 Monthly Report: "Speaking Engagements," "The Poplarville Incident," and "May 17th Celebration"

MAY 21, 1959

SPEAKING ENGAGEMENTS

The 8th Annual Meeting of the Regional Council of Negro Leadership, held in Mound Bayou, Mississippi, had, as one of its principal speakers, the Field Secretary for the State of Mississippi, Medgar W. Evers, who urged Negroes in attendance from the various counties to take advantage of their constitutional guarantees—the right to vote; the right of our children to receive the best education in the best public schools—in their prospective communities.

The attendance at the Regional Council was comparatively fair, however, the response to the address by the Field Secretary was very good.

Other speaking engagements were at the Mississippi Medical-Pharmaceutical Society (annual meeting) in Greenville, Mississippi, April 29–30th, and the Jackson Alumni Chapter of the Delta Sigma Theta Sorority on May 3rd.

The Clarksdale Branch N.A.A.C.P. held a very successful Freedom Fund Dinner, May 15th, at the Haven Methodist Church, at which time the Field Secretary was the principal speaker. The dinner was well attended. Everyone was quite attentive as the Field Secretary unveiled fifty years of progress through the efforts of the National Association for the Advancement of Colored People. Presentation of awards were given to officials and members of the Clarksdale Branch N.A.A.C.P. from the office of our Southeast Regional Secretary.

THE POPLARVILLE INCIDENT

From the very beginning of the Poplarville incident, shortly after the arrest of Mack Charles Parker for the alleged crime of rape, the Field Secretary has been on the scene. On Saturday, March 7, approximately eleven days after the alleged rape occurred, and some seven or eight days after Parker had been arrested, the Field Secretary had the opportunity to talk with the mother, Mrs. Eliza Parker, and discovered that no lawyer in the area had agreed to defend her son. Upon this revelation by Mrs. Parker, it was suggested that there were Negro lawyers in Jackson who would possibly be happy to defend her son because of the apparent innocence she had expressed in her son's case. The names of several Negro lawyers were mentioned and she finally chose one, R. Jess Brown, who seemed to have been proceeding along the legal line that since Negroes were excluded from jury duty in Pearl River County, the case should have been dismissed. However, after having laid an apparent good legal foundation, in the early morning of April 25, about 1:00 a.m., young Parker was snatched from his jail cell in the Pearl River County jail in Poplarville. He was taken from the jail by some nine or ten masked white men; killed and dumped into the swollen Pearl River. Nine days later his body was discovered by the F.B.I. and state troopers, who had been in the case six hours after the incident occurred. Immediately after the recovery of the body, which was later sent to a Negro funeral home in Hattiesburg, Mississippi, the Field Secretary and a free lance photographer were able to get exclusive pictures of the body in its gruesome state. On the same day we attended the graveside funeral, which was held at Lumberton, Mississippi, the hometown of Parker.

Prior to the funeral, however, and the discovery of the body, the mother, Mrs. Eliza Parker, was en route to California with some of her children, after having received threats from anonymous individuals in the area. She is presently living in Merced, California with a sister, Mrs. Lola Peters, 215 West 14th Street.

The F.B.I. is still working intensively on a solution of the case. A number of suspects have accused the F.B.I. of using "Gestapo like" tactics during their interrogation. However, indications point to an early solution of the crime.

MAY 17TH CELEBRATION

The celebration of the Fifth Anniversary of the Supreme Court Decision of May 17, 1954 was a complete success, and the Mother of the Year phase of our celebration was also a success. Mr. Wilkins, our Executive Secretary, was at his best, when he addressed a crowd of 2,500–2,900 people on this very memorable day. Our finances for this occasion exceeded $4,200, which was possibly the best financial effort ever staged in Mississippi by the Association. Our Mother of the Year is Mrs. Connley of Gulfport, Mississippi, who reported a whopping $843.00. As winner of the contest, she will attend our National Convention at the expense of the State Conference.

The highlight of our meeting was the fact that there were officers sitting in the vast audience with warrants for Mr. Wilkins and the Field Secretary, Medgar W. Evers. However, the warrants were not served, and according to the newspapers there were a number of state and local officials who prevented the execution of said warrants. The warrants were issued after a member of the Jackson White Citizens Council swore out affidavits for our arrest.

On Monday, the following day, the newspapers, radio and television stations, throughout the state, on every newscast remarked that our arrest was imminent, but nevertheless averted. Our pictures were photographed on the front pages of some of the Jackson papers. The effect this had on the Negro community was favorable to the NAACP.

Mack Charles Parker—A black resident of Poplarville, he was charged with raping a white woman. While waiting for trial in jail, he was abducted by a white mob and eventually shot to death in Louisiana. A grand jury returned no indictment on the known suspects, as the judge, Sebe Dale, himself a member of the all-white Citizens' Council, urged the jury to ignore evidence collected by the FBI. For more details of the case, see Howard Smead's *Blood Justice: The Lynching of Mack Charles Parker* (New York: Oxford University Press, 1988).

36 Medgar Evers, Address to Los Angeles Branch of the NAACP

MAY 31, 1959
LOS ANGELES, CA

Medgar Evers: Thank you, Mr. Newson, president, board members, members of the NAACP, friends of NAACP, ladies and gentlemen. I consider it a great honor to have this opportunity to visit with you today, and may I take this opportunity to bring to you greetings from the national office, the Mississippi State Conference of NAACP Branches, its president, Mr. C.R. Darden, members of our great organization throughout the state, and all the citizens of Mississippi who believe in justice and equality for all Americans, regardless to race, creed, or color.

You know, there was an article written in the November issue of *Ebony*, and it said about me that "These are the reasons why Medgar Evers lived in Mississippi." However, since I've been here in California, I wonder why do I live there. [audience laughter] But despite all of that, we must continue to fight for justice and equality in Mississippi, where justice does not ring out for people of color in most of the counties; in fact, the entire state.

However, before going into what I have to say here today, I would like for you to have a word, or hear a word, from the person who has suffered most from the occasion that we now memorialize; Mrs. Parker. Mrs. Parker, will you come and just say a word, just one word to the audience, please? [audience applause]

Mrs. Parker: First I want to say hi to everybody. Honestly, I tried to get around talking, but looked like to me I had to say something anyhow. I want to thank everybody that ever done anything for me. I appreciate everything you done for me. First, again, I want to let you all know that I'm not no sinner. I'm going to let you all know I am a Christian. I'm asking the prayers of whoever's praying for me that I may continue on. [audience applause]

Medgar Evers: Thank you, Mrs. Parker.

Now, ladies and gentlemen, it is not my purpose here today to malign the state of my birth, but the many obnoxious bills passed by the state and local legislatures and governments for the obvious purpose of keeping me and my posterity second-class citizens make it compelling that I should at this time unfold the truth about the conditions under which Americans of African descent live here in this great country during the century of wonders: the United Nations, Sputnik, explorers, space, atoms, the twentieth century.

Certainly many of the incidents mentioned herein will doubtless appear to be fantasies to you, but I can assure you that I shall not falsify against the state of my birth. To enumerate all of the injustices against Negro Americans in Mississippi would be next to impossible, so I shall make mention of the injustices that are most permanent— prominent, along with others less prominent, which will give some background to the state from whence I've come.

Many of the cries that are now heard echoing throughout the United States by white southerners for more time to equalize schools were never heard before 1954, the Supreme Court decision declaring segregation unconstitutional. There was hardly a whisper for adequate schools for Negroes, let alone equal schools.

There is still in existence today, less than twenty-five miles from Jackson, the state capital of Mississippi, a two-room school with potbellied stoves, housing some forty-five students to the room, with most of the windowpanes out, and the responsibility for securing wood for fuel heat left to the students and teachers. There are many other such schools throughout the state, doubtless in each county. The number could be doubled, certainly in most of them.

Mississippi started its ambitious equalization program after the May 17 decision declaring segregation unconstitutional. However, the $120 million program has come too late and it is certainly too little. Negroes in Mississippi want for their children the quality of education that will make them first-class scientists, top diplomats, and top engineers of tomorrow, and it cannot be done under the so-called separate-but-equal doctrine.

Negro teachers are brow-beaten into acquiescence by being forced to sign an affidavit stating that they do not "belong nor contribute to any organization whose purpose it is to overthrow the Constitution of the United States or the State of Mississippi." This requirement passed by the Mississippi legislature in 1956 was designed to prevent teachers, Negro teachers, from working with or contributing to the NAACP.

So we in Mississippi cannot understand why it is that Negroes in places like Los Angeles, places like New York City, places like San Francisco we have so few people who are interested in the cause for which we struggle in Mississippi. The campaign that is under way now here in your great city, there shouldn't be enough room for the people who should want to work in the campaign to get more members, to get more finances, so that we might quickly end this injustice that is perpetrated against 10 million Negroes in the southland.

I hasten to say that the program that was instituted by the legislature to prevent Negro teachers from participating with the NAACP has served its purpose well, not that the purpose of the NAACP is to overthrow the Constitution of the United States nor the State of Mississippi, except where the laws of the State of Mississippi do conflict with the supreme laws of our land as it relates to the rights of Negro Americans.

The month of May 1955, in the community of Belzoni, Mississippi, was probably the beginning of an intensified campaign of violence and economic pressures against Negro citizens who wanted the right to vote and be respected by their fellow men. It was in this community that the Reverend G.W. Lee, a militant minister for civil rights, was shotgunned to death by unknown assailants as he was en route home on this particular Saturday night. Officers tried to claim that he lost control of his car and rammed onto the porch of a house, where a piece of two-by-four was to have pierced the windshield, striking the Reverend Lee in the face, killing him almost instantly.

During the coroner's inquest there was an attempt made to say that the lead which was discovered in the Reverend Lee's jaw was filling from his teeth. This was later disproved after sending several pellets to the FBI laboratory in Washington, which revealed that the lead was that of buckshots, and classified thusly.

In August of 1955, there was the, in fact, infamous [Emmett] Till case, with which I'm sure most of you are familiar. But to briefly recapitulate, a young fourteen-year-old Negro boy from Chicago, Illinois, came down to visit some relatives in Money, Mississippi, where he was alleged to have wolf-whistled at a white woman, which irritated her husband and brother-in-law, to the extent that young Till was taken from his home early one morning, beaten, shot, and his weighted body dumped into the murky Tallahatchie River. The body was later discovered by a young white fisherman, who saw the form of a human being bobbing up and down in the water.

The men responsible for this heinous crime were apprehended, brought to trial, and as is typical of Mississippi justice, were released and today are free.

Ladies and gentlemen, at this point it is imperative that we citizens of this great country call upon our federal government to enact into law strong civil rights legislation which would include an antilynch law, to make it possible that men of color and women of color in the southland of this great country can live like decent Americans, can live like citizens, without being fearful that in driving down Highway 11 or Highway 51 or Highway 61, across the Magnolia State of Mississippi, being accused of rape, and then maliciously taken out of an unguarded jail and eventually wind up in some murky river that goes across the width and breadth of that state. It is necessary that civil rights legislation be enacted in this Congress, that will help to protect the rights of the many citizens who live below the Mason-Dixon line. [audience applause]

During the same month of August 1955, in the county of Lincoln, the city of Brookhaven, a Negro citizen by the name of Lamar Smith was busily encouraging Negroes in his community to vote, either in person or by absentee ballot. As he proceeded to get more absentee ballot forms for neighbors, several white men accosted him on the lawn of the county courthouse, beat him, and shot him to death because of his activities. The guilty parties were apprehended, later released on $20,000 bond, each, and never brought to trial, even until this day. That happened in 1955.

I am now bringing you up to date on many of the things that have happened in Mississippi. Certainly you have read about them, but many, I'm sure, you're not fully acquainted with. For example, the Reverend Gus Courts of Belzoni, Mississippi, was making change in his small grocery store late one Saturday evening in December 1955 when he heard a crashing window before him, and felt a sting in his left arm, only to look down and see blood streaming on the floor. It was then that he knew he had been shot by a load of buckshots, with only a portion of the load inflicting personal injury.

These acts of violence, coupled with economic pressures, have been the chief tactics used to discourage Negroes from seeking justice and equality in Mississippi. I'd just like to briefly give you the activities of Mr. Courts, just very briefly, during this time. He had a truck. He had a store, also. But now, with this truck he would carry tenants out to various plantations for the purpose of chopping cotton or for the purpose of picking cotton.

And, of course, each time he would make one of these trips to these plantations, some member of the Citizens Council would trail him wherever he went, and as soon as he got there and unloaded his truck with the persons who were going to work, this white member of the Citizens Council would go to the plantation owner and tell him, "You can't hire those people, because that's Gus Courts who is carrying them, and he is a member of the NAACP. He's one of those—," well, I'll say *Negroes*, "who—," he didn't say Negro, but, "He's one of those Negroes who has his name on the registration book down in Humphrey County, and we cannot support these people, because they want to take over the county."

Consequently, Mr. Courts would lose his business. He'd have to refill his truck with his people and take them back. So eventually, the people quit going with Mr. Courts, because they were fearful that the retaliations would not only be on Mr. Courts, but would also be on them. So those are some of the injustices that we encounter in Mississippi.

However, despite these and many other acts of intimidation, people around the world have an unquenchable desire to be free men and women, even in the State of Mississippi. Negro citizens in most Mississippi counties are barred from actively participating in local, state, or federal elections by Gestapo-like actions similar to the ones referred to in the cases above, in addition to the legal barriers, such as the poll tax and the twenty-one questions, which are prerequisites to voting.

And if I might just briefly, at this juncture, show you a typed form that has to be filled out before you can be a registered voter in Mississippi, it has twenty-one questions to it. Listed all the way down here, one specifically, I'd like to say, number six, "By whom are you employed?" Now, the purpose of that is to find out who your employer is, and if you go down and register, they can bring economic pressure through your employer. Consequently, we don't get the number of registered voters that we want.

Number sixteen I liked especially. "Are you a minister of the gospel in charge of an organized church, or the wife of such a minister?" That question has a twofold purpose. Number one, it is for the purpose of determining whether or not a minister presides over a flock of people who could very well be potential voters, and if so, we want to make certain that this minister does not influence those people. Consequently, we'll give him maybe fifty dollars or a hundred dollars, or we'll give him a contribution for his church and say to him, "Now, you cannot allow the NAACP to meet in your church. You cannot make contributions to the NAACP," etc., etc.

Number two to that, "If the answer to question sixteen is yes, state the length of residence in the election district." Of course, that particular one refers to the fact that each minister is entitled to vote after he or she is in the election district for at least six months.

So the first purpose that I mention to you is the one that is most prominently used. However, there are two questions on the back of this form. One says, "Write and copy in the space below Section—," it might be six or eighteen of the Constitution of Mississippi. Now, you're supposed to write that exactly as it is. Of course, you have the book itself and you write it as it is. Now, if you fail to cross a *t* or dot an *i*, you have automatically failed that course. [audience laughter] That sounds funny. I said in the beginning that it would sound like fantasies to you, but it's fact.

All right. Number nineteen says, "Write in the space below a reasonable interpretation of the section of the Constitution of Mississippi which you have just copied." Now, all the circuit clerks who are the registrars of voters in Mississippi are white. Consequently, I'd say 99 percent of them are prejudiced. Now, of course, you know what that means when a Negro goes to be registered. If you do not interpret the section that you've written to the satisfaction of this circuit clerk, then you have failed, if you manage to get beyond number eighteen.

So these are the obstacles, ladies and gentlemen, that we have to go through to register and vote. That is one of the reasons why in Mrs. Parker's community of Lumberton, which, of course, is in Lamar County—but in Poplarville, which is in Pearl River County, there are no registered Negro voters. In the county, there are approximately five to six thousand potential voters among Negroes, with not a single registered Negro voter. And in her county of Lamar, there are approximately three thousand potential registered voters. There aren't any voters at all in her particular county, and there are many other such counties where you have no registered voters.

However, out of a potential of 494,653 registered potential voters among Negroes, we have less than 30,000 qualified in the entire State of Mississippi. So when we think in terms of the people in Los Angeles, with the great opportunity that you have here to register and to vote, without any obstacles, it is really amazing to us to realize that you, in many instances, fail to take advantage of your situation out here, because to take advantage of it out here would help us in Mississippi. It would help us in Belzoni. It would help us down in

Poplarville, many of the other places, because we could get some civil rights legislation on the books that would prove profitable to all of us across the southland.

While the white man is responsible, to a great degree, for this one-sided situation, the Negro himself has not contributed all that he or she could to change the picture that has been brought before you. To illustrate, in cities like Jackson, Meridian, Morrow, Gulfport, Biloxi, Greenville, Clarksdale, a few others where Negroes are permitted to register and vote without molestation, we find that there is a considerable amount of apathy and reluctance on the part of Negroes to take advantage of the situation, which would make it easier for our fellow men to live in places like Belzoni, etc.

So often we find Negroes of means—of course, I imagine that applies to Los Angeles as well as Mississippi. So often we find Negroes of means able to do it, who could and well afford to lead our people out of the present state, but are nevertheless content with things as they are because of the personal profit that they receive from segregation and human misery. These people have been selected in Mississippi as leaders of the Negro community, in an effort to stamp out any semblance of fight for justice and equality by the more militant Negro people.

Many of these—quote—"Uncle Toms"—end quote—are given high educational posts such as principals, superintendents, and even college presidents, to bolster their community prestige. In the case of principals, there seems to be a conspiracy on the part of some of the state and county officials to name all Negro schools that are now being built after the principal, to further his or her prestige in the community.

A number of principals have assumed the role of community dictator, to the extent that they have totally discouraged the formation of Parent-Teacher Associations to work with the schools. They have expelled students who expressed an opinion or action favorable to the Supreme Court's decision declaring segregation unconstitutional, and in some instances have refused to permit student governments to function in school because of the political training it would provide some of the more aggressive students, making them—quote—"incorrigible"—end quote—to the brainwashing techniques to which the curriculums ascribe—subscribe.

I'd like to point out to you, at this particular time, two cases that are important, as far as I'm concerned. Number one, Mr. Darden, president of our Mississippi State Conference of NAACP Branches, has two sons. His two sons belong to the Youth Council of the Meridian branch NAACP. As a result of their having belonged to the Meridian branch Youth Council, they decided on one occasion, among themselves, that they were going to take some action. Well, it wasn't really any action; it was just a decision. They had decided to wear some badges commemorating the Supreme Court's decision of May 17, 1954.

Now, these badges merely had on them "U.S. Supreme Court decision, 1954," and, of course, it had the stamp of NAACP on it. These young people went to school this morning, this particular morning, with the badges on. As a result, the principal told them they'd have to pull them off. And they, of course, refused to pull them off. Excuse me. The principal insisted that they pull them off. They again refused to pull them off. So the principal suspended the students for insubordination.

So the children went home, and as a result, the parents met with the children and decided to go down and have a conference with the teacher, or the principal. As a result of this action of having this conference, the principal swore out an affidavit against Mr. Darden, who is president of our State Conference of NAACP Branches, charging him with disturbing a session of a classroom; had him arrested and fined—rather, he was released on $100 bond. He went to court, of course, and was later fined $50, which is now on appeal.

These tactics, ladies and gentlemen, are being employed against those of us in Mississippi who fight for justice and equality, basic justice, simple justice, the right to vote, a constitutional guarantee. These are many of the outstanding examples that we have where justice is not carried out.

There is one final case that I'd like to mention in this connection, a Mr. Amos Brown, who is a very bright young man, who is a senior at one of the Negro high schools in Mississippi, in Jackson. Young Mr. Brown is also president of the State Conference of Youth Councils for NAACP. He's also president of the student body, or he was, of this particular school. In addition to that, he was president of the Southeast Region of NAACP Youth Councils.

Mr. Brown attended our convention in Cleveland, Ohio, last year. As a result of his attending this convention, he made certain statements while there at the convention which got into the newspaper. As a result of these reports going back to the superintendent of education and the principal, Mr. Brown was called in when he returned. Though school was out, he was called in by the principal, and he asked him why did he make such statements while he was in Ohio.

He, of course, gave him his reasons for making the statements. He felt that this is a country where freedom of expression is guaranteed, and what he said was not contradictory to what the Supreme Court of the United States had said. And as a result, Mr. Brown was kept out of school by the principal, Negro principal, because of his action, because he felt the way that he did.

Those are two examples, ladies and gentlemen, of what we encounter in Mississippi. And we encounter it, that's why I say not from altogether the white man. We encounter it a great deal from some of our people, some of our people who are way up there, those people who feel that they have too much to lose than to get into this fight so that we can all become free men and women in a matter of no time.

During the Korean War we often read in our newspapers how the Communists were brainwashing our troops. Well, if that technique was used, it could very well have been that such a scheme was a copy that was, and still is, used on southern Negroes by whites who attempt to make the Negro believe that he is nobody, or at best, inferior to every other racial group.

Charity begins at home and spreads abroad. The hypocrisy that is practiced at home and preached abroad has begun to fall on deaf ears. For as it is often said, the things you do speak so loudly, until the things you say cannot be heard. Which brings me to this phase for which many of us have come. Ladies and gentlemen, the savagery dealt Mack Charles Parker in a—quote—"civilized society"—end quote—makes a mockery out of so-called cannibalism in the most remote areas of the world.

It appears that the only time Mississippi makes national or international headlines is when a bunch of cowards like those at Poplarville, Mississippi, take an unarmed Negro who is already at their mercy, out of an unguarded jail cell, beat him, shoot him, and throw his lifeless body into the Pearl River or some other body of water.

I'd like to say at this time, when I heard the incident relative to this terrible thing, I was moved with great compassion. You know, I lost my father in 1954, and my mother, at the time of this incident, had had a stroke, and she later died. I lost my sister earlier. But then, having lost my close relatives, as close as they were, it didn't strike me as hard as the loss of this young man, who had not been given an opportunity for justice and equality that he was due.

It was necessary for me, when I heard the newscast that morning, to go into my room, and I closed the door, and it was necessary for me to shed tears, because the injustice that had wrought this young man was not done, as I see it, by God, but it was done by ungodly men who don't believe in justice, who don't believe in equality, who believe as Walker, the sheriff, the man who's running for sheriff now, when he said, "I was interrogated by the FBI as though I were a nigger or a dog." In other words, they put us on the same basis with a dog. And in some instances, the dog is better than we are; in many instances.

Ladies and gentlemen, that is why, as long as God grants breath in my body, as long as I have two sons and a wife, and there are others in Mississippi, we're going to fight for justice and equality. [audience applause] This is not to say that all white people in Mississippi are hoodlums. Quite the contrary is true. There exists a predominance of white citizens of Mississippi who believe in law and order, justice, and a semblance of fair play. However, this group does not have the Christian courage to stand up against the lawless elements of Mississippi and demand that the laws of God, the United States, as well as many of our state laws, be complied with as moral, human obligations, placed upon our democratic society.

There is a tendency toward allowing the irresponsible to occupy high positions of trust, public trust, which has nothing less than a disastrous effect on a state as backward as Mississippi. I'd just like at this time to say this. The NAACP, from the very beginning, has been in on this case. We're going to stay in the case. [audience applause]

On Saturday, eleven days after this man had been abducted— rather, less than eleven days after this young man had been abducted, I traveled from Jackson to Lumberton. I searched around, without anyone knowing who I was, until I found Mrs. Parker. At that time I talked with her at length, and I asked her if she had secured a lawyer for her son's defense. She indicated to me that no white lawyer in that vicinity would take his case. I said, "Well, then, what do you intend to do, ma'am?"

And she indicated to me that she would like to do whatever she could, but she didn't know what to do. At that point—you know, in Mississippi they have what you call a barristry [phonetic] statute, and also they have laws to prevent, as much as possible, solicitation, should I say, of cases. Also, they have passed a law in Mississippi making it possible for them to outlaw the NAACP if they find that we are out stirring up litigation.

So, consequently, I said to Mrs. Parker, "I know of some lawyers who are in Jackson who would be happy to help you in your situation." And I gave her the list of about three Negro lawyers in Jackson, and, of course, she chose one R. Jess Brown. She came to Jackson the following Monday and, of course, we had some time getting together, because apparently we couldn't make connections. But she employed Mr. Brown to represent her. All the while, the NAACP was in on the case.

As a result of Mr. Brown's employment, at a later date the trial was set. And Mr. Brown and another attorney, Attorney Jack H. Young, who assisted Mr. Brown in this case, went down to Poplarville and apparently laid a very good foundation, so much so until there was rumored around the community that Mr. Brown and Attorney Young had a very good chance of freeing young Parker, at least establishing the fact that he did not commit this crime that they accused him of.

Now, this might be of interest to you. Not a single—there was not a positive identification of the attacker of this alleged victim who was supposed to have been raped. She never positively identified anybody. In the very beginning she said that the man who attacked her was a middle-aged man. She said he was approximately forty or fifty years old and he was rather tall and thin.

Well, when, of course, they lined these young men up and she picked Parker out as being the one, she said, "Well, I'm not sure." She said, "He looks like—he doesn't look like the one, but he—." No, she said, "He doesn't sound like the one." She said, "He kind of looked like the one, but he doesn't sound like the one." But now, Mr. Parker is a fairly dark man, according to his picture, and it was night when this was supposed to have occurred. And I would imagine it would be rather difficult for anyone to say just how a dark person looked in pitch-black dark. So, but she said, "He looked like the one, but he doesn't sound like the one." So there was never a positive identification of this young man or of any alleged attacker.

But getting back to the trial, Mr. Brown and Young laid a very solid foundation, to the extent that they were going to disprove this woman's testimony. So the rednecks, if you'll allow me to use this expression, in—and I'm going back to Mississippi. [audience laughter] I have something to go back to Mississippi for, and defend. The rednecks in this particular area met. Some thirty-five of them met, according to a report out of Washington, which is supposed to have been released by the FBI; met in a farmhouse out in the community of Pearl River County. And as a result of this meeting, thirty-five of them said that, "Now, we're going to do something about this crime. We can't allow this white woman to be cross-examined by a Negro lawyer." As a result of that, they decided on doing away with this young man.

So what happened was that they took thirty-five pieces of paper, and on ten slips of that paper they marked an *x* or some sort of mark, and the ten men who drew those pieces of paper were the ones to carry out this heinous crime. They drew the paper. The next night they carried out their mission.

According to a WDSU-TV report from New Orleans, Louisiana, these lynchers took young Parker to the Pearl River bridge which divides Bogalusa and Mississippi; Louisiana, that is. As a result of that, they were fixing to kill him. However, a car, an oncoming car came with the lights shining on them, and they decided not to carry out their mission then. Instead they drove across to the Louisiana side. They stopped at a cattle station. This is according to a report made by WDSU-TV. And, of course, after a pause of some three or four minutes, they came back to about the center of the bridge, at which time they carried out their heinous crime.

Ladies and gentlemen, I have here, and I will not show them, but I have here pictures of that heinous crime, the body of this young man. I will not show these, only to maybe some of you who might come to see them. But it was the most atrocious thing that I'd ever seen. It was something that would make any sensible Negro know that until every Negro in Pearl River County is free, we have no freedom in this country. [audience applause]

And it is necessary, it is necessary that we put forth every effort, every effort to do what we can to make freedom a reality for everybody here in this great country. [audience applause] Actually, the segregationists are losing, and they know it. That is why they are resorting to these irrational tactics. The movement today for freedom cannot be pushed back, any more than a tidal wave can be pushed back by hand.

That which seeks to destroy the freedom of man, seeks to destroy the soul of man. Man wants to be free. Yes, even in Mississippi. And we will continue to struggle for freedom. The eyes of the world are upon America. To treasure the traditions of hate and fear and cling to the traditional customs will surely lead to the destruction of our democratic way of life.

It is appalling to observe the unethical folly of men in government who think the outside world will continue to look up to America as a symbol of democracy, as long as the lynchings of Parkers and Tills and Lees and other Negroes ring out across this great continent and across the continent of Africa, Asia, and all the other countries who believe in freedom and justice and equality. [audience applause]

Theoretically, we are the greatest exponents of democracy of any nation in the world, but this on paper, and not in the hearts of men who control the policies of this great country. We cannot wait until the hearts of men are changed, to enjoy our constitutional rights. We have been patient, and remain patient, because we believe enough in our country to press vigorously for our rights, with the conviction that we will someday win first-class citizenship. [audience applause]

We are confident that we will achieve victory, not through violence, but through the channels provided by the Constitution of the United States of America, through the courts, political action, and education. If we work with sufficient dedication, we will be able to achieve in the not-too-distant future a society in which no one is discriminated against because of race, creed, or color. Our faith is invested in a law that is over and above manmade laws. We are dedicated to the cause of freedom, and will continue to fight under God's laws, without fear of consequences.

He has said—and I quote—"Blessed are ye when men shall revile you and shall persecute you, and shall say all manner of evil against you falsely, for my sake. Rejoice and be exceedingly glad, for great is your reward in heaven, for so persecuted they the prophets who were before you."

Ladies and gentlemen, I am happy to be a part of an organization that has uncompromisingly fought for justice and equality of Negro Americans, for Negro Americans. [audience applause] The NAACP has in its fifty years fought without hesitation, for all of our rights, for all of the colored people of America, and, as far as that goes, for the colored people of the world. So we should be, if we're not proud of the NAACP, proud to contribute whatever we have to offer to its continued success.

I'd just like to say this before closing, that the White Citizens Councils get their money from the taxpayers of Mississippi, my taxes and other people's taxes, and they're able to have at their disposal— for example, the first year they had $250,000 for the purpose of maintaining segregation, for the purpose of keeping your relatives second-class citizens, and keeping mine second-class citizens. So we should make sacrificial efforts to help an organization that has done more, I'd say, than any other organization, outside of the church, to help make first-class citizenship a reality here in this country. [audience applause]

In closing, I am reminded of the writings of James Weldon Johnson, who wrote, "God of our weary years, God of our silent tears, Thou who hast brought us thus far on the way; Thou who hast by Thy might, Led us into the light, Keep us forever in Thy path, we pray. Lest our feet stray from the places, our God, where we met Thee, Lest our hearts, drunk with the wine of the world, we forget Thee, Shadowed beneath Thy hand, May we forever stand, true to our God, true to our native land."

Thank you.

*

37 Monthly Report: "Speaking Engagements"

JUNE 22, 1959

SPEAKING ENGAGEMENTS

The Field Secretary visited the West Coast Region of the N.A.A.C.P. and State of California at the invitation of the president of the Los Angeles Branch, Attorney James Akers. The occasion was the protesting of the lynching of M. C. Parker, at which time the Field Secretary spoke on conditions as they exist in Mississippi. The following is an excerpt from the address:

"So often we find Negroes of means who could well afford to lead our people out of our present state but are nevertheless content with things as they are, because of the personal profit they receive from segregation and human misery. These people have been selected by whites as leaders of the Negro communities in an effort to stamp out any semblance of our fight for justice and equality by the more militant Negro people. Many of these 'Uncle Toms' are given high educational posts, such as principals, superintendents, and even college presidents, to bolster their community prestige. In the case of principals there seems to be a conspiracy, on the part of some state and county officials, to name all Negro schools that are now being built after the principal, to further his or her prestige in the community. A number of principals have assumed the role of community dictator to the extent that they have totally discouraged the formation of Parent-Teacher Associations to work with the schools; they have expelled students who expressed an opinion or action favorable to the Supreme Court Decision declaring segregation unconstitutional, and, in some instances, refused to permit student governments to function in school because of the political training it would provide some of the more aggressive students, making them 'incorrigible' to the brainwashing techniques to which the curriculum subscribes."

Also on the program was Mrs. Eliza Parker, mother of M. C. Parker. The Ward A.M.E. Church auditorium, in which the rally was held, was filled to capacity. It was also the occasion for the kick-off of the Los Angeles Branch N.A.A.C.P. membership drive, during which a number of memberships were secured and life membership pledges made.

While in Los Angeles the Field Secretary was interviewed by Lew Irwin for A.B.C. News over station KABC-TV, Los Angeles. There was also a half hour feature of Mrs. Eliza Parker and Field Secretary Evers on the Paul Coates Show over KT-TV, Sunset Blvd. Hollywood.

Following my stay in Los Angeles, the Regional Secretary-Counsel, Mr. Franklin Williams, urged that I come to the San Francisco Bay Area for a series of radio, television, and public appearances, which I did. On Thursday morning, June 4, a news conference was called. Representatives from the Chronicle, Examiner, and other news reporters, along with KRON-TV, were on hand for what was to have been a thirty minute interview, which lasted for more than an hour. At six o'clock, June 4, KRON-TV carried a filmed interview of the Field Secretary over the Shell News. Altogether, there were four taped radio interviews of the Field Secretary while in the Bay area, with a considerable amount of newspaper coverage. The Regional Office staff made it possible for me to tour the state capitol of California while the legislature was in session, and to watch the energetic action of Everett Brandon as he conversed with various assemblymen and senators in an effort to get favorable legislation through the state legislature.

Other speaking engagements were to the Men of Tomorrow Club; the West Coast Regional meeting of branch and area presidents; and finally to the Palo Alto Branch N.A.A.C.P., June 8, at the Unitarian Church, Palo Alto, California. Mr. Williams, as usual, was superb in his presentation of the Field Secretary. A question and answer period, which was full of enthusiasm, followed the address. At the conclusion the audience responded with a one minute standing ovation.

The trip was inspiring to me and I hope helpful to our West Coast Region of the N.A.A.C.P.

Franklin H. Williams (1918–1990)—After serving in the U.S. Army during World War II, Williams joined the NAACP and became an assistant to the

Association's special counsel in 1945. He was appointed as the NAACP's regional secretary-counsel, and in 1959 became the assistant attorney general of California. In 1967 he was appointed U.S. ambassador to Ghana, and three years later upon his return, he assumed the post of president of the Phelps-Stokes Fund. See Glenn Fowler, "Franklin H. Williams Dies at 72; Lawyer and Former Ambassador," *New York Times*, May 22, 1990. B11.

Everett P. Brandon—NAACP field secretary of the West Coast Regional Office. Brandon worked closely with Franklin Williams during the late 1950s and early '60s in conducting voter registration and planning boycotts of Woolworth stores. He has written commentary articles for San Francisco's *Sun Reporter* newspaper. See microfilm Guide to NAACP Papers, Part 25; Branch and Department Files; Series B, Regional Files and Special Reports, 1956–1965, available online at www.lexisnexis.com/academic/guides/Aaas/naacp2502.pdf.

38 Medgar W. Evers, Address (Excerpts)

SUNDAY, SEPTEMBER 6, 1959, 3:00 P.M.
AREA CONFERENCE OF THE FLORIDA STATE
CONFERENCE OF N.A.A.C.P BRANCHES
PANAMA CITY, FLORIDA.

Ladies and Gentlemen:

I bring you greetings from the Mississippi State Conference of N.A.A.C.P. Branches, its president, Mr. C. R. Darden, and many of the fine people who constitute this great organization. The opportunity of visiting with you and sharing the many common experiences, which we encounter during these periods of change, is indeed inspiring. It gives one to know that where there is unity there is strength—strength to overcome the seemingly impossible, and the courage to press on to the ultimate goal of first-class citizenship, even in the State of Mississippi.

While on the subject of Mississippi, recently the people of the state elected a new Governor, who is supposed to represent all of the people of this great state, but who has already begun to show his colors by proposing to speak to a Fascist-like group of White Citizens' Council members and friends at a dinner for the stated purpose of raising funds, obviously to spread race hatred and the dissemination of vile propaganda and to arouse the emotions of the illiterate and borderline whites who thrive on bigotry and race prejudice. We fervently hope, work, and pray that the time will come when, in the Governors' mansions across the Southland, there will be elected to the highest offices of our states persons who will represent the people; not white or black, but all people who live and love the Southland as we do.

You know, as dear as we are to our native Southland, we have not as a group contributed as much as we could have toward making the South the ideal place in which to live and rear our families. It is now necessary that we put forth strenuous efforts to secure economic and political strength in order to bolster our status in our respective communities. We have, for too long, overlooked our economic potential; we have likewise failed to grasp and utilize our great political potential. It is positively necessary that Negroes vote in every election, regardless; even if there is only a race for dog catcher.

While voting is important, it is more important that we register, otherwise we cannot vote.

We are concerned about our Foreign Policy and Radio Free Europe, or Voice of America as it is popularly called, but we are equally more concerned about the fact that freedom of speech is fast becoming something of the past, and the right to freely assemble, as guaranteed by the Constitution of the United States of America, is being threatened by Fascist-like elements and groups which have sprung up throughout the Southland and, in many instances, individuals occupying high places in federal, state, county and municipal governments.

We are concerned about the fact that the lynchers of Mack Charles Parker are known to the F.B.I. and state officials, however, despite this knowledge not a single person has been arrested, which raises this question. Is it excusable to lynch a person to death and inexcusable to murder one? For when one is murdered, the guilty is immediately pursued, and if apprehended, arrested; but not so with the lynchers, they are still free, though they are known.

We are making steady progress across the South with the integration of public schools. We shall continue that progress until every public school is opened to every child, regardless of race, creed or color—and this includes Mississippi.

———————————————————————————————————— *

39 Medgar W. Evers, Address, "Our Need for Political Participation"

SUNDAY, OCTOBER 25, 1959
VESPER SERVICES OF THE J. P. CAMPBELL COLLEGE

OUR NEED FOR POLITICAL PARTICIPATION
Under the American system of government, the vote is the basic tool for all citizens who would "promote the general welfare, and secure the blessings of liberty," set forth in the preamble to the Constitution.

In recent years, with increasing attention directed to the American ideal of equality for all, the access of Negro citizens to the ballot has assumed new importance.

The ballot is one of the keys to the solution of the myriad problems of segregation. Through our vote, the Negro citizens can be heard and given equal consideration along with other groups representing business, labor, veterans, and farmers.

Due in large part to the power of the Negro vote, both major political parties have included in their platforms stronger resolutions aimed at improving the lot of the Negro citizen.

This is not to imply that only practical considerations will focus attention on the plight of the nation's 18 million non-white citizens. A kind of national soul-searching began with World War II. While fighting a war against forces proclaiming a doctrine of racial superiority, it became increasingly difficult to justify racial discrimination at home. Since then, the difficulty has mounted as questions about discrimination have been raised with each new court case, whether involving school desegregation or other efforts to obtain civic justice, with each publicized case of violence against Negro citizens.

At the same time, there has been a new awareness of the threat to all citizens in the denial of individual liberties to some.

During the same period, as the United States became the leader of the free world, racial injustice at home has been an ever-growing source of embarrassment. In emerging areas of Africa and Asia it is one of our greatest liberties.

No one has understood this better than the Negro citizens of the United States. World opinion, as well as individual rights, have been stressed repeatedly in their demands for political equality.

Any study of the political behavior of the Negro voter must begin with the recognition that he is an American citizen first and is basically influenced by the same kind of political considerations which motivate other American voters. But because of disabilities peculiar to the Negro as a racial group, there are additional factors which condition his voting habits. Other groups, of course, are also influenced by considerations affecting their special interests. Each believes that a government that gives due consideration to his special interest is good government for the whole American people.

Race is no factor in registration or voting in many states and in some counties in Mississippi, but, as is the case, Negroes have been slothful in asserting the privilege that is theirs. Registration and voting have lagged to some extent because we have no political machines to herd voters to the registrar or to the polls. That task must be assumed by organizations interested in the welfare of Negro citizens.

The enhanced position of the Negro in the political life of the nation is bound to sharpen up competition for our vote. Politicians with little or no personal concern with civil rights want our vote in order to use public office to cope with other pressing problems.

The future of the Negro voter is very large in the hands of the Negro citizen and voter. The burden of improvement rests primarily with the Negro himself. Negro citizens must prepare to present themselves in numbers to be qualified, and that preparation is their responsibility. There is no attempt here to underestimate the forces of resistance, the ignorance, trickery, fear, threats, and physical assaults that have been employed and will continue to be employed. But their eradication will not be accomplished by some miracle out of the sky, some wished-for relief from a far-off place: it will be downed primarily through the intelligence, diligence, persistence and courage of the population presently disfranchised. This population as a whole must be like the lone colored woman who presented herself on seven successive Saturday mornings to be registered and was finally enrolled. Let no man say that it is somehow unfair or unethical for Negro citizens to push politically for their rights as citizens. If it is legitimate to lobby and use political pressure to secure wider markets and fatter profits, what is so wrong with using political power to secure human rights? The answer is "nothing" and Negro Americans should proceed on that basis.

All the effort will have been wasted in a sense if, after the battle has been won and the right to vote freely has been secured, the Negro citizen uses his ballot in a purely selfish and narrowly racial manner. To the degree that Negro Americans use their ballot for the maintenance for all citizens of the constitutional guarantees of liberty, i.e., for the preservation and strengthening of the American ideal, they will demonstrate the maturity which must be the end product of citizenship in a democratic society.

✳

40 Medgar W. Evers, Field Secretary, Comments on Mississippi NAACP Operations

JANUARY 1960

The influential work of the National Association for the Advancement of Colored People, on a national scope as well as local, has made its everlasting impression in many areas of Mississippi life; to be specific:

(1) The Association's program on registration and voting has created an awareness of the Mississippi Negro vote potential to the extent that wherever there is a gathering of individuals, particularly urban, it is becoming normal to discuss before departing the importance of voting. Many Negro owned businesses, particularly in the City of Jackson, are stipulating that in order to work one must be a registered voter, if otherwise qualified.

Organizations, such as the Crusade for Voters and similar names, have been formed through the guidance of the N.A.A.C.P. for the specific purpose of registration and voting.

The year of 1960 should see a tremendous increase in the number of Negro voters in the State of Mississippi.

(2) Segregation was attacked in two (2) areas in Mississippi during 1959, both in the field of Education and Recreation. In education, Mr. Clyde Kennard of Hattiesburg, Mississippi, filed an application for undergraduate work at Mississippi Southern College. His application was turned down. Legal action is now pending.

A petition to the Harrison County, Mississippi Board of Supervisors by Negro citizens of said county to "open the beaches on an unrestricted basis" provoked deep feelings between the citizenry of Harrison County. Compromises offered by the Board were refused by Negroes who are not interested in "a portion" of the beach front. The coming year, 1960, promises more attacks on segregation in Mississippi.

(3) Membership and Fund Raising. There was an increase in membership and fund raising during the year of 1959, chiefly because of early planning and conscientious work. For example, our Laurel, Mississippi Branch NAACP membership increase is a result of planning and conscientious work on the part of the members. Other areas produced good plans for membership but they were not carried out.

During the month of January, 1959, the Mississippi State Conference Board approved a state-wide fund raising project—Mother of the Year—which was very successful. The second year for this same project promises to be even more successful. In fact, the overall NAACP program has an outstanding outlook for the future.

State Conferences: Action. Enumerate all activities with State Conferences during the year, such as program developments, obtaining speakers, notices, press releases, etc. Be sure to include your impressions, suggestions and observations.

The Mississippi Field Secretary for the N.A.A.C.P. worked with the State Conference in a state-wide fund raising drive—Mother of the Year Contest, May 17th Celebration Program; State Conference Board Meetings; the 14th Annual Conference and the voting program.

Speakers for the Mississippi State Conference for 1959 included: Mr. Roy Wilkins, Executive Secretary, May 17; Mr. Kelly M. Alexander, Pres., North Carolina State Conference; Rev. W. P. Taylor, District Supt., Hattiesburg District of the Methodist Church; and Attorney R. B. Sugarmon, all participating on the program of the 14th Annual Mississippi State Conference of NAACP Branches. Press Releases were in excess of twenty-five (25) for the year of 1959.

Impressions: My impression is that there is a change in attitude of many of the would be "die-hards" in the state. This is not to say, however, that the fight is won, but, rather, that we are winning it faster than I think we even realize. The election of Ross Barnett for Governor, for the next four years, created a state of apprehension in the minds of many, but even Barnett sees the handwriting on the wall.

Observations: In observing the three-day trial of Robert Lee Goldsby, which was apparently without tension—despite the fact that a Negro had killed a white woman—might be an indication, particularly in Jackson, of the change that is taking place in the struggle for human rights.

Suggestions: There must be, however, an intensification of our work in the state, if we are to reach our goal of being free by 1963.

Clyde Kennard (?–1963)—A former US paratrooper, Kennard in 1956 and 1958 applied for admission to the Mississippi Southern College, and after his rejection in 1959, he was arrested with the charge of allegedly stealing $25 worth of chicken feed from a white neighbor. Despite no real evidence, Kennard was convicted and sentenced for seven years in prison, where his health deteriorated beyond recovery. Kennard died in 1963 shortly after being released from prison. Subsequent investigations completely exonerated Kennard, and one of the buildings of the University of Southern Mississippi is today named after him. See Myrlie Evers, *For Us the Living* (Garden City, NY: Doubleday, 1967), 214–223; and Katagiri, *The Mississippi State Sovereignty Commission*, 55–61, 127–128.

Kelly Miller Alexander (1915–1980)—Alexander joined the Charlotte NAACP in 1940 and succeeded in revitalizing the dormant branch. For this success he was elected president of the North Carolina State Conference of the NAACP in 1948. In 1950, Alexander was elected to the National NAACP Board of Directors and became a Life Member in 1954. Under his leadership, the North Carolina NAACP witnessed a remarkable increase in membership and branch activities during the 1950s and 1960s. See http://www.library.uncc.edu/display/?dept=special&format=open&page=386#BiographicalNote.

Russell B. Sugarmon (1929–?)—A native of Memphis, Sugarmon became the first African American to run for public works commissioner in Memphis. In 1964, Sugarmon won election to the Tennessee Democratic Party Executive Committee, and two years later ran successfully for the State Senate. He has retained the elected post in General Sessions bench from 1988 to the present. See http://www.thehistorymakers.com/biography/biography.asp?bioindex=622&category=lawMakers.

---

*

41 "Race Sentencing Hit, NAACP Compares Terms of Negroes and Whites," United Press International
New York Times

JANUARY 23, 1960

JACKSON, Miss. (UPI)—The actions taken against white youths at Corinth in the killing of a Negro boy and the penalties given Negro teen-agers at Tupelo for the stabbings of three white men were compared today by the National Association for the Advancement of Colored People.

The cases "indicate the inconsistency of Mississippi justice for Negroes and whites," said Medgar Evers, Mississippi field secretary of the N.A.A.C.P.

At Corinth, one white teenager was indicted on a reduced charge of manslaughter for the shotgun slaying of a Negro boy Halloween night.

Last month at Tupelo, one Negro teen-ager was sentenced to life imprisonment, another was sentenced to twenty-five years in prison and a third to twenty years for stabbing three white men. They were charged with armed robbery, a capital offense.

---

*

42 Medgar W. Evers, Address, Men's Day Program of the Freemont A.M.E.

SUNDAY, FEBRUARY 28, 1960, 3:00 P.M.
MILES, MISSISSIPPI

Christian friends, brothers and sisters, ladies and gentlemen. I consider it a blessing from almighty God to have this very spiritual pleasure to fellowship with you on this men's day program and to be able to acknowledge the very presence of God within me.

All that I have said thus far leads us to here. Today is "Man's Obligation to God and Man." *Obligation to God.* You know we are not as grateful and obliging to God as he would have us be. We men often take our being too much for granted. We often feel that our responsibility and obligation to God ends when we make a liberal church contribution and attend services regularly. Granted, both are essentials in our daily Christian lives, but an equally important factor is often expressed in the "negative" by the following quotation.

"Man's inhumanity to man makes countless thousands mourn." As I remember from my youth being taught the Golden Rule of "Do unto others as you would have them do unto you," that part of the Golden Rule is now in many instances being shelved as being obsolete or outdated and therefore no longer usable in this day and time, which is possibly the saddest mistake we find ourselves making.

Man is, I would say, God's chosen creature on the face of the earth so much so until in creation God said, "Let us make man in our image, after our likeness and let them have dominion over the fish of the sea and over the fowl of the air, and over the cattle, and over the earth, and over every creeping thing that creepeth upon the earth." So God created man in His own image, in the image of God, created He him; male and female, created He them.

If we note with care the word image which means likeness or an imitation of any person or thing one is immediately impressed with the fact that we are God's children who possess His likeness and who consequently should do His will. That is unquestionably the obligation man owes to God—do His will.

Now we come to the other part of our topic, "Man's obligation to man." Certainly we cannot do the will of God without treating our fellow man as we would have him treat us. It is a biblical axiom that to say you love God and hate your fellow man is hypocrisy of possibly the greatest magnitude. So many of us fall into this category, either consciously or unconsciously, until it behooves each of us to check ourselves closely so as to avoid becoming a party to hate, or misunderstanding.

While we must not hate our fellow man, black, white, yellow, or what have you, we must nevertheless stand firmly on those principles we know are right, which brings us to the point of being reminded of the courage of Joshua and Caleb when after 40 years of bondage under the Egyptians and 40 years of freedom, there were many among the Israelites who wanted to go back into Egypt and slavery because they were not willing to suffer for a cause and for a principle. So it is today many people are not willing to stand up for a cause and a principle. Many persons are willing to sacrifice their birthright back into slavery, maintain segregation, and take the easy way out rather than to suffer a little and gain what is rightfully theirs. In this instance, we find history repeating itself.

We, as men, owe it to our fellow man and to our children to stand firm and stand out for those things that we are entitled to. I count it a blessing from God that I am able to withstand ridicule and abuse because I am willing to take a stand for my fellow man though many show no appreciation for the work that we are trying to do in their behalf. But let it not be said in the final analysis when history will only record those glorious moments. And when your grandchildren will invariably ask: "Granddaddy, what role did you play in helping to make us free men and free women? Did you actively participate in the struggle or was your support only a moral one?" Certainly each person here, and man in particular, should be in a position to say, "I was active in the struggle for all phases for your unrestricted privileges as an American citizen."

Christian friends, we are in a righteous struggle. We are living in a great day, a momentous day, a glorious day, a day that will be forever inscribed in the annals of history and in the minds of men.

Now, my friends, I have one or two requests to make and I feel that these requests should be the paramount objective of each person here today: Number one—let us vow to treat our fellow man as we would like him [to] treat us. Two, let us be in a spirit of coopera-

Medgar in high school, about 1946 or 1947.

Twenty-year-old Medgar,
posing in his Army uniform;
taken in Paris, early 1946.

Medgar during his college years at Alcorn State.

Alcorn A&M College football team. Medgar is second from right in front row; 1950 or 1951.

Medgar and Myrlie cut their wedding cake. Vicksburg, Mississippi, December 24, 1951.

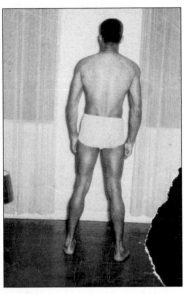

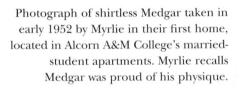

Photograph of shirtless Medgar taken in early 1952 by Myrlie in their first home, located in Alcorn A&M College's married-student apartments. Myrlie recalls Medgar was proud of his physique.

Medgar and Myrlie relax on the couch in their Mound Bayou home.

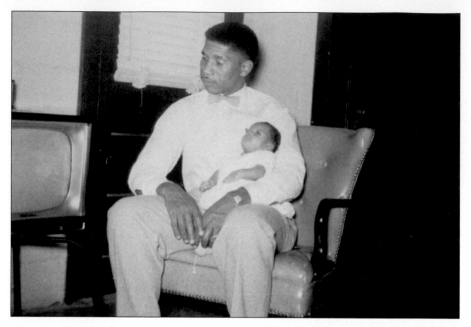

Medgar holds infant daughter Reena on his lap while watching television; Mound Bayou, Mississippi, 1954.

Medgar playing with son, Darrell, at home in Mound Bayou, Mississippi, about 1954. Myrlie took this photograph.

Evers family portrait taken by Farish Street News Stand and Studio, Jackson, about 1956. Reena Denise sits on Myrlie's lap; Darrell Kenyatta is in the center.

Medgar sitting on a speakers' platform at a mass desegregation rally held at the Masonic Temple, Jackson, Mississippi, in 1963. NAACP leader Roy Wilkins is seated at extreme right.

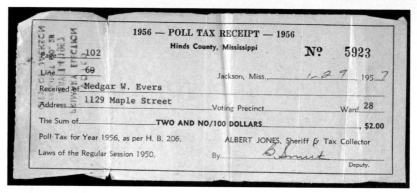

Medgar's poll-tax receipt, representing his eligibility to vote. Address indicates the first home of the Evers family when they moved from Mound Bayou to Jackson, Mississippi.

1963 strategy session of Mississippi's NAACP leadership. Meeting held at an African American church in Jackson, Mississippi.

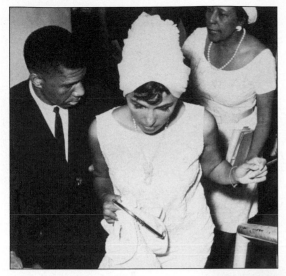

Medgar with actress Lena Horne, appearing at a civil-rights rally in Jackson, June 1963. Medgar appears extremely fatigued, Myrlie observes. Horne would later state that throughout her visits to Mississippi she felt "safe because of Medgar."

Medgar with a young girl who was a victim of police brutality; Jackson, Mississippi, 1963.

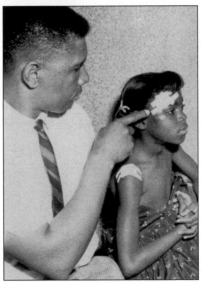

Mass meeting organized by the NAACP at a church in Jackson, Mississippi; probably taken in 1963.

Press conference of desegregation campaign's leadership in Jackson, Mississippi, during 1963. NAACP national leader Roy Wilkins is seated at left; Medgar is seated in center.

Medgar's NAACP membership card.

Address By Medgar W. Evers, Mississippi Field Secretary
of the National Association for the Advancement of
Colored People

MASTER OF CEREMONIES, DEDICATED MEMBERS OF THE NATIONAL ASSOCIATION
FOR THE ADVANCEMENT OF COLORED PEOPLE, FRIENDS, LADIES AND GENTLEMEN:

I BRING YOU GREETINGS FROM THE MISSISSIPPI STATE CONFERENCE OF NAACP
BRANCHES, IT'S PRESIDENT DR. AARON E. HENRY, AND MANY OF THE FINE
PEOPLE WHO CONSTITUTE THIS GREAT ORGANIZATION. THE OPPORTUNITY OF
VISITING WITH YOU AND SHARING THE MANY COMMON EXPERIENCES, WHICH WE
ENCOUNTER DURING THESE PERIODS OF CHANGE, IS INDEED INSPIRING, IT
GIVES ONE TO KNOW THAT WHERE THERE IS UNITY THERE IS STRENGTH--
STRENGTH TO OVERCOME THE SEEMINGLY IMPOSSIBLE, AND THE COURAGE TO
PRESS ON TO THE ULTIMATE GOAL OF FIRST-CLASS CITIZENSHIP, EVEN IN
THE STATE OF MISSISSIPPI.

THIS FIGHT FOR FREEDOM, JUSTICE AND EQUALITY IS NOT A NEW FIGHT.
THE NEGRO HAS ALWAYS FOUGHT AGAINST ENSLAVEMENT. THE FIGHT WAS
CARRIED ON BY A FEW NEGROES DURING THE DAYS OF DRED SCOTT AND
FREDERICK DOUGLAS, WHEN THE COURTS WERE AGAINST US. THE COURTS
WERE STILL AGAINST US IN 1896, WHEN THE CASE OF PLESSY vs FERGUSON
WAS RENDERED. WE CONTINUED TO FIGHT UNTIL WE GOT A FAIR DECISION MAY
17, 1954, AND NOW WE MUST WORK AND SACRIFICE FOR THE IMPLEMENTATION OF
THAT HISTORIC DECISION. WE CALL UPON ALL WHO BELIEVE IN EQUALITY AND
JUSTICE TO WORK FOR MAKING THIS GREAT NATION THE SYMBOL OF DEMOCRACY
THAT OUR FOREFATHERS INTENDED IT TO BE.

THESE ARE TROUBLED TIMES. SELDOM, IN A LIFETIME, HAS A MAN SEEN A
CRISIS SO DEEP AS THIS. AMERICA'S TROUBLES ARE DOUBLED. THE POWER'S
THAT BE CANNOT CONCENTRATE ON DEFENSE MEASURES, NOR CAN THEY DEPEND
ON THE STATES TO COOPERATE IN SELLING DEMOCRACY TO OTHER NATIONS OF
THE WORLD IN AN EFFORT TO ESTABLISH WORLD PEACE, UNTIL ALL PEOPLE WITH-
IN THEIR BORDERS ARE GIVEN EQUAL OPPORTUNITY TO LIFE, LIBERTY AND THE
PURSUIT TO HAPPINESS.
WE WILL NEED ALL OF OUR BEST MINDS, REGARDLESS OF RACE, CREED OR
COLOR, TO PREPARE FOR THE NEW AND AWESOME AGE IN WHICH WE ARE LIVING.
MANY THOUGHTFUL AMERICANS ARE SHOCKED BY THE REALIZATION, THAT WHILE

Text of one of Medgar's speeches, with handwritten notes. Medgar usually prepared
texts for formal, public presentations, but he often departed from his prepared
remarks. Medgar primarily excelled as an informal speaker with smaller, intimate
audiences.

file, and 74 per cent of the leaders.

These lower ratings do not reflect opposition, however. What they signify is simply that one-third to three-quarters of the Negro rank and file are unsure of what these organizations are and what they have done. Even Martin Luther King's Southern Christian Leadership Conference goes unrecognized by a third of Negroes polled. Clearly the roots of the Negro revolution lie not so much in the strength of its leadership as in the consciousness of the rank and file.

Some findings on other individual Negro leaders:

▶Harlem Rep. Adam Clayton Powell got plus marks from 51 per cent of the rank and file, 52 per cent of the leaders. But some down-rate him. New York piano mover Raymond Telefair says: "When things get thick he thins out."

▶U.S. Circuit Judge Thurgood Marshall wins 64 per cent approval among the rank and file and a sky-high 94 per cent among the leaders. Basil Wilmington Brown of Highland Park, Mich., assessed him this way: "He was great because of the many, many years of legal work culminating in the segregation decision in the Supreme Court."

▶Best-selling writer James Baldwin, high priest of the Negro's anguish, gets a favorable reading from only 40 per cent of the rank and file but goes up to 67 per cent among the leaders.

▶Among Negro entertainers, it is the militant ones who get the highest marks. A relative newcomer like Chicago comedian Dick Gregory, who was conspicuously jailed during the Birmingham riots, scores higher (62 per cent favorable) than such an internationally known name as Harry Belafonte (58 per cent).

In short, it is a dictate of this social revolution that the leaders must prove themselves on the civil-rights battlefields —and the poll statistics make it clear that the leaders have won their spurs the hard way. Compared with 4 per cent of the rank and file, 21 per cent of the leadership or their families have gone to jail sometime during the fight for civil rights. Thirty-nine per cent have joined in sit-ins; 54 per cent have picketed a store; 62 per cent have marched in a demonstration; and 70 per cent have boycotted stores. Mrs. Ruby Hurley, the NAACP's Southeastern regional director in Atlanta says: "There are easier ways to make a living."

All through the leadership interviews ran the common theme of urgency. "Progress shouldn't be made yesterday," said Massachusetts' Attorney General Edward W. Brooke. "You don't stop beating your wife with all deliberate speed, you stop right now," added Philadelphia Councilman-at-Large Marshall L. Shepard. Seven out of ten Negro

Who Are the Leaders—How They Rate

Ratings by Rank and File			Ratings by the Leaders	
Favorable	Poor		Favorable	Poor
88	1	Martin Luther King Jr.	95	1
80	1	Jackie Robinson	82	2
79	1	James Meredith	81	1
78	1	Medgar Evers	92	1
68	1	Roy Wilkins	92	0
64	*	Thurgood Marshall	94	1
62	2	Ralph Bunche	87	2
60	1	Dick Gregory	80	3
56	3	Harry Belafonte	73	2
55	3	Lena Horne	68	2
53	3	Floyd Patterson	50	9
51	7	Adam Clayton Powell	52	16
40	1	James Baldwin	67	3
15	29	Elijah Muhammad	17	65

*Less than 1 per cent

July 29, 1963

Newsweek public-opinion poll of African Americans' rankings of black national leaders and public personalities; appeared in the July 29, 1963 issue. Evers is ranked among the top tier of African American leadership, including Dr. Martin Luther King, Jr., Jackie Robinson, James Meredith, Roy Wilkins.

Photograph taken in front of Evers home, 1963. In front, son James Van Dyke Evers. In rear, left to right: James Meredith, Medgar, and James Baldwin.

Photo of Evers addressing a desegregation rally, in 1963.

The last formal portrait of
Medgar; taken in Jackson
in 1962 or 1963.

Medgar and Myrlie at work in the NAACP office in Jackson, Mississippi. No date.

STATE OF MISS. OPERATOR'S LICENSE NO.	PERSONAL DESCRIPTION			
	DATE OF BIRTH			
7 2 2 1 8 6	7 0 2 2 5			MEDGAR W EVERS
RESTRICTION CODE NUMBERS (SEE OTHER SIDE FOR EXPLANATION)	RACE	SEX	EYES	HAIR
	C M		BR	BK	2 3 3 2 GUYNES ST
MO. DAY YR.	WEIGHT		HEIGHT FT. INS.	
6 3 0 6 4	1 6 0		5 1 1	JACKSON

↑ EXPIRES ↑

Medgar W Evers

SIGN ON THIS LINE — VOID
UNLESS SIGNED IN INK

LEWIS 3118

MISS.

Medgar's driver's license bears the blood from his assassination on June 12, 1963.

Funeral procession of Medgar Wiley Evers in downtown Jackson; June 15, 1963.

Evers family meeting with President John F. Kennedy in the White House Oval Office following Medgar's burial at Arlington National Cemetery; June 19, 1963. Left to right: Myrlie, daughter Reena, President Kennedy, son Darrell Kenyatta, a D.C. NAACP leader, Medgar's brother Charles. President Kennedy informed Myrlie at this occasion that her husband's death would help to ensure the passage of the Civil Rights Act he had just submitted to Congress.

Float at Watts, Los Angeles, annual parade; Myrlie was one of the parade's honorary marshals. Photograph was taken by Rolland "Speedy" Curtis, late 1960s or early 1970s.

Press conference held following the guilty verdict handed down against Medgar's assassin, segregationist Byron De La Beckwith; Jackson, Mississippi, February 5, 1994. Myrlie at left center with son Darrell Kenyatta standing behind and above.

tiveness. For example, the Rev. Dr. Martin Luther King and others in Montgomery, Alabama have to me set an example of cooperation that has been unexcelled in my lifetime and possibly yours.

Those Christian people in Montgomery have really demonstrated cooperation, and how effective it can be in a community. Certainly Rev. King and others demonstrating through actual practice what they preach from the pulpit can be used in other forms of protest such as registering and voting, which is my third request: that you select a committee in your community to teach the importance and use of the ballot, so that every person twenty-one years and above is provided with transportation to go down and register in order to vote.

My last request is that you support more earnestly the *National Association for the Advancement of Colored People*, an organization that has contributed more than any other in our struggle for first class citizenship. Just think where we would have been today had it not been for the work of the *National Association for the Advancement of Colored People*. Many of the achievements of the organization have been forgotten or ignored. For example, the grandfather clause and the white primaries were declared unconstitutional through the legal maneuvering of the organization. Restrictive covenants, discrimination in public education, and the separate but equal doctrine, have all been declared contrary to the U.S. Constitution and the American way of life, and even here in our state where sickness knows no color. Veterans Hospitals have been integrated, and in Mississippi.

Furthermore the average member of the organization is a member of some church, which strengthens our ties with the churches, almighty God, and this great nation of ours.

As men living in as highly a diversified and complex society as ours, it is our duty and responsibility to our fellow men and our children to tackle the problems that lie ahead with faith and courage. Faith that is spoken of in the Bible, which in paraphrase says: "Only possess the faith of a small mustard seed and you will be able to move mountains, and then the courage to withstand the greatest onslaught the enemy can muster and you are bound to succeed." No, it will not be easy, but neither does one find it altogether easy to be a Christian in this very sin-sick world.

I am reminded here of a secular song, the lyrics of which are as follows: "Give me some men who are stout-hearted men, who will fight for the rights they adore. Start me with ten who are stout-hearted men, and I will soon give you ten thousand more. Oh, shoulder to shoulder and bolder and bolder, they grow as they go to meet the foe. Then! There is nothing in this world that can halt or mar a plan when we stick together man to man." I have no doubt in my mind that the lyrics to that song have a very appropriate meaning in this day and time.

Then it was Samuel Garth who said, "When honor is lost it is a threat to die; death; but a sure retreat from infamy."

* * *

43 (1) Medgar Evers to Gloster B. Current

March 9, 1960

Dear Mr. Current:

In reply to your memorandum dated March 2, 1960, I wish to report that presently no demonstrations have taken place in Miss., however, plans are being made to make protests in various cities in the state. On Sunday, March 13th, the Miss. State Board of the NAACP is meeting in a special session to discuss plans for activities relative to strikes, boycotts, etc. I shall report to you immediately following the Board's action.

The unrest of young people throughout the southland and the nation has had its influence on the young people at Tougaloo College and Campbell College here in the Jackson area. I am scheduled to speak at Tougaloo and organize a chapter there Friday, March 11th.

I am presently negotiating with the administration of J. P. Campbell College, an A.M.E. school here in Jackson, for the possibility of organizing a chapter there. I will also report on the outcome of these activities.

Sincerely yours,

Medgar W. Evers
Field Secretary
MWE:gb

(2) C. R. Darden, President, Mississippi State Conference Branches, NAACP, to Medgar Evers

March 14, 1960
P.O. Box 109
Meridian, Mississippi

Mr. Medgar Evers
1072 W. Lynch
Jackson, Mississippi

Dear Medgar:

I have had ample time to meditate and to pray over the most unpleasant meeting that I have attended of any kind. I am reminded of your influence, in that you took your American Legion and took over the Jackson Branch, which by its record has proved to be a miserable failure. Now, after many conflicts you have proven that this old adage is true, "It is human to error, but to persist is devilish." Your conduct has forced me to inform you that this matter is not rested.

Regretfully yours,

C. R. Darden, State President

(3) C. R. Darden to Gloster B. Current

March 14, 1960
P.O. Box 109
Meridian, Mississippi

Mr. Gloster Current
20 W. 40th Street
New York, New York

Dear Gloster:

I regret having to bring this matter to your attention again but I have had enough. Medgar Evers is too much of an antagonist in the board meetings to be tolerated. He took his American Legion of Jackson, Mississippi, took over the Jackson Branch of NAACP, and there has been nothing in the Jackson Branch but confusion since that election of American Legion to NAACP Branch officers. A conference with you is necessary when I come up for the April Board Meeting.

Very sincerely yours,

Mississippi State Conference Branches, NAACP

C. R. Darden, Pres.

(4) Medgar Evers to Gloster B. Current

March 15, 1960

Mr. Gloster B. Current
Director of Branches
20 West 40th Street
New York 18, New York

Dear Mr. Current:

On Sunday, March 13th, at 3:45 P.M., the Mississippi State Conference of Branches met in special session at the request of President

C. R. Darden, chairman of the board. The agenda for the meeting is enclosed and the first item is the report of the President, who attempted to reprimand you, Mrs. Hurley, Herb Wright, and myself as national officers for attempting to go over his head and the authority of the board by discussing, in Memphis during our regional meeting, ways and means of permitting Mississippi youth to participate in nation-wide protests against racial segregation and discrimination.

His accusations were to the effect that: "Gloster B. Current has no right to tell Mississippi what to do."

His emphasis was that we were interested in organizing sit-downs in Woolworth's and Kress stores in the Jackson and Greenville areas. However, after some length he permitted me to make explanation of our position, which was to the effect that no sit-down strikes in Mississippi were advisable, but rather some form of brief protests to indicate to the rest of the nation that Governor Coleman's pronouncement that negroes are satisfied would not be augmented by complete silence, while everyone else is protesting Jim Crow. This explanation registered with the members of the board, however, his attitude became even more belligerent and he accused the national office of trying to dictate the internal affairs of the Mississippi State Conference of Branches.

The President's original position, that there would be no protest in Mississippi of young people, particularly if the NAACP was to be part of it, prevailed. His contention was if members of our Youth Council were involved in protest movements of any sorts, hatred for the organization would be more pronounced than ever before.

Many of the board members demanded an apology from him when he launched a personal, unprovoked attack on the Field Secretary. Despite a rather hectic meeting, plans for our Mother of the Year seem inevitably to be more successful this year than last. Also out of the meeting came a committee set up to work out a program of action to be submitted to the State Board which meets again on the morning of May 15th at 11:00 A.M. in Jackson.

Sincerely yours,

Medgar W. Evers
Field Secretary
MWE:gb
encl.
cc: Mrs. Ruby Hurley

James Plemon Coleman (1914–1991)—The fifty-second governor of the state of Mississippi (1956–1960), Colemán was the first governor to be elected after the 1954 *Brown* decision. The state legislature during his tenure passed various resolutions prohibiting school integration and created the infamous State Sovereignty Commission. Coleman used the SSC to put various NAACP members under surveillance. In 1967, Coleman was appointed to the United States Fifth Circuit Court of Appeals, the position he held until his retirement in 1984. See Katagiri ——http://mshistory.k12.ms.us/features/feature48/governors/coleman.htm.

 44 Monthly Report: "Branch Activity" and "Sit-Down Protests"

MARCH 22, 1960

BRANCH ACTIVITY
The southwide student protest has generated a deal of activity on the part of Mississippi Branches; we have begun to get more activity out of branches that were on the verge of collapsing. An example of one of these branches is that of the Hattiesburg Branch who with a change of president has launched a campaign to secure five hundred members and two hundred and fifty youth members. Previously Hattiesburg has had no youth council, however, in a mass

meeting held Monday, March 21, at which time the Laurel Youth Council choir sang and Dr. B. E. Murph of Laurel spoke, the Hattiesburg Branch organized its first Youth Council with thirty-three young people joining, making their selection of officers and committee chairmen.

The Laurel Branch of NAACP kicked off its campaign to get five hundred adult members and six hundred and fifty youth members during 1960, and under Dr. Murph's dynamic leadership it is very likely that their goal will be attained.

In a meeting with members of the Moss Point–Pascagoula Branch Friday, March 18th, a goal of some three hundred members was set with plans for organizing a youth council within the next month outlined. In this small community enthusiasm for the program of NAACP was quite apparent. Meeting with the Gulfport and Pass Christian Branches indicated a revitalization of these two branches. The Gulfport Branch membership goal is two hundred and the Pass Christian Branch's goal is one hundred. The Vicksburg Branch met with the Field Secretary March 4th in the second of a series of meetings leading up to the kick-off of their membership campaign which is set for Sunday, April 10th; their goal is five hundred members.

SIT-DOWN PROTESTS

In the State Board meeting Sunday, March 13th, the question was raised by a number of board members as to why Mississippi was apparently "dragging its feet" in the protest demonstrations. The President, chairman of the board, Mr. C. R. Darden indicated that there were things far more important that the State Conference should engage itself in, especially registration and voting. It was his feeling that the NAACP in Mississippi should not encourage demonstrations of any kind, because in his words, "It would create more hate by whites for the NAACP." Despite the fact that there were others of the board who disagreed with the chairman's position, his wishes prevailed.

The general attitude in Mississippi, especially among our Branches on the coast and in the Delta, is that the State Conference is being too cautious, thereby creating a situation which would make it difficult to get a desired number of members or more participation in general, financially, etc. However, in accordance with the national program of NAACP we are getting out to each of our branches a memorandum from the State Office, suggesting that they abstain from the purchase of items from the stores named by the national board of directors and others that discriminate against negro patrons.

[...]

Respectfully submitted,

Medgar W. Evers
Field Secretary
MWE:gb

Benjamin E. Murph (?–1972)—A Laurel dentist and leader of the Jones County NAACP, Murph served in the integrated Laurel School Board and joined the Laurel Urban Renewal Agency. See Dittmer, 275, 342; and the on-line State Sovereignty Commission File, [1–29–0–1–1–1–1], http://mdah. state.ms.us/arlib/contents/er/

---

*

CHAPTER V

KEEP YOUR

EYES

ON THE PRIZE

Documents 45–55
(April 19, 1960–December 20, 1960)

. . . Freedom's name is mighty sweet,

soon one day we're gonna meet.

. . . Got my hand on the Gospel plow

I wouldn't take nothing for my journey now.

The only chain that a man can stand,

Is that chain of hand in hand . . . .

CHORUS

Hold on, hold on,

Keep your eyes on the prize,

Hold on, hold on . . . .

Keep your eyes on the prize

Freedom Song, 1960s.
"Keep Your Eyes on the Prize," adapted from the traditional spiritual and reprinted in Guy Carawan and Candie Carawan, eds., Sing for Freedom: The Story of the Civil Rights Movement through its Songs *(Bethlehem, PA: Sing Out Publications, 1990), 111.*

THROUGHOUT THE SPRING of 1960, a wave of largely student-led, nonviolent demonstrations occurred in hundreds of Southern cities and towns. By the end of April over 60,000 young people, black and white, had been arrested challenging racial-segregation laws denying blacks access to public accommodations. That month, SCLC director Ella Baker coordinated a youth conference in Raleigh, North Carolina, leading to the creation of a new, militant civil-rights organization, the Student Nonviolent Coordinating Committee (SNCC). Many of SNCC's leaders and field organizers—Marion Barry, Robert Moses, Julian Bond, John Lewis, Stokely Carmichael (Kwame Ture), Fannie Lou Hamer—would play enormously important roles in the Black Freedom Movement throughout the decade of the sixties. The insurgence of African American youth and student activism in the South inspired similar protests throughout the country. In Las Vegas, Nevada, for example, threats of an NAACP-led boycott and protests forced casino and gambling-club owners to abandon the practice of segregating black customers. In May, pressure by the Urban League led to the hiring of African Americans as bus drivers by the public-transportation company in Kansas City, Missouri.[1]

As the level of civil-rights insurgency rose, the retaliation of white-racist violence and political harassment also increased. On February 18, 1960, King was arrested and falsely charged with failing to report over $30,000 on his federal income tax return. On March 8, a twenty-seven-year-old black man was tortured by white youths, who beat him with chains and carved six *K*s one-inch deep into his stomach and chest. The racist attack was in response to nonviolent demonstrations by black students at Texas Southern University to desegregate Houston lunch counters. In April, the Nashville home of

NAACP attorney Alexander Looby was firebombed, in retaliation for his role in defending sit-in demonstrations. As the protests increased, activists in SNCC and another liberal civil-rights group, the Congress of Racial Equality (CORE), voiced criticisms of the NAACP for its reluctance to engage in civil-disobedience tactics, or to provide sufficient financial support for the new protest mobilizations. At the June 1960 NAACP national convention in St. Paul, Minnesota, a two-day private caucus was held with representatives of the sit-in demonstrators, who explicitly condemned Wilkins's lukewarm response. Thurgood Marshall confessed that the Association had at best approached the nonviolent protests favored by King at "a snail's pace," and finally recognized that the traditional legal strategy of reform within the courts was insufficient in challenging racial segregation.[2]

Evers found himself politically somewhere between the militant, youthful insurgents and the moderate leaders of his own national organization. As the documents here show, as early as 1959 Evers contemplated enrolling in law school, to prepare himself for a career in politics. He could foresee the inevitability of African Americans winning full voting rights across the South, which was finally achieved in 1965 with the passage of the Voting Rights Act. "He believed in the NAACP and what it stood for, and what it had been able to do over the years," Myrlie states. Yet he may have also been trying to "formulate his exit" strategy from the Association. "Personally, he wanted to be a legislator," Myrlie states. "He knew that there was power in making positive changes there, and he also knew for himself that it would be the culmination of his work, and moving on into another arena." There were also personal considerations concerning the economic situation of his growing family, with the birth of a third child. "He was thinking down the road. And it was like, 'Do I dare think that far? When at any moment, my life may be snatched away from me'," Myrlie reflects. "'What else do I do to benefit myself and my family?'"[3]

Evers admired the courage of the young sit-in demonstrators, but worried that this tactic might not be appropriate for Mississippi, given its repressive political environment. From a practical standpoint, there were only a handful of African American lawyers in the state, and the local branch organizations had few financial resources. The only African American newspaper in Mississippi, the *Jackson Advocate*, defended Jim Crow segregation, and was controlled by whites. Students and teachers who attended public schools and were arrested in desegregation demonstrations would certainly be expelled or fired. These factors prompted Evers to promote another tactic of resistance that, he believed, could be more effective: economic boycotts of segregated, white-owned businesses.

In early April, hundreds of African American students in Jackson visited the homes of an estimated seven thousand black families throughout the city, urging them not to buy from local merchants who discriminated in their hiring policies or practices towards customers. Black families were urged not to purchase their customary Easter Sunday clothing that year. Within weeks, Jackson merchants experienced a loss of up to 75 percent of their business.[4] Myrlie estimates that the 1960 boycott was 90 to 95 percent effective among blacks in Jackson. There were, however, a good number of local blacks who resisted the boycott and continued to patronize white establishments. "So you get the names, the addresses, the phone numbers, the car tags" of those blacks who opposed the boycott "and you announce it at the mass rally," Myrlie recalls. "And the people knew; they would take it down, they'd call and harass [them]." In some instances, when African Americans were seen leaving white-owned stores after making purchases, another kind of intimidation was required. "There would be [black] men and some women in the back alleys" at the rear entrances of stores, watching for black customers. When one was spotted, his or her clothing items would be seized and destroyed. Myrlie admits proudly, "We took knives and ripped those clothes, let me tell you. We almost got 100 percent."[5]

Evers continued his frenetic routine of extensively traveling across the state, meeting with branch organizations and investigating crimes throughout 1960. In late April, he traveled to Biloxi to establish an NAACP local, in the aftermath of a bloody struggle to desegregate a local beach; from June 10 to 13, he spoke and participated in the conference of Mississippi Independent Beauticians, encouraging its members to become active in civil-rights efforts; from July 19 to 21, at a conference of the General Baptist Convention, he urged black ministers to use their influence to support the NAACP's activities; in August, he investigated charges of police brutality and misconduct in Brookhaven; on September 19 he spoke before the U.S. Civil Rights Commission meeting in Jackson to protest police harassment of blacks who refused to sit in segregated seats on buses; in November, he urged federal housing authorities to investigate policies of racial discrimination by the West Point Urban Renewal Program. The state of Mississippi responded to this new level of black activism by increased surveillance, illegal wiretapping of telephones of NAACP members, and planting black covert agents inside their organizations. The Mississippi Sovereignty Commission, a state-funded agency, maintained an extensive surveillance network to monitor the activities of Evers and others, looking for any pretext to arrest them.

Their opportunity to move against Evers finally occurred in late 1960, with the bizarre case of Clyde Kennard. An army veteran, born in Hattiesburg, Mississippi, Kennard had attended the University of Chicago for several years. After returning to Mississippi, he applied for admission to the all-white Mississippi Southern College to complete his undergraduate degree. Although he had attended NAACP-sponsored activities, Kennard was not a civil-rights activist. Nevertheless, segregationists viewed Kennard as a militant, and filed spurious charges against him on the grounds that he had stolen $25 worth of chicken feed from a white neighbor. In November 1960, Kennard was convicted by an all-white jury of burglary, and sentenced to serve seven years in prison. Kennard would ultimately have his sentence reduced and would be released in 1963, but would die several months later. Evers was intensely involved in the Kennard trial, and was outraged by his conviction. In a statement to the *Hattiesburg American* newspaper, Evers declared: "The greatest mockery [to judicial] justice took place Monday, November 21, in the Forrest County courthouse, when despite the overwhelming evidence in Clyde Kennard's favor, he was convicted and sentenced to seven years in the state penitentiary. . . . In a courtroom of segregationists apparently resolved to put Kennard 'legally away,' the all-white jury found Kennard guilty as charged in only ten minutes." Evers was subsequently charged with "constructive contempt of court" because of his public statement. On December 2, Evers was convicted, sentenced to serve thirty days in jail, and given a $100 fine. In 1961, this conviction was overturned on appeal.[6]

The tragic Kennard case touched Medgar emotionally and profoundly. In a memoir of civil-rights activist John R. Salter, the "only time that I ever saw [Evers] break down came in the fall of 1961, at an evening dinner session of the annual convention of the Mississippi NAACP" in Jackson, as he spoke about Kennard. Medgar's "voice shook and, with what was obviously deep sorrow and frustration, he wept openly. With one accord and with many others weeping by this time all arose and began singing 'We Are Climbing Jacob's Ladder.'"[7] The burden of leadership for Medgar was enormous, and would grow even heavier during the next two difficult years.

45 Report to Mrs. Ruby Hurley from Medgar W. Evers, Field Secretary

APRIL 19, 1960

SACRIFICE FOR HUMAN DIGNITY

The Jackson, Mississippi Sacrifice for Human Dignity, which began April 10, 1960, and was reported on through April 12th, earlier, was very successful. Cooperation from the Negro community reached its maximum Wednesday and Thursday, at which time it was difficult to find Negroes on Capitol Street or many of the other areas where there is usually a heavy traffic of Negro customers. Estimates of eighty (80) to ninety (90) percent cooperation is believed to have taken place.

Local newspapers refused to make mention of the protest except to say in one article that police officials and merchants reported, "The boycott had apparently fizzled out." Along with such pronouncements coming from these individuals, Percy Green, local editor of the Jackson Advocate, Negro Newspaper, was constantly flashed on television saying that the boycott had fizzled out, which gave indication that the sacrifice was affecting the white merchants. Definite proof lies in the fact that Negro businesses, particularly groceries and millineries, witnessed tremendous increase in cash sales, further the fact that on Easter Sunday many of the Church ministers made comments to the effect that this was the first Easter in recent years to see so many female members of the congregation in their seeming "old" clothes, bears witness of a favorable end to Jackson's "Negro Boycott." We're happy to report at this time that the Sacrifice for Human Dignity was a success, it ended Saturday, April 16, 1960.

Enclosed is a news release which followed the demonstration, which, of course, was not carried in the city newspapers.

Respectfully submitted,

Medgar W. Evers
Field Secretary
MWE:gb, Encl.

*

46 Monthly Report: "Branch Activity" and "Anti-Segregation Demonstrations"

APRIL 21, 1960

BRANCH ACTIVITY

The Jackson Branch N.A.A.C.P. in a very enthusiastic meeting Sunday, April 3rd, began its spring membership campaign. The meeting was held at Anderson's Chapel Methodist Church, on Page and Whitfield Mill's Road, under the usual surveillance of the Jackson Police Department and other city officials. Some fifty (50) or more memberships were turned in at the membership kickoff. The speaker for the occasion was Rev. John D. Mangrum, Chaplain of Tougaloo Southern Christian College, and a member of the Jackson Branch Board of Directors of the N.A.A.C.P. Among many of the things Rev. Mangrum spoke of were the following excerpts: "At a time when our country needs to be unified, when we need to be teaching our youth the very best that we know, not only to keep in the race of democracy against totalitarianism, but to win friends and influence people who can and would come into our camp, our State, through its representatives, both in the State Government and in the National Government seem to go out of their way to prevent democracy." "They pass laws which are insulting to human beings and blasphemous and idolatrous before God. At a time in the life of our part of the country, when every experience seems to point out the utter stupidity of segregation, they preach it and write about it as though this were the highest and most wholesome way of life known. It is an attitude of defiance, of hatred, of flouting laws that are for the justice of all so that the privileged few might continue to bask in the sunlight of an ignominious idolatry which dubs Mississippi as the hinterland of the Nation." "There can be no justice in a segregated community. Negroes have known this for a long time, and white people have known it, too." "If you agree when the enemies of democracy tell you that the N.A.A.C.P. is a communist front organization, you are asleep, if you want to awaken from your long sleep and join and become active in an organization dedicated to making all America Free and Decent, Join the N.A.A.C.P. I am not going to tell you that people in this organization are perfect or that they are all even good. I will tell you that those who have eyes to see, and ears to hear, know that it is the one organization that has done more to help make America the land of the free and the home of the brave than any other."

The Omega Psi Phi student choral group along with Pearl Street A.M.E. Church Youth Choir furnished music for the program. The goal for the Jackson Branch is fifteen hundred (1,500) members. It is evident that the campaign will be extended in order to achieve this goal.

[. . .]

ANTI-SEGREGATION DEMONSTRATIONS

Negro citizens of Jackson, Mississippi gave a beautiful show of unity during the Easter week "Sacrifice for Human Dignity", when each Negro citizen was asked to refrain from purchasing anything from white merchants from the 10th through the 17th of April in the metropolitan city of Jackson. This movement, sparked by the desires on the part of young people from the various colleges and high schools in the immediate Jackson vicinity, was an expression of dissatisfaction with segregation and discrimination as is practiced in Miss. More than seven hundred (700) students, combined, participated in a door to door canvas, urging Negro citizens to cooperate in this "Sacrifice for Human Dignity."

Dean Charles A. Jones, of the Lampton Theological Seminary, Campbell College, along with the Field Secretary, coordinated the activities of this protest movement. Preliminary meetings with barbers, beauticians, doctors, dentists, businessmen, civic leaders, ministers, teachers, fraternal groups, and students preceded the actual demonstration. Most of the groups mentioned pledged their cooperation.

Because of the blackout given our movement by the newspapers, it was necessary that more exhaustive work be done as to getting the word across the Negro communities, which made it necessary that some ten thousand, five hundred (10,500) handbills be distributed. This was done by students from the colleges in the immediate vicinity of Jackson. The participation in our "Sacrifice for Human Dignity" reached its optimum of possibly eighty (80) to ninety (90) per cent from the 11th through the 14th of April, with an average participation of seventy (70) per cent of the Negro community throughout the "Sacrifice."

Newspapers, policemen, and some merchants tried to give the impression that the boycott was a failure, however, other merchants admitted that they were hard hit. One store in particular, a downtown store which caters principally to Negro trade, indicated on Friday, one day after the boycott began, that it had lost seventy-five (75) per cent of its trade. During this same period, other merchants (white) indicated they had felt the effect of the shortage of the Negro market. Further indication of the success of the program is the fact that Negro businesses, to the contrary, were over-run by the Negro market, particularly in the field of foods and millineries. The "Sacrifice for Human Dignity" was a success.

Other protests against segregation are taking place on the Gulf of Mexico, in Gulfport and Biloxi along the twenty-six (26) mile man-made beach, whose beautiful sand dunes have been opened to every other racial group but the American Negro. This protest is taking the form of direct action in that individuals of the Negro group, particularly members of our Gulfport Branch, under the leadership of Dr. Felix H. Dunn, President of the Branch, and Dr. Gilbert Mason of Biloxi, a life member of the N.A.A.C.P., who was arrested on Sunday, April 17th as he swam on the beach within the city limits of Biloxi. Dr. Mason's case is in City Court with a decision to be rendered Monday, April 25th. He is being represented by a local attorney. Dr. Dunn and his family were taken to City Hall in Gulfport, but were not arrested, the mayor of Gulfport explained to them that they had a perfect right on the beach, and that they could go any time they chose without being molested by the police department of Gulfport. So as a follow-up, on Sunday, April 24th, from Biloxi through Pass Christian, which includes Gulfport, Negro citizens plan to swim in the Gulf of Mexico. There will be more to report on the outcome of this situation, in the near future.

Respectfully submitted,

Medgar W. Evers
Field Secretary
MWE:gb

Rev. John D. Mangrum—Chaplain of Tougaloo College and adviser to the college's youth council, Mangrum was one of the activists who embraced the Jackson student movement. He later extablished the Freedom Summer Collection archives at the University of Southern Mississippi. See Payne, 89.

Charles A. Jones—Chaplain of Campbell College, Jackson. In 1960, Jones and other black businessmen and clergy formed the Citizens Committee for Human Rights to provide support for the Jackson students' boycott movement led by John Salter. Campbell College later closed and merged with Jackson College. See Payne, 161.

 Monthly Report: "Biloxi Anti-Segregation Demonstration"

MAY 23, 1960

BILOXI ANTI-SEGREGATION DEMONSTRATION

As a follow-up to the report of April 24, 1960, in regard to the Biloxi, Gulfport, Pass Christian, and Gulf Coast demonstrations, I'm happy to report that members of our Gulfport and Pass Christian Branches participated on Sunday, April 24, 1960, in a movement to desegregate the beaches on the Gulf Coast.

A special report has been submitted on the outcome of the April 24th demonstration. The fact that Negroes actually swam and relaxed on the beaches of Biloxi prompted hoodlums to attack them with chains, clubs, and other instruments.

The quick action of the members of the Gulfport Branch, under the leadership of Dr. Felix H. Dunn, and Dr. Gilbert R. Mason, prompted an immediate inquiry from the Federal Bureau of Investigation after they had called Mr. Clarence Mitchell, who was at the time in the state, over at Meridian, Mississippi, and told him what was taking place at that very moment. Instantly Mr. Mitchell began to put in calls to key people, including our Executive Secretary, Mr. Roy Wilkins, our Regional Secretary, Mrs. Ruby Hurley, and a direct call to the Federal Bureau of Investigation. These calls brought instant results in the form of FBI investigation.

The Field Secretary's follow-up investigation and affidavits from individuals who were injured in the violence were forwarded to Mr. Robert L. Carter, and in turn forwarded to our Washington Bureau. These complaints, along with the insistence of our Director of the Washington Bureau, Mr. Mitchell, brought very favorable action from the Department of Justice, in that on Tuesday, May 17, 1960, the 6th Anniversary of the United States Supreme Court decision, the Federal Government filed suit in Vicksburg, Mississippi, against Harrison County officials charging that they had violated the Federal contractual agreement between Harrison County and the United States Government of 1948, when they refused to permit Negroes to use the Gulf Coast beaches on a non-segregated basis. This action also came after the N.A.A.C.P. had publicly announced its assistance to the Negro citizens of Harrison County to gain admittance to the beaches. Mr. Carter, our General Counsel for the N.A.A.C.P., conferred with Dr. F. H. Dunn, Dr. G. R. Mason, Attorney Knox Walker, and myself, on April 29th and 30th, as to the legal action that could be taken. This strategy meeting preceded the announcement by the Federal Government of its intervention, which was heartily greeted by the Negro group.

Dr. Mason and other members of the Negro citizenry of Biloxi, would like for the N.A.A.C.P. to act in their behalf, as a friend to the court, in the suit to open the beaches to all.

United States Judge Sidney Mize, in whose court the case will be heard, indicated, in a news release, that it would come up during the regular court term in June, 1960.

$*$

48 Monthly Report: "Action"

JUNE 29, 1960

ACTION

An investigation was made into reports of police brutality in Oakland, Mississippi, which occurred earlier in this year. The incident involved a teen-age Negro youth, who was reportedly disorderly, and the night-watchman, (white), both of Oakland, Mississippi.

The young Negro was alleged to have been drinking and disorderly, and was later set upon by the white night-watchman and beaten without any indications of resisting arrest.

With regards to other violence which has been reported to the Washington Bureau of N.A.A.C.P., and the Department of Justice, the Field Secretary appeared before the Mississippi Advisory Committee on Civil Rights to prevent further complaints during the month of June.

As a continuation of the investigation and the proposed Legal Action of the Biloxi Beach situation, the Field Secretary, along with Mrs. Ruby Hurley, Southeast Regional Secretary for N.A.A.C.P. and Mr. Robert Carter, General Counsel for N.A.A.C.P., conferred with Negro residents of Biloxi and Gulfport, relative to proposed Legal Action in an effort to open the Gulf Coast Beaches to Negro citizens.

This action is contemplated even though the Federal Government has filed suit to desegregate the Gulf Coast Beaches.

49 Monthly Report: "Branch Activities" and "Investigations"

JULY 22, 1960

BRANCH ACTIVITIES

The fact that the State Sovereignty Commission announced that $20,000.00 of public funds was being made available by the Commission to the White Citizens Council, prompted the Field Secretary to issue a statement to each Branch urging that an immediate protest be voiced against the action of the Sovereignty Commission. Several Branches responded with mass protest meetings. These Branches were Clarksdale (Coahoma County), Greenville, and Jackson. Other Branches have indicated that similar protest meetings will be staged.

The Mississippi State Conference of N.A.A.C.P. Branches Board of Directors met Sunday, July 17, 1960 and issued the following statement with regards to public funds granted to the White Citizens Council by the State Sovereignty Commission:

"The Board of Directors of the Mississippi State Conference of N.A.A.C.P. Branches deplores the actions of the State Sovereignty Commission, an agency of the State of Mississippi, in granting $20,000 in public funds to the private organization—White Citizens Council. The Board unanimously approved taking steps toward legal action against this crime perpetrated on the State Treasury and the Negro and White citizens of the State of Mississippi. We seek the co-operation of all other citizens who are outraged by this travesty against the law to join hands with us in seeking to cause an immediate halt to this type of conduct."

In a meeting with the executive officers and members of the Greenville, Mississippi Chapter of N.A.A.C.P., it was greatly emphasized that inaction on the part of Branches in times as critical as the present is paramount to downfall in our struggle, that it is necessary that each Branch of N.A.A.C.P. do more than the bare minimum of existing. It was further emphasized that we must encourage our people to greater action, rather than discourage them into inaction. Each officer and member present pledged a double determination to make the presence of a N.A.A.C.P. Chapter in Greenville, Mississippi known.

Meetings with members of the Cleveland and Mound Bayou Branches, which are in Bolivar County, Mississippi, revealed that plans are underway to reactivate the two Branches under dynamic leadership.

INVESTIGATIONS

Newspaper reports of one Jerry Dawson having been found emasculated in Amite County on the morning of July 9, 1960, prompted the Field Secretary to make an investigation, which was done Sunday, July 10th, with the President of the McComb Branch, a photographer, and an interested party from the area.

Jerry Dawson, a forty-four (44) year old Negro laborer, was found early Saturday morning by a county supervisor of Amite County, who was en route to the National Democratic Convention. Dawson was found lying dying in the middle of Mississippi Highway 568, some two and one half miles east of Gillsburg, Mississippi. He had apparently been cut under the neck with a dull instrument. He had bruises on his chest and knuckles which indicated that he could possibly have been dragged.

The officers of Amite County immediately rounded up three Negroes who had been in the company of Dawson on the previous day.

In checking with individuals, Negroes, in the area, it was hard for them to believe that a Negro would do such a dastardly crime. The

Field Secretary shares the very same opinion as the residents in question. Further investigation is being made into this recent killing. To further indicate that this was not an ordinary murder between Negroes, a Negro man, about sixty (60) years old, who lives in the immediate area of this crime, has been mysteriously missing for approximately one week as of this writing. We shall continue to probe these incidents.

The President of our Tougaloo Chapter of N.A.A.C.P., Rev. Otis Smith, was arrested and lodged in Madison County jail on July 8, 1960, charged with disturbing the peace. He is alleged to have been "stealing cars on the Natchez Trace Lover's Lane."

We have been able to obtain his release on $1,000 bond, and his case is scheduled for hearing on September 19, 1960 before the Mississippi Circuit Court in Hinds County. Further investigation is being made into this incident in view of the fact that this is the second time Smith has been arrested for a similar offense within the past three months, notably since the Easter boycott of Jackson stores.

———————————————————————————————————— *

50 Memorandum to Roy Wilkins from Gloster B. Current

AUGUST 29, 1960

REGARDING THE BEATING OF JOHNNY FRAZIER, STATE
PRESIDENT, NAACP MISSISSIPPI YOUTH COUNCIL

Medgar Evers called Sunday, August 28, to report that Johnny Frazier, state president, Mississippi Youth Council was arrested in Wenona, Mississippi, Saturday, August 27, en route from the Youth Conference in Georgia.

He was beaten by the police because he refused to move to the rear of the bus and charged with disturbing the peace and resisting arrest. Mr. Evers was on his way up there to try to get him out of jail.

He was unable to obtain the services of any Negro lawyer because apparently they were all out of the State attending the Bar Association meeting in Philadelphia.

Frazier lives in Greenville, Mississippi.

GBC:jw
cc: Mr. Randy White
Mr. Herbert Wright

Johnny Frazier—The leader of the Jackson NAACP Youth Council, Frazier was arrested in 1960 after he tried to desegregate a Winona bus station. He then tried to desegregate a white Episcopal church. He was later expelled from his high school when he brought a placard declaring segregation to be "outlawed" by the Supreme Court. See the State Sovereignty Commission Files online, 1–70–0–9–2–1–1, and 2–49–0–38–2–1–1, at http://mdah.state.ms.us/arlib/contents/er/.

51 Report of Medgar Evers (Press Release)

AUGUST 30, 1960

The Mississippi State Conference of NAACP Branches vigorously condemns the extreme police brutality against Johnny Frazier of Greenville, Mississippi, because he refused to move to the rear of a Trailways Bus in Winona, Mississippi, August 27, 1960.

The sheriff and deputy of Montgomery County, violated their oath of office and Frazier's constitutional rights, when he was beaten by the officers into a state of semi-consciousness, even though there was no provocation on his part.

Only in Nazi Germany has such inhuman cruelty been equaled.

52 Monthly Report: "Investigation"

AUGUST 30, 1960

INVESTIGATION

An investigation was made into the complaint forwarded to this office by the President of the McComb Branch Mr. C. C. Bryant, who stated that three (3) young ladies from Brookhaven, Mississippi had been taken from a Greyhound Bus by police officers at McComb and placed in the city jail.

Traveling to Brookhaven on August 13, 1960, the Field Secretary interviewed two (2) of the three (3) persons involved in the incident whose names are Miss Ruth Mae Merchant, 827 Railroad Avenue, and Miss Mattie Mae Maxwell, 828 Railroad Avenue, both of Brookhaven, Mississippi. These young women gave a full account of the action of the McComb police because they were riding near the front of the bus. It was indicated that they had to remain in jail for approximately two (2) hours, during which time there were lectures regarding segregation. At one time an officer indicated to Miss Maxwell, "You think you're white, don't you?" Many other such remarks were made during the course of the conversation.

These young ladies promised to make out affidavits to be turned over to the N.A.A.C.P., however, up until this point we have not been able to obtain said affidavits. We shall talk with these individuals again for possible results.

Immediately upon return from a ten (10) day stay at Keysville, Georgia, attending the Southeast Region N.A.A.C.P. Youth Retreat, the Field Secretary received a telephone call from Mr. Johnny Frazier, President of the Mississippi State Conference of Youth Councils, stating that he was in jail at Winona, Mississippi, and his bond was set at $2,000, and that he wanted me to come up and get him out. This message reached me about 5:30 P.M. Saturday, August 27, 1960. Realizing that there was very little that could be done before Monday, the Field Secretary notified the family of Mr. Frazier, the Southeast Region Secretary, Mrs. Hurley, and the Director of Branches, Mr. Current. He was also in communication with the State Conference President, Mr. Darden.

Monday morning, early, after having conference most of Sunday by telephone, the Field Secretary, along with a youth member, motored to Winona, Mississippi, approximately one hundred (100) miles north of Jackson. It was after we had arrived in Winona that we were made aware of the fact that a Justice of the Peace hearing was to be held that morning at 10:00 A.M. We proceeded to the sheriff's office hoping to be able to confer with Johnny before the hearing, but the sheriff denied us that opportunity stating that only the family or a lawyer would be allowed that privilege even though neither relative nor lawyer was present. After being denied the opportunity to see Mr. Frazier, the youth member with me, Mr. Meredith C. Anding, Jr., and I had proceeded to get some breakfast when we came in contact with Mr. Amzie Moore who had come over for the hearing.

Returning to the courthouse where the hearing was to take place we were confronted by a sullen crowd of white men, mostly farmers in overalls, who stared menacingly at the three of us as we talked among ourselves. At about 10:15 A.M. the Judge proceeded toward the courthouse to carry out an assignment which was scheduled for fifteen (15) minutes earlier, 10:00 A.M. Whites were directed downstairs, Negroes were directed to the balcony of the courtroom. At about 10:25 A.M. young Frazier was brought into the courtroom handcuffed, in full view of the white spectators who were apparently enjoying the circus scene. Mr. Frazier, who was without an attorney, was asked if he wanted to speak to anyone, his answer was "Yes." The sheriff asked, "Who?" and the reply was "Mr. Evers," at which time there were more menacing stares and taunts coming from the main floor of the courtroom. After having conferred with Mr. Frazier he indicated that he would not plead guilty so as to appeal to a higher court of record where the facts would all be brought out in the light in which they are. He further indicated to me the extent to which he had been beaten by the sheriff and his deputies, despite a denial on their parts. At one point during the cross-examination of the sheriff's deputy by Mr. Frazier, the question was asked, "Are you a Christian?" This appeared to have shaken the man's conscience, as he began to stammer. The Judge came to his rescue by ruling out the question as being unrelated to the case. At another point in the cross-examination by Johnny Frazier, serving as his own defense counsel, he asked the sheriff if he did not call him (Frazier) a nigger, and the sheriff, who uses the word as freely as water, replied, "Yes, I called you a nigger, that's what you are, a nigger." To this remark an echo in the audience was "second the motion." Johnny was convicted by the Justice of the Peace, fined $25.00 on two counts, one for disorderly conduct, and the other, resisting arrest, plus court costs, $23.00, a total fine of $73. We immediately indicated to the Judge that we wanted an appeal from his decision to a higher court. This was granted after having made arrangements for an appeal bond. The appeal bond was secured after having to return to Jackson.

The distance between Jackson and Winona, including the matter of transacting the procurement of the security bond made it impossible for me to return to Winona until after office hours were over. We nevertheless returned to Winona and found it rather difficult to get cooperation from the sheriff in releasing young Frazier. After finally being released Frazier was told by the sheriff to "get out of town." Before we could get out of town, three cars made it their business to check our every move, and as we proceeded to the city limits, we were followed quite some distance by these cars.

We're in the process now of preparing affidavits to be forwarded to our Washington Bureau and the Department of Justice.

Curtis Conway Bryant (1917–?)—Pike County NAACP president, he invited Robert Moses and worked with SNCC in the early 1960s on voter registration efforts. His long career in civil rights and community activism were commended by Mississippi state legislature in 2001. See Payne, 85, 101–104; http://billstatus.ls.state.ms.us/documents/2001/html/SR/SR0051PS.htm.

---

*

53 Monthly Report: "Civil Rights Commission"

OCTOBER 19, 1960

CIVIL RIGHTS COMMISSION

On September 19, 1960, the Field Secretary appeared before the Civil Rights Advisory Commission in Jackson protesting through a prepared statement the harassment of Negro citizens who choose to ride on interstate buses near the front seat, by local law enforcement officers in practically every town in the state and urged that the Commission make a study of this practice and recommend the appropriate steps to eliminate these injustices. To substantiate our claim Mr. Johnny Frazier, of Greenville, Mississippi had been beaten and arrested at Winona, Mississippi, ostensibly because he was riding near the front of the bus. He had been asked several times by the driver to move to the rear, which of course he refused to do.

Other instances of police harassment of citizens traveling interstate and intrastate has occurred in McComb and other towns which were pointed out to the Commission.

Mr. Aaron R. Henry, President of our Clarksdale, Mississippi Branch, made a very complimentary report of Negroes attempting to register in the eighty-two (82) counties that make up the State of Mississippi. His confidence rests in the Civil Rights committee directing letters to the Registrars across the state requesting that they send to Dr. Henry's office the status of Negro voters in the eighty-two (82) respective counties, which drew condemnation through newspapers by the Attorney General of the State of Mississippi. The Attorney General accused the Civil Rights Commission of being a "pawn" of the NAACP.

*

54 Monthly Report: "The Clyde Kennard and Medgar Evers Cases"

DECEMBER 20, 1960

THE CLYDE KENNARD AND MEDGAR EVERS CASES

The case of Clyde Kennard has become widely known and discussed in and out of the State of Mississippi; to appreciate the deep implications of the Kennard case it is necessary that we review the activities of Mr. Kennard up to November 21, 1960, beginning with the year of 1959.

Mr. Kennard, a young Negro man and ex-paratrooper, who lives some seven or eight miles from the town of Hattiesburg, Mississippi, attempted to enroll at Mississippi Southern College, in September of 1959. His attempt to enroll at Mississippi Southern, at the time brought forth accusations and conviction in the Justice of Peace Court of Forrest County, of possession of whiskey. Mr. Kennard neither smokes nor drinks, and at the time his prosperous chicken farm made it unnecessary to deal in the illicit traffic of alcoholic beverages (Mississippi is a "dry" state). Nevertheless, whiskey was planted in his car, and with him being alone on the campus, made it easy for officials to make such a "plant" and get away with it; and later to be sustained in a Mississippi court. This case is still on appeal to the Mississippi Supreme Court.

The case in point had its beginning when Kennard was alleged to have conspired to steal and receive stolen goods, from the Forrest County Cooperative in October of 1960.

His trial in Circuit Court on November 21, 1960 at which time he was represented by Attorneys R. Jess Brown and Jack H. Young, ended with the judge sentencing Kennard to seven years in the penitentiary, allegedly for "conspiring" to burglarize the Forrest County Cooperative.

The evidence presented by the defense bore every semblance of innocence; however, the evidence presented by the State was so inconclusive that even a layman like myself was able to observe the "flaws."

The Circuit Judge in this case was Stanton Hall, who was formerly Chairman of the General Legislative Investigation Committee for the State Senate, and whose avowed purpose it was to help maintain segregation in the State of Mississippi. Judge Stanton Hall was elected Circuit Judge of Forrest County within the last two years.

During the entire proceedings of the trial of November 21, 1960, the Field Secretary for Mississippi sat attentively in the "balcony" of the court room and observed this trial. The Field Secretary was pointed out while sitting in the balcony, by a news reporter from one of the local radio stations of Hattiesburg.

On the day after the trial of Clyde Kennard, November 22, the Field Secretary released the following statement to United Press International, and the Associated Press: "The greatest mockery to Judicial Justice took place Monday, November the 21st in the Forrest County Court House, when despite the overwhelming evidence in Clyde Kennard's favor, he was convicted and sentenced to seven years in the State Penitentiary for alleged burglary. In a court room of segregationists apparently resolved to put Kennard 'legally away,' the all-white jury found Kennard guilty as charged, in only ten minutes."

As a result of this statement, the Field Secretary was served with a subpoena to appear in the Forrest County Circuit Court to show cause why he should not be cited for contempt of court. The Field Secretary immediately got in touch with our Regional Office and was advised to get in touch with General Counsel, which I did. I also obtained the services of a local attorney, Jack H. Young, of Jackson, Mississippi. This provided the legal preparation for my defense in court, for Friday, December 2, 1960.

Mrs. Ruby Hurley, our Regional Secretary, came to Jackson, Thursday, December 1, 1960, in order to be in the court room during the trial. In the meantime, interest from across the State had showered the Office and home of the Field Secretary, in the form of telephone calls and letters, many indicating that they would be present at the trial.

On Friday, the second, in a courtroom filled almost to capacity, of both Negroes and whites, more or less evenly divided as was anticipated, a verdict of guilty was pronounced by Judge Hall, as was anticipated. Immediately the sentence of thirty days in jail and one hundred dollars ($100) fine was imposed, and due mainly to the thoroughness of Attorney Jack H. Young in having prepared before leaving Jackson, appearance and cost bonds, approved by the sheriff of Hinds County, was the Field Secretary spared from experiencing some time actually in jail.

An appeal to the Mississippi Supreme Court was made immediately, by attorneys Jack H. Young and R. Jess Brown. My bondsmen were two very prominent Jackson citizens, Mr. I. S. Sanders, a former principal of one of the State High Schools and now a real estate agent and businessman, and Mr. John ____ley Dixon, Treasurer of the Mississippi State Conference of NAACP and member of the Board and local Branch, businessman and civic leader.

A considerable amount of publicity was given this trial, before and after. There were strong editorials written in both the Delta Democrat Times of Greenville, Mississippi, and the State Times of Jackson, Mississippi, relative to this attempt to abridge Freedom of Speech. There was a small article also appearing in the Jackson Daily News, relative to the same question.

Jack H. Young (1908–?)—A founder of the Magnolia Bar Association, which was founded in 1955 to help the state's black lawyers who had to obtain law degrees outside Mississippi and other Jim Crow states. He was one of the key civil-rights lawyers offering legal services to civil-rights workers such as the 1961 Freedom Riders, whom Young was authorized by the NAACP to defend in court. In 1975, the NAACP awarded him the first William Robert Ming Advocacy Award. See George Alexander Swell, "Jack H. Young, Sr.: Distinguished Civil Rights Lawyer," *Mississippi Black History Makers* (Jackson: University Press of Mississippi, 1977), 276–282.

✳

55 ". . . with Liberty and Justice for All . . . ," Mississippi NAACP Branch Newsletter

DECEMBER 20, 1960

FOREWORD

"With malice toward none; with charity for all; with firmness in the right, as God gives us to see the right, let us strive on to finish the work we are in, to bind up the Nation's wounds, to care for him who shall have borne the battle and for his widow and his orphan, to do all which may achieve and cherish a just and lasting peace among ourselves and with all mankind."

This is our creed.

RACIAL SELF DEFENSE PROGRAM

Negro Citizens of Jackson, Mississippi, gave a beautiful show of unity, during the Easter Week "Sacrifice for Human Dignity," when each Negro Citizen was asked to refrain from purchasing anything from white merchants from the 10th to the 17th of April, in the metropolitan area of Jackson. This movement sparked by the desires on the part of young people from various colleges and high schools, in the immediate Jackson vicinity, was an expression of dissatisfaction with segregation and discrimination as is practiced in Mississippi. More than 700 students combined and participated in a door-to-door canvas urging Negro citizens to cooperate in this "Sacrifice for Human Dignity."

The success of the boycott was a controversial issue, but it is generally agreed that 70 percent of Jackson participated. Newspaper headlines and editorials read, "It's Goldfish Gulping Time," "Threatened Negro Boycott Discussed," "The Big Jackson Boycott." Jackson business leaders and the Chamber of Commerce denied charges that business was affected. A news release from the Mississippi State Office, NAACP, early termed the success of this boycott, which caused to be released by the White Citizens Council editor a statement, "Nothing apparently is happening." However, later indications were that 75 percent of the trade of two stores was lost, the first day of the Easter boycott the success of this boycott drove trade to Negro business.

A general program, called "Racial Self Defense," was launched in November, asking and reminding friends of freedom that, as much as we have accomplished in the past, it gives no reason to let up now. To that end, we feel that a program in favor of recognition of the dignity of all manhood is *imperative now!* We urged support and cooperation in a movement of withholding our patronage from all stores that do not accord the Negro citizens all of the courtesies and privileges they accord any other customer. Stores that do not recognize Negroes as Miss, Mrs. or Mr. do not deserve to have Negroes trade with them. Stores that do not employ Negroes are likewise not worthy of our patronage. We can, by this method, use the same items and clothes that we already have, as a step toward our contribution to Human Dignity, and create for the Negro a new respect and appreciation.

A letter went out to all branches of the NAACP and most organizations throughout the state over the signature of Dr. Aaron E. Henry, President of the Mississippi State Conference of NAACP, urging participation in this worthy cause.

REGISTRATION AND VOTING

Registration and voting has been constantly emphasized in speaking engagements, conferences with branches, at mass meetings, and in small informal groups. Commendable progress has been made during the year in getting more registered voters.

Negro citizens, complaining of not being allowed to register in order to vote, were later questioned by the Department of Justice, which had the Federal Bureau of Investigation inspect registration records.

Inspection of the records was expected to be a preliminary step toward establishing a pattern of discrimination whereby the federal government could appoint referees to supervise registration as provided by the Civil Rights Act which was passed earlier this year.

Attorney General Joe Patterson, who advised circuit clerks last year against letting the FBI agents poke into their voter registration records, declined to comment, "Until I look my hand over. This is the first I've heard about it." In the meantime, Negro citizens have been urged to continue to register and to report any denials which are ostensibly based on racial discrimination.

On Tuesday, November 8, Mississippi voters inserted into their state constitution an amendment designed to limit Negro suffrage by denying the ballot to anyone "not of good moral character." The measure, recommended by Citizens Council leaders and Mississippi's governor Ross Barnett, received a near three-to-one vote of approval. Another racial amendment, one to eliminate a requirement that the state provide free public schools, was given an even stronger endorsement.

Also approved overwhelmingly was an amendment eliminating a requirement that jurors be registered voters.

The amendment allowing non-voters to serve on juries was proposed after the U.S. Fifth Circuit Court of Appeals, Carroll County, Mississippi, "systematically excluded" Negroes from juries. Negro Robert Lee Goldsby's murder conviction was overturned by the high court on such grounds. Goldsby was convicted in Carroll County where there were no Negro voters.

DESEGREGATION

No attempts have been made in Mississippi to desegregate the public school systems since 1955, however, a young Negro farmer of Hattiesburg, Mississippi, Mr. Clyde Kennard, who attempted to enter Mississippi Southern College at Hattiesburg, Mississippi on three previous occasions, was sentenced on November 21, 1960 in the Forrest County Courthouse to seven years in the state penitentiary for alleged burglary.

The Field Secretary attended the trial of Mr. Kennard and released a news article, which read, "The greatest mockery to judicial justice took place Monday, November 21st in the Forrest County Courthouse, when despite the overwhelming evidence in Clyde Kennard's favor, he was convicted and sentenced to seven years in the state penitentiary for alleged burglary. In a courtroom of seg-regationists who apparently were resolved to put Kennard 'legally away,' the all-white jury found Kennard guilty as charged, in only 10 minutes."

For the above news release the Field Secretary has been cited for contempt of court and was found guilty as charged. The case is on appeal.

DESEGREGATION AND RECREATION
Other protests against segregation took place on the Mississippi Gulf Coast. In Gulfport and Biloxi, Mississippi along the 26 miles of man-made beaches. These beautiful sand dunes have been opened to every other racial group but the American Negro. Negro citizens became weary and started a protest. This protest took the form of direct action, in that individuals of the Negro group, particularly members of the Gulfport NAACP, under the leadership of Dr. Felix H. Dunn, Branch President, and Dr. Gilbert Mason of Biloxi. Dr. Mason was arrested on April 17 at Biloxi, Mississippi and was later referred to as the "leader" of the Beach Incident. Dr. Dunn and his family were taken to Gulfport city hall, but were not arrested on the same date as above. The mayor of Gulfport explained to them that they had a perfect right to be on the beach, and that they could go any time they chose without being molested by the police depart-ment of the city. As a follow-up, on April 24th Negroes from Biloxi, Gulfport, and the immediate areas swam in the segregated beaches of the Gulf Coast. This, however, prompted hoodlums to attack the Negroes who swam on the Biloxi beaches with chains and other in-struments. The quick action of Drs. Dunn and Mason prompted an immediate inquiry from the Federal Bureau of Investigation after making contact with Mr. Clarence Mitchell, of our Washington Bu-reau NAACP who was in the state at that time making an address for the Meridian Branch.

The beach incident prompted a rather thorough investigation by the federal government who on May 17, 1960, six years after the historic school desegregation decision, filed suit in federal district court in Vicksburg, Mississippi for the purpose of opening the beaches to all persons without regard to race.

The suit, under federal district judge Sidney Mize, is still pending.

FUND-RAISING

The Biloxi Branch of NAACP sponsored a rather successful Freedom Fund Banquet, September 30, 1960 at which a Dr. Goode from Mobile, Alabama, was the guest speaker, and the Mississippi Field Secretary made remarks about the "NAACP's nationwide program, the NAACP's interest in the Biloxi Beach suit," and the fact that more people, particularly more Negroes, should support the NAACP and its program. The crowd of approximately 130 individuals, at $5 per plate, gave the Biloxi chapter a gross of about $600 or more. This Freedom Fund Banquet was the first such event to take place in the Biloxi area. Despite the counter-action of a very vocal Citizens Council, the Branch gained immense prestige.

The Jackson, Mississippi Branch of NAACP took a cue from the Biloxi Branch of NAACP and sponsored its Freedom Fund Banquet on Saturday, October 22, 1960 at the Masonic Temple Building, at which time the Rev. John D. Mangram, Chaplain at Tougaloo College and advisor to our chapter of NAACP at Tougaloo was the speaker. The banquet was a success.

The traditional "Mother of the Year" program was held in May; for various reasons, it was not as successful as the previous one (1959).

At this writing plans are underway for a Brother Joe May Program, December 18th, to benefit our Fighting Funds for Freedom.

INVESTIGATIONS

An investigation was made into reports of police brutality in Oakland, Mississippi, which occurred earlier this year. The incident involved a teenage Negro youth who was reported disorderly, and the night marshal (white), both of Oakland, Mississippi. The young Negro was alleged to have been drinking and disorderly, and was later set upon by the night watchman and beaten without any indications of resisting arrest. Efforts to get affidavits against the law officer were unsuccessful.

Jerry Dawson, a 44-year-old Negro laborer was found early Saturday morning, July 16, 1960, by a county supervisor of Amite County, who was en route to the National Democratic Convention. Dawson was found dying in the middle of Mississippi Highway 568, some two and one-half miles east of Gillsburg, Mississippi. He had apparently been emasculated with a dull instrument. He had bruises on his chest and knuckles which indicated that he could possibly have been dragged.

The officers of Amite County immediately found three Negroes who had been in the company of Dawson the previous day. During the same time a Negro man of about 60 years of age was reported to have been missing about one week.

The Negroes apprehended in the round-up were released with speculation that the victim had met his death at the hands of a lynch mob; however, no further evidence has been forthcoming.

Police brutality is one of our most frequent acts of violence that is perpetrated upon Negro citizens. It occurs much too often. Many cases investigated have not been carried to court because of absence of witnesses and fear.

An appeal was made to the Governor of the state of Mississippi on November 27, 1960, by the President of the National Association for the Advancement of Colored People, for the State of Mississippi, Dr. Aaron E. Henry. The delicate situation concerned was an incident that took place in Batesville, Mississippi, when a young Negro girl, 12 years of age, named Lynda Faye Kuykendall, was brutally beaten by a variety store owner and a law marshal, after being falsely accused of stealing candy, Saturday, November 19, 1960. Mr. Willie Kuykendall, the child's father, has been an active NAACP'er and explains that his difficulty began with the white people in Panola County, after he attempted to register to vote some time ago.

Mr. Kuykendall and his family have received numerous threats and the Governor of the state has promised to personally instigate an investigation of the incident. Mr. Kuykendall has also sought help from the President of the United States, the U.S. Supreme Court, Federal Bureau of Investigation, the National Association for the Advancement of Colored People, Civil Rights Commission and others. In a notarized statement, Mr. Kuykendall states the following: "I cannot . . . cope with the lawless element of the white group alone, I feel that no act is beneath their dignity, even murdering me."

In a letter from Mr. Kuykendall dated December 1, 1960, he lists his address now as 2032 Missouri Street, Gary, Indiana. He indicated that pressure on him and his family had become so great that it became unbearable for them to continue to live there.

The latest report in this matter is that the Governor, Ross Barnett, has completed his investigation into the incident and will release his findings to the public soon.

CIVIL RIGHTS COMMISSION

Investigations have played a major role in the activities of the Field Secretary during this year. Registration and voting complaints have been investigated and affidavits were forwarded to the Civil Rights Commission and the Washington Bureau. Some of the counties were visited by members of the Commission where denial to register to vote has occurred.

In September of this year the Field Secretary made an appearance before the Civil Rights Advisory Commission relating complaints of harassment of Negro citizens on public conveyances, reporting that the majority of Negro citizens who travel on interstate or intrastate buses, have encountered numerous threats, insults and even violence, when they have dared to take a seat anywhere near the front of the bus, even though having paid the same fare that other passengers have paid.

It was further revealed that it has become increasingly inconvenient for Negro citizens passing through McComb and Winona, Mississippi towns.

The tactics used by police when a bus arrives in either of those towns are illustrated by what happened to five persons who were en route from Jackson, Mississippi to New Orleans, Louisiana in September, 1960. Upon arrival in McComb, Mississippi the police boarded the bus, ordered all Negroes to the rear, and those who were slow about moving were struck with nightsticks by the police, and told to move along faster. Another incident occurred in Winona, Mississippi in August of this year, when a young Negro lad by the name of Johnny Frazier of Greenville, Mississippi, was beaten into a state of semi-consciousness by the sheriff and the deputy of Montgomery County, because he was riding near the front of the bus. These are only a few of the many incidents that take place throughout Mississippi as Negro citizens pay their peaceful way through to their destinations and are molested by police and others.

It is the feeling of this group that this harassment Negroes in Mississippi are receiving on these buses is the result of an organized effort to intimidate Negro citizens and subject them to inferior seating arrangements on public conveyances.

The Civil Rights Commission was strongly urged by the Field Secretary to make on the spot investigations and cause to be prosecuted those guilty of violating the law they are sworn to uphold.

Dr. Aaron E. Henry, president of our Clarksdale, Mississippi Branch of NAACP, and now State Conference President, made a very complimentary report of Negroes attempting to register in the 82 counties that make up the state of Mississippi. His competence resulted in the Civil Rights Advisory Committee directing letters to the registrars across the State requesting that they send to Dr. Henry's office the status of Negro voters in the 82 respective counties. This drew condemnation through newspapers, by the Attorney General of the state of Mississippi. The Attorney General accused the Civil Rights Commission of being a "pawn" of the National Association for the Advancement of Colored People.

[Pages 17 and 18 are missing from the original document.]

PUBLIC RELATIONS

Speaking Engagements in the State

Other than NAACP Branches, the Field Secretary addressed the following organizations:

84th Annual Session of the M. W. Stringer Grand Lodge

Vesper Services, J. P. Campbell College

Emancipation Day Program, Prentiss, Mississippi

Reactivation of NAACP College Chapter, Tougaloo Southern Christian College, Tougaloo, Mississippi

Pre-membership Campaign Meeting, Vicksburg, Mississippi

Central Methodist Church, Jackson, Mississippi

Old Strangers Home Church, Jackson, Mississippi

Meridian, Mississippi Membership Committee

Membership Committee, Canton, Mississippi

Crusade for Voters Dinner

Membership Committee, Vicksburg

Tougaloo Southern Christian College, Tougaloo, Mississippi, Alpha Phi Alpha Fraternity

Student Political Actions Committee, Tougaloo Southern Christian College, Tougaloo, Mississippi

Fremont AME Church, Hinds County, Myles, Mississippi

Engagements out of State

Special NAACP Meeting, Atlanta, Georgia

Guest of American Veterans Committee Convention, Atlantic City, New Jersey

First Southeast Youth Retreat, Boggs Academy

Mass Meeting of North Carolina State Conference, Charlotte, North Carolina

Annual S. E. Regional Conference, Memphis, Tennessee

Springfield, Ohio Branch NAACP

Lima, Ohio Branch NAACP

East Liverpool, Ohio Branch NAACP

Press releases 78

Incoming mail 990

Outgoing mail 2,871

Miles traveled 16,295

Branches visited (some more than once) 40

New branches organized 1

New college chapters 1

Joe T. Patterson (1907–1965)—Mississippi state attorney general in the 1950s, Patterson staunchly opposed federal civil-rights laws and court decisions in the name of the "state rights." He unsuccessfully defended the state against the suit filed by James Meredith seeking admission from the University of Mississippi. Patterson died of a massive heart attack in 1965. "Joe T. Patterson Is Dead," *New York Times*, April 22, 1965, pg. 47.

Dr. Felix H. Dunn—A private practitioner in Gulfport, Mississippi, he became actively involved in desegregation movement in the fifties and sixties. Dunn served as president of the Biloxi local NAACP between 1954 and 1966. See Payne, 179.

Dr. Gilbert Mason (1928–)—A native of Jackson and medical practitioner in Biloxi, Mason organized a "wade-in" protest against a federally funded part of Gulf Port beach in 1959, which later caused a bloody white riot. He was vice president of Mississippi NAACP for thirty-three years. See Mason, *Beaches, Blood, and Ballots: A Black Doctor's Civil Rights Struggle* (Jackson: University Press of Mississippi, 2000).

Aaron R. Henry (1922–1997)—Pharmacist and highly active member of the NAACP, Henry organized a boycott of Clarksdale stores in 1961 and was arrested with six others for "withholding trade." Henry spearheaded the formation of the Mississippi Freedom Democratic Party (MFDP) and the Council of Federated Organizations (COFO). He played a central role in unification of MFDP and the National Democratic Party, and was elected to the Mississippi House of Representatives in 1982, holding the seat until 1996. See *Aaron Henry: The Fire Ever Burning* (Jackson: University Press of Mississippi, 2000); and Payne, 56–66.

*

CHAPTER VI

TAKING

FREEDOM FOR

OURSELVES

Documents 56–69

(February 12, 1961–October 14, 1962)

"The question for black people is not, when is the white man going to give us our rights, or when is he going to give us good education for our children, or when is he going to give us jobs—if the white man gives you anything— just remember when he gets ready he will take it right back. We have to take for ourselves."

Fannie Lou Hamer, "To Praise Our Bridges," in Clayborne Carson, et al., eds., Eyes on the Prize Civil Rights Reader: Documents, Speeches and Firsthand Accounts from the Black Freedom Struggle, 1954–1990 *(New York: Penguin, 1991), 179.*

B Y THE EARLY 1960s the friends and political associates of Medgar Evers were convinced that his life was in jeopardy, and that it was no longer a question of whether he would be murdered, but only a matter of when the political assassination would occur. There was a general consensus that Evers would be more useful to the movement if he relocated somewhere else. Wilkins and Current broached the subject with Evers on several occasions. The possibility of relocating Evers to an NAACP field secretary post in California was seriously explored.

As far as Myrlie was concerned, it was both irresponsible and suicidal for her husband to remain in Mississippi. They did not speak often about the problem directly. But when they did discuss it, Myrlie was direct and to the point. "Medgar, the children and I would rather eat bread and drink water some other place, than to have you stay here and continue this fight and be killed," Myrlie recalls explaining to her husband. On several occasions the tensions between the couple reached a breaking point, and Myrlie questioned whether her marriage could be maintained. Myrlie confesses frankly that she worried whether they were "going to work this through and stay together. But it was all out of fear that he might lose his life and that we might lose him. It was really out of love, all of us who truly cared about him."[1] John R. Salter recalls visiting the Evers home with his wife in 1962 on a Saturday night:

"There was no answer to our knock and I knocked again. Then the door opened, only a crack, and I could see a gun. I called my name and Medgar opened the door, instantly apologetic. He had come to Jackson for the weekend. Inside the Evers home, furniture was piled in front of all the windows. At least half a dozen firearms were in the living room and kitchen. The children were in bed and

Medgar and his wife and Eldri and myself visited for a good while. The barricaded nature of the Evers home was not uncommon for a civil rights person in Mississippi; what was uncommon was the fact that both Medgar and his wife were mighty calm. It was a very pleasant visit—unusually so, considering the fact that . . . no one was any more prime a target in the Deep South at that time than was Medgar."[2]

Medgar finally came to the difficult decision that he would stay and fight the segregationists and white supremacists, come what may. Myrlie explains that her husband's attitude was: "Come hell or high water, he was going to remain." Evers explained to his wife that he could not ask others to sacrifice for the struggle if he was not prepared to make the ultimate sacrifice, and that she would have to understand and support his decision. "He said, 'You're either with me or not. I cannot leave home and fight white folk, fight my folk and try to bring them along, and come home and fight with you. You have a decision to make, Myrlie.'" In making this choice, Evers still wanted to avoid the political limelight. "He was a 'servant leader,'" Myrlie relates. "Medgar all but ran away from being characterized [as] acting in any way where he would be seen as the [leader]. . . . He knew he was the one who was going to be killed, with the hope of those who wanted to see him dead, of getting rid of him and the movement at the same time." Evers believed that the freedom struggle must not be halted solely by his own death; consequently, he owed it to the movement to downplay his own centrality and significance. Evers's refusal to promote himself became a major issue for Myrlie:

"I would encourage Medgar to, you know, in the press releases that went out, 'mention yourself' . . . in terms of speaking other places. Hey, you can make some money, supplement our income. Build yourself up. Let's get some coverage on you. . . . And that man would give me one of his stares. 'That's not what I am about. I'm about doing the job that needs to be done. Let others get the glory if they want it.'"[3]

In late 1960, James Meredith, a native Mississippian and African American who had served nine years in the U.S. Air Force, contacted Evers regarding his intention to apply for admission to the all-white University of Mississippi. Meredith knew of Evers's reputation of integrity and respected him, but he seriously questioned the ability of the NAACP, in his words, "[to] command the needed following among Mississippians to seriously attack the system of 'White Supremacy.'" Evers consulted with Marshall in the NAACP national office, and the chief counsel questioned Meredith's background and motives. From Evers's home, Meredith and Evers spoke with Marshall, who according to Meredith's accounts, "wanted some documents to prove that I was legitimate . . . I had never allowed anyone to question my integrity in any way, and as far as I was concerned the case was closed. Other alternatives would have to be pursued." With great difficulty, Medgar explained to the frustrated and angry Meredith that Marshall's requests weren't unusual, and represented no challenge to the truthfulness of his desire to attend college; rather, to win the struggle to desegregate "Ole Miss" it was necessary to prepare their case comprehensively. "I must give sole credit to Medgar Evers, his expert knowledge of human nature and his ability to deal with people, for the case moving beyond this point," Meredith wrote in 1966.[4] With Evers's help, Meredith secured the NAACP's backing, and on January 31, 1961, he formally applied for admission to the University of Mississippi. Meredith's subsequent admission and enrollment, in the fall of 1962, sparked massive white rioting and demonstrations on the campus, which were quelled only by the presence of federal marshals and military police.[5]

In May 1961, CORE initiated the "Freedom Rides," a series of nonviolent demonstrations challenging racial segregation on public buses and at transportation centers, without the formal endorsement or participation of the NAACP. By late June 1961, over 160 Freedom Riders had been arrested and incarcerated in Jackson alone. Many were brutally beaten by police and were physically abused by guards in the state penitentiary and in municipal jail.

The NAACP offered legal assistance to the demonstrators, but attempted to make it abundantly clear to the press that it "has not been involved directly in the Freedom Rides in Jackson."[6] As the SCLC and SNCC also developed constituencies and desegregation projects in Mississippi, Evers found himself increasingly called upon to be a negotiator among rival groups with frequently competing interests [see Document 65].

"In general, Medgar's attitude toward these organizations was one of hearty welcome," Myrlie observed in *For Us, The Living*. "He knew the volume of work to be done; he knew the need of numbers of dedicated workers."[7] Yet Evers made it plain that he questioned many of the organizing tactics of the groups, particularly King's SCLC. "At first Medgar did not take kindly to the idea of demonstrations. He had seen them accomplish results in some places, but he felt that the time and place had to be chosen carefully." He was critical of the SCLC's "tactics that had too often meant the total organization of a community to precipitate a crisis and win concessions and then the collapse of everything as the organization moved to another city, leaving the local Negroes to suffer the inevitable consequences," Myrlie asserted.[8] In some areas of the state, many activists who had been members of the NAACP but who favored a more militant approach in challenging segregation were recruited into the new organizations. In several Mississippi towns, the core membership of the NAACP would be "recruited away." Evers would be forced "to drop what he was doing and go to these towns to rebuild a branch that had been raided for both membership and loyalty," according to Myrlie.[9] Everyone understood, however, that such factional disputes and rivalries undermined the entire movement. Finally, the different groups formed a united front in Mississippi called COFO, the Council of Federated Organizations. In 1962, Henry became COFO's president; in its leadership structure, Bob Moses represented SNCC and CORE was represented by David Dennis. Amzie Moore and other civil-rights veterans provided invaluable contacts and assistance to the newcomers.[10]

Evers continued to build the NAACP on the ground, addressing the demands of members, recruiting new memberships, investigating crimes—but now under quite different circumstances. As the documents in this chapter outline, Evers continued to be enormously busy. On February 12, 1961, Evers addressed Jackson's New Mt. Zion Baptist Church, declaring that while "we have made great strides in the field of human rights we cannot let up now!" [See Document 56.] On March 28, 1961, he participated in a mass rally at Jackson's College Hill Baptist Church, protesting the arrest of NAACP youth members from Jackson State College [see Document 60]; the following day he led a demonstration in front of the Jackson courthouse to protest being denied access to the trial of the student protestors; on March 30 he helped to organize a mass rally of 1,500 people. Medgar was again a featured speaker at a mass protest rally in Jackson on April 20, where he militantly declared, "We are here to indicate to the world that so long as there is segregation and discrimination anywhere in the state of Mississippi or the United States of America, for that matter, we are not and shall not be satisfied" [see Document 59]. On June 7, 1961, with Roy Wilkins as the keynote speaker, Evers coordinated a "gigantic rally" that attracted 2,000 supporters in Jackson [see Documents 61 and 63]. On July 28, 1961, Evers demanded that the FBI investigate the murder of Jerry Jefferson, who was killed by a law-enforcement officer in Batesville. On October 10, 1961, Evers spoke at a protest rally held at the Masonic Temple in McComb, pledging the NAACP's support for students who were expelled from a local high school after they had participated in sit-in demonstrations. Evers maintained a similar schedule throughout 1962, culminating in October with his coordination of a black boycott of the racially segregated state fair in Jackson.

56 Medgar W. Evers, Address

SUNDAY, FEBRUARY 12, 1961
JACKSON BRANCH, NEW MT. ZION BAPTIST

The occasion for which we are assembled here today is a glorious one. It symbolizes a long struggle for human rights in this great country and it commemorates the beginning of an organization that has uncompromisingly led in the fight for total democracy.

It was well said by an early American patriot that "These are times that try men's souls; the summer soldier and the sunshine patriot in the time of trouble will shrink from the service of his country, but those who stand it now deserve the love and admiration of men and women alike." Those words were spoken in part by Tom Paine during the crisis of the early history of this country. Today, those same words accurately describe the National Association for the Advancement of Colored People. For certainly, the NAACP has not shrunk from the call of duty in this day of crisis; to the contrary, it has waged a righteous battle for Americans of all racial groups, especially that of the American Negro.

Our job is not complete and because we have made great strides in the field of human rights we cannot let up now! But rather, it is necessary from this day forward that we take increased devotion, lest those precious rights we have gained be taken away. Let it not be said of us when history records these momentous times, that we slept while our rights were being taken by those who would keep us in slavery and by those who say that we are doing all right, for you and I know that we are doing all right.

Today we live in an age in which man has accomplished scientifically the unbelievable. Leontyne Price sang at the Metropolitan Opera in New York City while at the same time she was seen in her hometown of Laurel, Mississippi on television. Spaceships read about in Buck Rogers comic strips 20 years ago are realities today. Even with this amazing advance in science and technology, man has not until this day done what God would have us do and that is, love our neighbor as ourselves, especially if your neighbor happens to be black and the other neighbor white.

There are many examples to justify such a statement which we will not attempt to go into here, for certainly we feel that our ministers can do a much better job.

However, ladies and gentlemen, we have a great challenge before us here in the city of Jackson, Hinds County, and Mississippi. There is much for us to do and it can be done if we but set our sights on our objectives and continue to work toward their completion.

I shall list for us some of the things here in the city of Jackson which should require our immediate attention:

1. More and varied jobs for Negroes
   a. Factories:
      Vickers
      General Electric
   b. City employment
      Policemen
      Policewomen
      Firemen
   c. Federal
      Internal Revenue personnel
      Postal clerks
      Typists
      Office personnel at the Veterans Administration
2. More registered voters
      Progressive Voters League doing good job as well as the Community Improvement Association
3. The implementation of the U.S. Supreme Court decision of May 17, 1954 with regards to schools (clipping)

4. The unrestricted use of public facilities, such as parks, libraries, etc.

5. The removal of segregation signs at the bus stations, train stations and city buses, as well as unrestricted seating arrangements for all passengers on the city bus lines.

These and many other opportunities belie the founding of the NAACP whose birthday we commemorate here. We must be ever-vigilant lest we lose sight of our objectives.

The NAACP is no stronger than its membership. If the membership is strong, the NAACP is strong. If the membership is weak, the NAACP is weak.

In closing, I will paraphrase some remarks of President John F. Kennedy during the campaign for president and his inauguration address: This is a great organization but it can be a greater organization; then, ask not what the NAACP can do for you, but what you can do for the NAACP.

[handwritten notes: "our young people," "Mrs. Blanche Moore"]

Leontyne Price (b. 1927)—A native of Laurel, Mississippi, Price studied music and singing at Central State University (Ohio) and the Juilliard School (New York). In 1955, NBC had Price sing the lead in its TV adaptation of *Tosca*, and despite strenuous objections from southern NBC affiliates, the show was broadcast and became a critical success. Price starred in various other TV musicals, followed by a hugely successful career at the Metropolitan Opera. See Dominique-Renè de Lerma, "Price, Leontyne," in Darlene Clark Hine, ed., *Black Women in America: An Historical Encyclopedia* (Brooklyn, NY: Carlson, 1993), 941–943.

"Buck Rogers"—A popular newspaper comic strip chronicling the adventures of an astronaut, William Rogers, who wakes after five hundred years of suspended animation.

---

*

57 Medgar Evers, "Yesterday—Today," Text Fragment

FEBRUARY 12, 1961

". . . We cannot let up now—it is necessary from this day forward that we take increased devotion lest those precious rights we have gained be taken away."

Medgar W. Evers
Mississippi Civil Rights Leader
February 12, 1961
Jackson, Mississippi

58 Medgar Evers to Roy Wilkins

March 29, 1961

Mr. Roy Wilkins
20 West 40th Street
New York 18, New York

Dear Mr. Wilkins:

The first "Sit-In" type demonstration in Mississippi, as I am sure you already know, took place Monday, March 27, 1961 at the Jackson Municipal Library, by nine young NAACP Members from our Tougaloo College Chapter.

These young people exhibited the greatest amount of courage in the face of mounting tension and were reported in our local newspapers as being "orderly, intelligent, and cooperative."

Their stay in jail was for approximately thirty-two (32) hours, primarily because the sheriff (J. R. Gilfoy) in Hinds County, conveniently made himself absent, rather than approve the property bonds which had been secured. Finally however, at 7:10 p.m. on Tuesday evening March 28, 1961 the young people were released.

This act of bravery and concern on the part of these nine young people has seemed to electrify Negroes' desire for Freedom here in Mississippi, which will doubtlessly be shown in increase in memberships and funds for 1961.

Mr. Wilkins, my main reason for writing this letter is that, it would be an inspirational gesture for these nine young people if we could arrange to have them attend our National Convention in Philadelphia, July 10–16. While we realize this would be an expensive item which is not necessarily included in the budget, it would give further inspiration and leadership to our cause, here in Mississippi.

Please consider having these young people attend our National Convention. I would appreciate an early reply.

Respectfully yours,

Medgar W. Evers
Field Secretary
MWE:11
cc: Hurley
Current
Wright

J. R. Gilfoy—The Hinds County sheriff. Gilfoy was an officer of the Jackson Police Department during the Jackson movement. When Beckwith was arrested as a suspect of the Medgar murder and was put in his custody, Gilfoy treated Beckwith with courtesy, allowing him to use official envelopes and see unlimited number of daily visitors. See Reed Massengill, *Portrait of a Racist: The Man Who Killed Medgar Evers?* (New York: St. Martin's Press, 1994), 164, 177.

✳

59 Medgar W. Evers, Address

APRIL 20, 1961
MASS PROTEST MEETING

The occasion for which we are assembled here tonight is a righteous one. It symbolizes a mere beachhead of a dedicated struggle to make possible the fulfillment of the American dream that is of justice and equality for all without regard to race, creed, or color.

It is significant that we are here tonight, for it indicates that at long last we here in Mississippi are determined to protest injustices through the courts and through such demonstrations as we are having here tonight.

Let it be known to those who say that Negroes in Mississippi are satisfied, that tonight we are here to indicate to the world that so long as there is segregation and discrimination anywhere in the state of Mississippi or the United States of America, for that matter, we are not and shall not be satisfied.

We are making gains in our struggle for first class citizenship, but it cannot be overemphasized that we have only begun this fight, and that there must be many sacrifices.

It was well said by an early American patriot that "These are the times that try men's souls. The summer soldier and the sunshine patriot in the time of trouble will shrink for the services of his country. But those who stand it now deserve the love and admiration of men and women alike."

Those words were spoken in part by Tom Paine during the crises of the early history of this country. Today, these same words describe these young people who have taken a giant step for freedom in the face of tremendous odds and impending crises. Americans and Mississippians of good will everywhere applaud the courage and foresight of these young people and are willing to stand behind them to the end that justice is done. Suffice it be said here, that while the majority of people here in Mississippi stand solidly behind the action taken by members of our Tougaloo College chapter NAACP, March 27, 1962, and the intercollegiate chapter NAACP of Jackson, April 19, 1961; the NAACP nationwide stands 100 percent behind you also.

Although great strides in the field of human relations have been made, we cannot let up now! But rather, it is necessary from this day forward that we take increased devotion lest those precious rights we have gained be taken away. Let it not be said of us when history records these momentous times that we slept while our rights were being taken by those who would keep us in slavery and by those who say that we are doing all right.

Today we live in an age in which man has accomplished scientifically the unbelievable. Leontyne Price sang at the Metropolitan Opera in New York City, while at the same time she was seen in her home town of Laurel, Mississippi on television. Spaceships read about in Buck Rogers comic strips 20 years ago are realities today. Even with this amazing advance in science and technology, man has not until this day done what God would have us do. That is, love our neighbor as ourselves; especially if one neighbor happens to be black and the other neighbor white.

However, ladies and gentlemen, we have a great challenge before us here in the city of Jackson, Hinds County, and Mississippi. There is much for us to do and it can be done if we but set our sights on our objectives and continue to work toward their completion.

I shall list for us some of the things here in the city of Jackson which should require our immediate attention:

1. More and varied jobs for Negroes
    a. Factories
       Vickers
       General Electric, etc.

b. City employment

Policemen and policewomen

Firemen

c. Federal

Internal Revenue personnel

Postal clerks

Typists

Office personnel at the Veterans Administration

2. More registered voters

3. The unrestricted use of public facilities, such as parks, libraries, etc.

4. The removal of segregation signs at the bus stations, train stations, and city buses, as well as segregated seating arrangements for all passengers on the city bus lines.

These and many other opportunities are available through persistent effort for their attainment. We must be ever-vigilant lest we lose sight of our objectives.

In closing, may I say, let men of good will and understanding change the old order, for this is a new day!

Thomas Paine (1737–1809)—An Anglo-American revolutionary writer, Paine was the author of *Common Sense* (1776) that denounced the British Monarchy and justified American independence. Paine also wrote several articles for *Pennsylvania Magazine*, one of which called for the abolition of slavery. After the American Revolutionary War, Paine left the United States and lived in England and France, taking part in the French Revolution and opposing the execution of Louis XVI. Medgar quotes from Paine's Revolutionary War pamphlet series, *The Crisis* (1776–83). See Eric Foner, *Tom Paine and Revolutionary America* (New York: Oxford University Press, 1976); and John Keane, *Tom Paine: A Political Life* (London: Bloomsbury, 1995).

*

60 Monthly Report: "Desegregation Activities"

APRIL 21, 1961

DESEGREGATION ACTIVITIES

Desegregation activities were set in motion March 27, 1961. When nine (9) members of our Tougaloo College Chapter of NAACP went to the main public library in the city of Jackson to do some research; and after about ten minutes' stay they were arrested for disturbing the peace, despite the fact that officers indicated that the group was very orderly. After spending thirty-two hours in jail, the nine were released on one thousand dollar bonds each. Their trial was set for March 29, 1961 for 4 o'clock p.m., in the Jackson Municipal court building.

A mass protest meeting was held Tuesday, March 28, 1961 at the College Hill Baptist Church. It drew a capacity crowd of some eight hundred people, as well as a large contingent of Jackson city policemen.

Many Negroes as well as whites were kept out of the courtroom across the street after it had been filled to capacity. The same one hundred or more Negroes who had gathered across the street anxiously awaiting the trial began applauding when members of the nine were being escorted into the court building. Instantly, there was a call from some police officers saying "get 'em out of here," and it was then that hoards of policemen and two vicious police dogs converged on Negro citizens only; and began whipping us with night sticks as well as extending the leashes on the dogs to the extent that Rev. S. Leon Whitney, pastor of Parish Street Baptist Church, was bitten on the arm (see picture of dog leaping at man in the newspapers). The Field Secretary was struck a number of times in the back by officers with billy clubs, and on the head with a pistol, by a man in plain clothes.

An eighty-one-year-old man, Mr. W. B. Wrenn, of 1523 Valley Street, Jackson, Mississippi, was beaten so brutally by the police that his left arm was broken above the wrist. The Field Secretary proceeded from the scene of the incident immediately, to his office on West Lynch Street, and called our National Office. The first call was not put through because of the line being busy, so immediately a call was made to the Department of Justice, to Mr. Burt Marshall, explaining what had taken place and asking that the young people who were on trial be given the fullest protection of the law. I was later able to put a call through to the National Office, at which time I talked with Mr. Wilkins and explained in detail what had taken place.

This act on the part of police officials brought on greater unity in the Negro community and projected the NAACP in a position of being the accepted spokesman for the Negro people.

The young people drew one hundred [dollar] fines and suspended sentences, which were immediately appealed.

On the night of March 29, 1961 the NAACP called for a Mass Meeting for March 30, 1961, at which time Mr. Clarence Mitchell, of the Washington Bureau NAACP spoke despite the presence of approximately thirty-six police men, tornado warnings, and torrential downpours. Approximately 1500 people came to this mass meeting to protest the brutality on the part of the police department of the city of Jackson. Similar mass meetings have been held since that time.

April 19, 1961 four members of our intercollegiate chapter of NAACP for the city of Jackson took seats on a city bus on Capitol Street in the section normally reserved for white passengers. They were arrested after refusing to move when ordered to do so. A mass meeting was called for April 20, 1961 at the Masonic Temple, at which time the Field Secretary was the principal speaker (speech attached). Approximately 700 people attended this mass meeting. The four young people involved in the bus incident were charged with "breach of the peace." The trial in city court is scheduled for Friday, April 21, 1961 at 4 o'clock p.m.

Mrs. Julie Wright, our Youth Secretary from Atlanta, was instrumental in organizing the intercollegiate chapter of NAACP for the city of Jackson and is now in the process of organizing a college chapter for Campbell College. All in all things look very bright, despite the brutality. We are appreciative to the National Office and to the Washington Bureau for the help that was and is given during these times of crises.

Respectfully submitted,

Medgar W. Evers
Field Secretary
MWE:11

(Dictated but not read)

---

61 Memorandum

JUNE 7, 1961
NAACP PLANS JACKSON, MISSISSIPPI, VOTER MEETING

The NAACP will hold a mass registration and vote rally here tonight at the Masonic Temple.

Medgar Evers, the Association's state field secretary, said that the meeting seeks to "stimulate a drive for more and better jobs" in addition to increased voting.

This is part of the NAACP's "Operation Mississippi" launched as a counter move to the utilization of trained police dogs on peacefully assembled Negroes here March 29.

The drive also seeks employment for Negroes at plants holding government contracts: police department employment in Jackson; Negro employment in the internal revenue bureau; and Negro office workers for the local VA hospital.

62 "NAACP Aide Is Freed, Supreme Court of Mississippi Upsets Contempt Finding," United Press International

New York Times

JUNE 13, 1961

JACKSON, Miss. (UPI)—The Mississippi Supreme Court overturned today the contempt conviction of Medgar Evers, state field representative for the National Association for the Advancement of Colored People.

Mr. Evers, who is 35 years old, was sentenced to a $100 fine and thirty days in jail in Forrest County Circuit Court last December for criticizing the conviction of another Negro for burglary.

The high court said today, "The Courts are subject to the same criticism as other people when a case is finished."

Mr. Evers, a Mississippi native and the association's only paid official in the state, said it was "encouraging that there is a court of law in our state that regards freedom of speech as a cornerstone of our American heritage."

Although it freed Mr. Evers from his sentence, the high court took issue with his statement calling the conviction of Clyde Kennard "a mockery of justice."

---

*

63 Monthly Report: "Branch Activity," "Legal Action," "Zoo Sit-In," and "Freedom Riders"

JUNE 21, 1961

BRANCH ACTIVITY

On June 5, 1961 the Field Secretary met with members of the Prentiss Branch of N.A.A.C.P. at which time there was an enthusiastic meeting and a number of memberships taken in. Reports were made relative to the "Freedom Riders" and "The NAACP Program and Policy" as they relate to our National goals.

Steps were taken as well as memberships to organize a Youth Council, to be connected with the Prentiss Branch. The council, we hope, will be completely organized in the near future.

The Jackson Branch of N.A.A.C.P. staged a gigantic rally, June 7, at which time our Executive Secretary, Mr. Roy Wilkins, was the principal speaker. The audience was most enthusiastic and the crowd numbered 2,000 or more. Mr. Wilkins gave a very inspiring address which captivated the people of the city. A total of one thousand dollars was taken up in the public offering at this rally, part of which will go to the Jackson branch Freedom Fund.

[...]

LEGAL ACTION

For the first time in the history of Mississippi, a Negro filed suit to enter the University of Mississippi. This suit was filed May 31, 1961, by the Legal Defense Educational Fund of NAACP, in behalf of Mr. J. B. Meredith, a member of the Jackson Branch of NAACP. Mr. Meredith is seeking admission to the summer session as well as the fall term on the undergraduate level. The present legal status of Mr. Meredith's suit is that a trial will be held on July 10, 1961. There was a hearing on a motion to admit Mr. Meredith, for the first session this summer. The hearing was not completed because of long drawn out testimony.

In rapid fire action on the heel of the suit to integrate "Ole Miss" came legal action again from Legal Defense Educational Fund of the NAACP, in behalf of Mr. Samuel Bailey, Vice president of the Jackson Branch; Mr. Joseph Broadwater, former President of the Jackson Branch and Mr. Burnett L. Jacobs, active member; to enjoin the city of Jackson, police department, the State of Mississippi et al., from continued arrest of inter as well as intrastate passengers; it is a sweeping injunction which after having been won will open up all transportation (interstate as well as intrastate) on a non-segregated basis, including the airport and restaurant.

ZOO SIT-IN

Members of our NAACP Youth Council and College Chapter on June 4, 1961 after the Mayor had gotten on Nation-wide television and said the zoo was integrated, sat in at the zoo. These young people led by Mr. Amos C. Brown, were arrested and detained for thirty minutes after Mr. Brown pointed out that the Mayor said the zoo was integrated.

On the following Tuesday, June 6, some of the same young people visited the zoo again, this time they were not arrested; however, again on June 14, 1961 while sitting on the benches at the zoo, Mr. Amos Brown and Mr. James Hopkins were arrested for "breach of the peace." They are presently out on five hundred [dollars] bail each. The contempt citation against the Field Secretary which was issued by the Forrest County Judge Stanton Hall, was reversed in the Mississippi Supreme Court, in a unanimous decision on June 12, 1961.

FREEDOM RIDERS

To date a total of one hundred thirty one "Freedom Riders" have been convicted for "breach of the peace." There has been a total of 43 released on bond; four have paid their fines, 40 in the penitentiary and 40 remain in the jails here in Jackson.

The Field Secretary spoke for the Columbia, South Carolina Branch of NAACP, on June 15, 1961 and the Nashville Tennessee Branch of NAACP on June 18, 1961. Both meetings were enthusiastically received.

James H. Meredith (1933–)—Native of Kosciusko, Mississippi, Meredith served in the US Air Force between 1951 and 1960, and in 1962 applied for admission to the University of Mississippi, which resulted in the 1963 Supreme Court decision in his favor and subsequent university-wide rioting on the campus. He was an organizer of the 1966 "Walk against Fear," and was shot in the stomach during the march from Memphis to Jackson, Mississippi. Described variously as "independent," "iconoclast," and "controversial," Meredith once worked as a staff for archconservative North Carolina Senator Jesse Helms, in the late 1980s. See James Meredith, *Three Years in Mississippi* (Bloomington, Indiana University Press, 1966); Peter Levy, *The Civil Rights Movement* (Westport, CT: Greenwood, 1998), 138–139; and Nadine Cohodas, "James Meredith and the Integration of Ole Miss," *Journal of Blacks in Higher Education* (Summer 1997), Issue 19, 112–122.

Samuel Bailey—A Jackson NAACP branch leader, Bailey was one of the major petitioners of desegregation suits against the Jackson City school board following the 1954 *Brown* decision. In 1963, he was a member of the Citizens Committee for Human Rights in Jackson during the rise in local mass demonstrations. See Payne, 161, 211.

Joseph Broadwater—He filed a 1961 federal suit to halt the city of Jackson from arresting Freedom Riders from their attempts at desegregating local public transportation facilities. Broadwater was also active in the Progressive Voter League in Jackson. See a 1961 investigative memo by the State Sovereignty Commission, online, http://mdah/state/ms/us/arlib/contents/er/imagelisting.php, [2–55–3–8–2–1–1].

Burnett L. Jacobs—He joined Bailey and Broadwater in a desegregation federal suit against the city of Jackson. Jacobs was an underwriter for a Jackson insurance company, and later moved to Mount Beulah to become the administrator for the conference center for Disciples of Christ. See State Sovereignty Commission file, [1–116–0–2–1–1–1], online at http://mdah.state.ms.us/arlib/contents/er/.

James Hopkins (1941–)—Alcorn College student who took part in a 1961 sit-in at local zoo. Hopkins later testified in court and argued that he had merely sat down to rest. See local newspaper clipping in the State Sovereignty Commission files, online [2–72–2–32–1–1–1] http://mdah.state.ms.us/arlib/contents/er/.

---

64 Monthly Report
"Direction Action"

SEPTEMBER 6, 1961

[…]

The Clarksdale Youth Council of NAACP stated its first demonstrating during the month of August, when three members of the Council attempted to buy an interstate train ticket in the "white" Illinois Central passenger train terminal. All three were arrested on breach of the peace charges. Their cases are on appeal to County Court.

The Vicksburg Youth Council staged their first demonstration when two youngsters picketed a segregated movie house. They, too, were arrested and charged with breach of peace.

After picketing variety stores in the city of Greenville, Mississippi, Johnnie Frazier, former president of the Greenville Youth Council of NAACP, was arrested for breach of the peace while picketing Wool-worth's on August 28, 1961. He was given a $100 fine and 90 days sentence. His case is presently on appeal.

      *

65 Memorandum to Roy Wilkins, Gloster B. Current, and Ruby Hurley from Medgar W. Evers

OCTOBER 12, 1961
OPERATION OF OTHER CIVIL RIGHTS ORGANIZATIONS
IN THE STATE OF MISSISSIPPI

This is the first report of the activities of other Civil Rights Organizations in Mississippi. Early in May of 1961, the Field Secretary from the Congress of Racial Equality (CORE) came to Jackson in the person of Mr. Tom Gaither. This was in connection with the proposed "Freedom Rides" which was scheduled to arrive here in Jackson on May 16, for a planned mass rally and then proceed to New Orleans, Louisiana. Of course, it is general knowledge that the Freedom Rides did not go beyond Jackson, and instead of arriving here as planned for the 16th of May, the first riders arrived here eight days late on May 24, 1961. After the first group of riders had arrived the CORE representative, Mr. Tom Gaither, was busy contacting ministers and other groups in the city of Jackson in a sympathetic mood to provide personal articles for the Freedom Riders who were being detained in jail. It was during this period that Mrs. Clarie Collins Harvey, a funeral directoress; Mrs. A. N. E. Logan, a cosmetic dealer; and Mrs. Thelma Sanders, owner of a millinery shop, formed an organization known as "Woman Power Unlimited." It has, as its primary objective, to aid the Freedom Riders with personal necessities and to locate housing for those that were released on bond.

During the course of time when the Freedom Riders were jailed, continuously coming and being bonded out, there were a series of workshops conducted on non-violence, as well as a movie shown on "The Nashville Story" (NBC White Paper) which were conducted by released Freedom Riders from Nashville Christian Leadership Conference. These workshops were presided over by Diane Nash, James Bevel, Marion Berry, Charles Sherrod, and Bernard Layafette [sic].

These hastily gotten together workshops were for the purpose of involving Jackson Citizens into the freedom ride movement, which had not been advocated by the NAACP. As a result of these series of meetings there was formed what is now called "The Jackson Non-Violent Movement" which opened [an] office at 1114–1/2 Lynch Street. It was there that their workshops intensified, which involved a number of young people in desegregation attempts at the various transportation facilities in the city of Jackson; also, sit-ins at the Walgreen Drug Store and picketing of a meeting of members of the Southern Governors' Conference, which was held here.

The organization was forced to move from that Lynch Street address by the landlord, due to economic pressures, to 1104 Lynch Street, where they presently are.

Since the Freedom movements began and the formation of the organizations mentioned there have been a number of mass meetings held. Several such meetings involved the personality Dr. Martin Luther King, Jr., which attracted a large number of people.

The next meeting was the return of the Freedom Riders when some 180 riders were returned to be arraigned. Mr. James Farmer,

Director of CORE was the guest speaker at this meeting; the attendance was estimated at 3,000 persons.

However, despite the large number of persons who turned out for this meeting of James Farmer, less than six hundred dollars was collected for the public offering. In the case of Dr. King, where some 2,500 to 3,000 were in attendance, less than eight hundred dollars was collected. These meetings were sponsored jointly by Student Non-Violent Coordinating Committee and Woman Power Unlimited.

Presently the Student Non-Violent Coordinating Committee is maintaining a skeleton operation here in the city of Jackson; with no direct action having taken place in several months. Most of the leaders of the organization mentioned earlier have been charged with "contributing to the delinquency of minors" and are out on heavy bonds, or have warrants out for their arrests when they return. Their activities here in Jackson at the present time are almost non-existent.

There was an attempt on the part of non-violent students to organize on Tougaloo College campus, however, due to our strong NAACP Chapter there, they have not made any headway. There have also been attempts to get an organization at J. P. Campbell College, which have not met with success, there again we have a strong NAACP College Chapter.

Members of Student Non-Violent Coordinating Committee set up offices in McComb, Mississippi, during the month of August, reportedly for the purpose of a pilot registration and voting project, as this first group moved into McComb, without my knowledge and through our McComb Branch they became established; in charge of this operation was Mr. Robert Moses, a young man of Manhattan, New York City, he was assisted by Travis Britt, John Hardy, Reginald Robinson and others.

These individuals fanned out into three counties, Pike, Amite, and Walthall. They made it clear that this was Student Non-Violent Coordinating Committee and the Southern Christian Leadership Conference, and they felt that the NAACP's name should not be brought in even though members of the NAACP were carrying out the operation. We, of course, had a conference with members of the board of the McComb Branch and the President, and this matter was quickly brought to a focus, so much so until rather than have this a joint operation with the NAACP, the non violent group broke away from the local NAACP. It was not until they began to run into difficulties securing bonds for young people they had caused to be arrested and until they themselves, Britt, Moses, and Hardy, became involved with some hoodlums, law enforcement officers and voter registrars which landed them either in jail or gave them severe beatings; did they ask for NAACP assistance publicly and cooperatively.

For instance, $2,500.00 was sent down by the National office for bail of Brenda Travis, Ike Lewis, Robert Talbert, Horace Watkins, and Elmer Hayes, as well as $100.00 bond placed on John Hardy, who became involved with the registrar in Walthall County. In each of these instances, Attorney Jack H. Young, has represented these individuals; frequently at the expense of the association and occasionally at the expense of other organizations.

The present demonstrations being conducted by the students at McComb's Burgland High School were instigated by this group, and as a result of the mass demonstrations which have taken place, some 119 students were arrested for protesting in front of the city hall. Our president of the McComb, Mississippi Branch of NAACP, Mr. Curtis C. Bryant, was picked up two days after attending a public meeting where he had made remarks and was charged with contributing to the delinquency of minors. Mr. Bryant is out on $200.00 bond.

Presently many of the students, who have been suspended from Burgland High School have returned to classes; after having signed a statement to the effect that they would not demonstrate again; subjected to expulsion from school for the rest of the year.

The Voter Registration pilot project of this movement has not netted more than twenty registered voters, in Pike county, none in Walthall and Amite Counties. In the case of Amite County, one member of our Branch, a Mr. Herbert Lee, was killed by a State Representative, allegedly because he was trying to attack him.

However, it is generally believed he was killed because of his activities in trying to get Negroes registered to vote. A memorial service is being planned for Mr. Lee, on October 29, 1961 at the Mt. Pilgrim Baptist church, near Gillsburg, Mississippi. The Field Secretary will be in attendance at this memorial service.

Other persons reported on the death list in Amite County for their Civil Rights Activities are the president of our Amite County Branch, Mr. E. W. Steptoe, Rev. Alfred Knox, and Rev. Cassie Tobias.

Respectfully submitted,

Medgar W. Evers
Field Secretary

Tom Gaither—A field secretary of CORE, and Gordon Carey, initiated the Freedom Rides in 1961 to challenge southern segregation on interstate buses and terminals. Gaither as a young college student had been involved in massive desegregation campaigns in Rock Hill, North Carolina, and Orangeburg, South Carolina. See August Meier and Elliot Rudwick, *CORE: A Study in the Civil Rights Movement, 1942–1968* (New York: Oxford University Press, 1973), 104, 116–119, 136; and J. Charles Jones, "Timeline: Rock Hill & Charlotte Sit-ins," http://www.crmvet.org/info/rockhill.htm.

CORE remained one of the crucial civil-rights groups in the movement, participating in Mississippi's 1964 Freedom Summer campaign and other important mobilizations. CORE began to support demands for "Black Power" in 1966–67, leading to the departure of most white activists from the group. Conservative black nationalists led by Roy Innis seized control of CORE's national leadership in 1968, and the goup splintered into political irrelevance by the early 1970s.

Clarie Collins Harvey (1916–1995)—A native of Jackson, Harvey was a successful business woman and owner of Collins Funeral Homes and Collins Insurance Companies. She was a member of the Mississippi Advisory Committee to the United States Commission on Civil Rights (1960–1970) and a life member of the NAACP and Urban League. As Medgar notes, she founded Woman Power Unlimited to help Freedom Riders held in Hinds County jail. See Mary Hamilton, et al., *Freedom Riders Speak for Themselves* (Detroit: News and Letters, 1961); George Alexander Swell, "Clarie Collins Harvey: An Involved Woman," *Mississippi Black History Makers* (Jackson: University Press of Mississippi, 1977), 267–275.

Diane Nash (1938–)—Nash participated in Fisk University students' sit-in campaign against Woolworth café in 1960 and soon emerged as a leader of the movement. When SNCC was formed in late 1961, she became a field secretary. In 1962 she was jailed in Jackson for teaching black children the philosophy of non-violence and direct action, and sentenced to two years in prison, which she later successfully appealed. Nash was an organizer for SCLC's Birmingham and Selma campaigns as well. See Jeanne Thesharis, "Diane Nash," in Darlene Clark Hine, ed., *Black Women in America: An Historical Encyclopedia* (Brooklyn, NY: Carlson, 1993), 834–836.

James Luther Bevel (1936–)—Originally an ordained Baptist minister in Nashville, Bevel was member of Nashville chapter of SCLC, and was a key organizer of the 1960 sit-in against Woolworth. He joined SNCC and married Diane Nash, and was also actively involved with many of Martin Luther King's campaigns in Selma, the March on Washington, D.C., and the Chicago open housing movement. See Ralph Luker, "Bevel, James Luther," *Historical Dictionary of the Civil Rights Movement* (Lanham, MD: Scarecrow Press, 1997), 25–26.

Marion Barry (1936–)—The first SNCC chairman, Barry was like Nash and Bevel actively involved in Nashville movement and later joined the Mississippi movement. After he moved to Washington, D.C., in 1965 to build a SNCC chapter, Barry became involved in district politics, and eventually was elected mayor in 1978, a position he held until 1990 (when he was arrested and tried for cocaine possession). Barry was reelected as Washington D.C. mayor in 1944. See Ralph Luker, "Barry, Marion," *Historical Dictionary of the Civil Rights Movement* (Lanham, MD: Scarecrow Press, 1997), 18–19.

Charles M. Sherrod (1937–)—A native of Virginia, Sherrod was SNCC field secretary from 1961 to 1967 in Albany, Georgia. After he left SNCC, he was a director of a cooperative farming project, New Communities, Inc., from 1969 to 1985. See Garrow, Bearing the Cross, 173–178; and Michael Fletcher, "Veterans of the Movement Find Time Outstripping Its Gains," *Washington Post*, July 17, 1996, A13.

Bernard LaFayette (193?–)—A leader of Nashville movement, Lafayette was cofounder of SNCC, and deeply involved in King's campaigns in Birmingham and Selma. He has been a member of International Nonviolence Executive Planning Board that seeks solutions to world problems through the philosophy of nonviolence. See Carson, 32–33, 56–58, 125–128; and "A nonviolence-training workshop with special guest trainer Dr. Bernard LaFayette, Jr," *Westside Gazette*, March 5, 2003, Volume 31, issue 48, pg.3.

James Farmer (1920–1999)—Farmer was an original founder of the Congress of Racial Equality in 1942. During the Second World War, with the belief in

Ghandian non-violence that was behind the founding of CORE, he refused to serve in the military for religious reasons. In 1961 he became CORE national director and led the organization's Freedom Ride campaign in 1961. In 1969, he was appointed Assistant Secretary of Health, Education, and Welfare by Richard Nixon. He was awarded the Freedom Medal by President Bill Clinton in 1998. For more details on his life and activities, see his autobiography, *Lay Bear the Heart: An autobiography of the Civil Rights Movement* (New York: Arbor Books, 1985); Richard Severo, "James Farmer, Civil Rights Giant in the 50's and 60's, Is Dead at 79," *New York Times,* July 10, 1999, A1; and Gary Younge, "Obituary: James Farmer," *The Guardian,* July 13, 1999, pg.20.

SNCC—Student Nonviolent Coordination Committee, was formed in October of 1960 by the southern students who had organized sit-ins and other desegregation protests, with the guidance of Ella Baker and modest financial support from the SCLC. It aimed to coordinate southern-wide activities with the philosophy of non-violence against Jim Crow, and emphasized youth leadership, local participation, and decentralized decision-making. The organization was involved in many important campaigns in Alabama, Georgia, and Mississippi. In the late sixties, SNCC's focus shifted to the Black Power and anti-Vietnam War movements, and in 1969 changed its name to Student National Coordination Committee. See Clayborne Carson, *In Struggle;* Howard Zinn, *SNCC: The New Abolitionist* (Boston: Beacon Press, 1964); and Emily Stoper, *The Student Nonviolent Coordinating Committee: The Growth of Radicalism in a Civil rights Organization* (Brooklyn, NY: Carlson, 1989).

Robert Parris Moses (1935–)—A New York native and math teacher, Moses first became involved in the civil-rights movement in 1960 when he participated in a mass rally organized by veteran activist and CORE founder Bayard Rustin. He joined the SCLC and subsequently SNCC. As a Field Secretary for SNCC and Director of its Mississippi Project, Moses was among many organizers who played important roles in the creation of umbrella organization, COFO, the Mississippi Summer Project, and Mississippi Freedom Democratic Party. After leaving the movement in late 1964 and teaching in Tanzania, he started the Algebra Project in the 1980s to enhance mathematical literacy for African American children. See Eric Burner, *And Gently He shall Lead Them: Robert Parris Moses and the Civil Rights in Mississippi* (New York: New York University Press, 1994); and Robert Moses, *Radical Equations: Math Literacy and Civil Rights* (Boston: Beacon Press, 2001).

Travis Britt—A member of CORE, SNCC, SCLC, NAACP during the early 1960s, Britt participated in 1961 Freedom Ride and was jailed in Jackson city jail. Britt was also severely beaten in the Liberty County courthouse during an attempt to register black voters. Among organizers, he had a great impact on black youths of the area in his teaching of non-violence and direct action. Britt is today married to Maryland State Senator Gwendolyn Britt. See Carson, 48; and Rebecca Dana, "History's Everyday Heroes; Project Collects Memories of Civil Rights Movement," *Washington Post*, August 4, 2004, C1.

John Hardy—An SNCC worker from Memphis, Hardy joined Moses and other members in McComb to help register black voters. He was arrested in 1962 at the office of registrar when he brought two farmers for registration. The Justice Department became involved in halting Hardy's prosecution on the grounds that the 1957 Civil Rights Act prohibited voter intimidation. See Carson, 48; and James Forman, *The Making of Black Revolutionaries* (New York: McMillan, 1972), 223–233.

Reginald Robinson—An SNCC worker from Baltimore, Maryland, Robinson joined Moses in McComb in 1961 to help local blacks register to vote. His and Moses's speeches in Ruleville in 1962 were said to have inspired Fannie Lou Hamer to become an active participant in the movement. After leaving SNCC, Robinson worked for federally funded anti-poverty programs in Boston and Washington, D.C., and has subsequently worked with victims of violent crimes to receive compensation from the Department of Employment Services. See Carson, 47, 73; and Terri Shaw, "SNCC Veterans, Remembering the Battle; Civil Rights Activists, When the Future Was Forged," *Washington Post*, January 2 1990, C1.

Brenda Travis—A high school student in McComb, Travis and four others were arrested in August of 1961 during what was the first direct-action sit-in in Mississippi against Woolworth restaurant. Travis also took part in the Mc-Comb Greyhound Bus station sit-in in the same year. She was expelled and re-fused re-admittance to the school, and 100 students walked away in protest. She became a symbol of McComb's youth movement. See Dittmer, 107–114; and [2–49–0–31–2–1–1] at the State Sovereignty Commission files, online http://mdah.state.ms.us/arlib/contents/er/.

Herbert Lee (1912–1961)—An Amite County native and farmer, Lee was a member of Amite NAACP and helped SNCC with voter registration. In September, 1961, local white politician, E. H. Hurst, shot and killed Lee in Liberty, Mississippi. He was acquitted after claiming self-defense. Payne, 121–123.

E. W. Steptoe—Born in the 1910s, Steptoe was an Amite County resident, owner of a dairy store and cotton farm. He was the leader of the Amite County NAACP and helped SNCC workers with voter registration. Steptoe became legendary among SNCC workers for his numerous arsenals of firearms in his house. He worked closely with Robert Moses and helped John Doar of Justice Department in the investigation of the murder of Herbert Lee in 1961. See Payne, 113–117.

*

66 "Seven Negroes Arrested for Boycott Role," United Press International

DECEMBER 8, 1961

CLARKSDALE, Miss. (UPI)—Seven Negroes were arrested today on charges of "withholding trade" from downtown merchants.

They were later released on their own recognizance.

The arrests followed a Negro boycott against white merchants for what the National Association for the Advancement of Colored People called discriminatory practices.

The seven, including Aaron Henry, state head of the N.A.A.C.P., were seized under a state law that prohibits "conspiracy to prevent others from exercising lawful trade or calling."

In Jackson, Medgar Evers, N.A.A.C.P. field secretary, called the arrests "a violation of our constitutional rights."

The charge is a misdemeanor. If convicted, each faces a minimum fine of $25 and a possible sentence of one to six months.

67 Medgar Evers to Alfred Baker Lewis

February 1, 1962

Mr. Alfred Baker Lewis
20 West 40 Street
New York 18, New York

Dear Mr. Lewis:

At the request of Mr. Current, Director of Branches, I am submitting an account of Voter Registration in the McComb, Mississippi area since July 1961.

During the month of August the Student Nonviolent Coordinating Committee moved into McComb, for the widely publicized purpose of Voter Registration in schools and clinics; during the remaining months of 1961 much was written, seen and heard about McComb and vicinity.

Out of all the publicity surrounding McComb, Amite County, and Walthall County, a total of not more than twenty (20) persons were registered, and this was in McComb alone.

Prior to the coming of SNCC the NAACP had quietly worked with local Voter Registration Committees in McComb to enroll more than 250 Negroes on the registration books, while in Walthall County the NAACP had worked through its branch members and had gotten them to file complaints with the Justice department for denial of registration who in turn filed suit early in 1961 to forbid such discriminatory practices against Negroes.

Amite County presented a much more difficult problem for us; however, through our unit there we had begun to eradicate the fear among Negroes and had gotten many Negroes to go down and attempt to register. The rash actions of some of the members of SNCC and the consequential shooting (to death) of Herbert Lee (a Negro), by a State Representative further embedded fear among Negroes that they should not try to register at this time.

So it is that we are not able to get Negroes in Amite County to do what they were otherwise trying to do for themselves, before the arrival of SNCC.

It is my hope that this sheds a bit of information on our situation here as it relates to the work that we are trying to do as well as our problems.

Sincerely yours,

Medgar W. Evers
Field Secretary

Alfred Baker Lewis (1897–1980)—Lewis was an active member of the American Socialist Party in Massachusetts, and managed the Party's Rand School in New York City. He began his association with the NAACP in 1924, and served the organization as treasurer and member of the board of directors for over forty years. See "Alfred Lewis Dead, Ex-NAACP Leader," *New York Times,* October 31, 1980, D17.

68 Medgar Evers, Address, Men's Day Program

JULY 22, 1962
SUBJECT: TODAY'S CHALLENGE FOR TODAY'S MEN
NEW JERUSALEM M. B. CHURCH, JACKSON, MISSISSIPPI

Pastor, Christian friends, brothers and sisters, ladies and gentlemen.

I consider it a blessing from almighty God to have this very spiritual opportunity and pleasure to fellowship with you on this men's day program and to be able to acknowledge the very presence of God within us.

Today we are witnessing a great transition. Things that were unimaginable 15 years ago are realities today. The cotton-picking machine was hardly thought of as being a remote possibility, spaceships were fantasies, only to be found in Buck Rogers cartoons or some other unrealistic place. Transmitting a live program from Broadway, in New York City, or Sunset Strip, in Hollywood, California, to the back woods of Amite County, Mississippi, could only be that of a miracle to happen once in a lifetime.

However, ladies and gentlemen and Christian friends, we have seen these things and many others come to pass, and doubtless there will be many, many others during your life span and mine. For example, man has been successful in landing an object on the moon, while during the same period descending to an ocean depth never before equaled by man. The fact that man travels faster than sound is history. It is no wonder then, that the title of our subject, "Today's Challenge for Today's Men" holds such significance for us today.

So that we might be placed in the right frame of mind, I have chosen at this time to read 121 Psalms:

1. I will lift up mine eyes unto the hills, from whence cometh my help.
2. My help cometh from the Lord which made heaven and earth.
3. He will not suffer thy foot to be moved; He that keepeth thee will not slumber.
4. Behold, He that keepeth Israel shall neither slumber nor sleep.
5. The Lord is thy keeper; the Lord is thy shade upon thy right hand.
6. The sun shall not smite thee by day, nor the moon by night.
7. The Lord shall preserve thee from all evil; He shall preserve thy soul.
8. The Lord shall preserve thy going out and thy coming in from this time forth and even for evermore.

As Negro Americans living in Mississippi today, it is imperative that we put forth extra effort to accomplish the desired goals of freedom for all. Doing just enough to get by is not enough. We must do our best. It is necessary that we become a part of this worldwide struggle for human dignity, for the world now recognizes the heights of those men and women who are willing to make a sacrifice for human betterment and dignity. Some of the signs that are most encouraging are the demonstrations in Africa, which are bringing about the independence of many of the hitherto subjected Africans and placing them beside men and nations as equals.

Yes, and it is heartening indeed to see how young Negroes in America, and especially throughout the deep south today, are willing to spend time in jail for a principle, rather than to accept as a "way of life" the old, outdated philosophy of "white supremacy" as we have known it in the south. As men shaped in the image of God, professing the faith of our fathers, and who often say, "Yea, though I walk through the valley of the shadow of death, I will fear no evil, for Thou are with me," what will you do to help overcome the evils of segregation and discrimination? That is a challenge to you, your faith and your religion, and your belief in the future security and happiness of your wife, children, and loved ones.

Court proceedings:

Samuel Baily vs. Patterson, Joe T.

Rev. L.A. Clark vs. City of Jackson.

J. H. Meredith vs. University of Mississippi.

Voting

Schools

We are making gains in our struggle for first class citizenship, but it cannot be overemphasized that we have only begun this fight which will ultimately require many sacrifices on our part which is the price one pays for freedom if he is to be free and remain free. Our forefathers wrote in the Declaration of Independence on or about July 4, 1976: "We hold these truths to be self-evident, that all men are created equal; that they are endowed by their creator with certain inalienable rights; that among these are life, liberty, and the pursuit of happiness." And as a result of this sentence and others as well as many sacrifices, America is what it is today. We can get our freedom, but today's challenge is for today's men.

I would like to leave with you a poem I think appropriate for the time. The author is unknown.

DO IT NOW!

    If you've got a job to do—do it now!

    If you're _____ you wish were through—do it now!

    If you're sure the job's your own, do not hem and haw and groan

    Do it now!

Don't put off a bit of work—do it now!

It doesn't pay to shirk—do it now!

If you want to fill a place, and be useful to the race, just get up and take a brace—do it now!

Don't linger by the way—do it now!

You'll lose if you delay—do it now!

If the other fellow waits, or postpones until it's late, you _____ up a faster gait—do it now!

Finally, as is quoted from the 6th chapter of Ephesians, beginning at the 11th through 13th verses:

11. Put on the whole armor of God, that ye may be able to stand against the wiles of the devil.

12. For we wrestle not against flesh and blood, but against principalities, against powers, against the rules of the darkness of this world, against spiritual wickedness in high places.

13. Wherefore take unto the whole armor of God, that ye may be able to withstand in the evil day, and having done all, to stand.

"Samuel Baily vs. Patterson"—*Samuel Bailey et al., Appellants, v. Joe T. Patterson, Attorney General of the State of Mississippi, et al., Appellees.* A federal suit brought in 1961 against the state's so-called "breach of peace" statutes intended against mass demonstrations. The plaintiffs contended that the statutes were being used against African Americans on the grounds of their race. The U.S. District Court, Southern District of Mississippi, Jackson Division, in 1962 decided against the plaintiffs. See 206 F. Supp. 67; 1962 U.S. Dist. LEXIS 3731; 6 Fed. R. Serv. 2d (Callaghan) 445, April 7, 1962. In 1963, the Court of Appeals Fifth Circuit reversed the ruling and granted injunctive relief in the complaints over segregated transportations. See 323 F.2d 201; 1963 U.S. App. LEXIS 4146; 7 Fed. R. Serv. 2d (Callaghan) 444, September 24, 1963.

"Rev. L.A. Clark vs. City of Jackson"—Civ. A. No. 3235. A federal desegregation suit brought by Rev. L. A. Clark, Mary A. Cox, and W. R. Wren against the mayor and city commissioners, demanding an injunction against the city of Jackson from prohibiting African Americans from using public facilities on the grounds of their race. In 1962, the United States District Court,

Southern District of Mississippi, Jackson Division, ruled against the plaintiffs, but affirmed its jurisdiction over matters of civil-rights violation. See Joel Friedman, "Desegregating the South: John Minor Wisdom's Role in Enforcing Brown's Mandate," *Tulane Law Review*, Volume 78, Issue 6, June 2004, 2207–2278.

"J. H. Meredith vs. University of Mississippi"—*Meredith v. Fair.* The case refers to the suit filed to the U.S. District Court by the NAACP Legal Defense Fund in 1961, arguing that James Meredith was denied admission to the University solely based on his race. In 1962, the Supreme Court upheld Meredith's right to admission. See 372 U.S. 916; 83 S. Ct. 722; 9 L. Ed. 2d 723; 1963 U.S. LEXIS 2171, Feb. 18, 1963. Final decision by U.S. Appeals Court, Fifth Circuit, 328 F.2d 586; 1962 U.S. App. LEXIS 3875. See Ralph Luker, "Meredith v. Fair," *Historical Dictionary of the Civil Rights Movement* (Lanham, MD: Scarecrow Press, 1997), 175.

---

69 "Mississippi Mood: Hope and Fear," Dorothy Giliam
Washington Post

OCTOBER 14, 1962

OXFORD, Miss.—Hope and fear are the moods of Negroes in Mississippi these anxious days.

You can spot these feelings in the hesitant words of a disfranchised Negro handyman in Oxford who hobbles heavily to a chair, hikes up his overalls, and talks.

Or in the bold words of a harassed Negro leader who, despite constant danger, declares that James H. Meredith's entry into the University of Mississippi "is a clear breakthrough" for Negroes and will be a springboard for other advances.

The hope is that Meredith signals the coming of the light for all of them. The fear is that the inevitable changes will bring further death, destruction, and repercussions.

WHAT HAPPENS NEXT?

These are impressions from a swing through Mississippi last week. People talked freely because they were talking to another Negro.

The major apprehension is about what will occur when the wrath of white Mississippians is no longer throttled by the Federal presence.

"Anything can happen," the Mississippi-born handyman declared darkly.

An Oxford-born woman who works in the tiny town's only Negro boarding house said she was saving her money so she could leave with the troops.

"I'm going to Ioway," is the way she put it. "I don't feel safe here with the soldiers out. But I still hope a lot more colored kids get in that school."

A DISTANT VISION

Behind these fears is the pride, the hope and the distant vision of change that exhilarates and scares them at the same time.

Their feelings are similar to those of Negroes all over the state in the wake of Meredith's desegregation of Ole Miss.

The extent of each of these moods depends on whether you live in Jackson or in the vast Delta; on whether you're a lawyer or a plow-boy or a man who loses his job because of James H. Meredith.

In Oxford, a 29-year-old man who moved there from Chicago last February lost his $6-a-day job in the grill at Ole Miss last week.

"The younger bus boys heard 'nigger' once too often. They walked off. I had to go, too. But the boss came after me later that night and I went back. Then he fired me. I was glad. It was a rather small contribution.

"When a white man first called me 'boy' down here, it was like a slap in the eye. Then you get used to it. When the odds are this much against you, you get to the place where you don't hurt no more."

THE LONG TRADITION

Like Gov. Ross R. Barnett, many Negroes had said "never" to deseg-regation in their lifetimes. But in their heads, not in their hearts.

Why did they believe, like the whites, that Barnett could buck the whole might and majesty of the Federal Government?

Negroes familiar with the state's history and politics explain that Mississippi's devotion to white supremacy and segregation is kept alive by politicians, ministers and big business. Until blood flowed on the streets of Oxford, there was no break in this pattern.

All these elements, said Memphis attorney A. W. Willis, have cooperated since the Civil War to advance black inferiority and separation.

Those who didn't like it, he continued, got out if they could; the others acquiesced.

"Mississippi," offered Russell B. Sugarman, another Memphis attorney, "is now a controlled state."

The success of the technique is reflected both in Negroes' incredulity and in the frank admission by one of Oxford's few Negro businessmen.

"One of our greatest handicaps here is getting over that inferior feeling."

NEGRO FRUSTRATIONS

Ironically, a slim Negro student in Jackson suggested that Ebony magazine editor Lerone Bennett's recent description of Southern Negroes at the turn of the century captures many of Mississippi's present-day frustrations.

Bennett wrote:

". . . to be powerless and to curse one's self for cowardice, to be conditioned to dirt and fear and shame and signs, to become a part of these signs and to feel them in the deepest recesses of the spirit . . . to be a plaything of judges and courts and policemen, to be black in a white fire and to believe finally in one's own unworthiness, to be without books and words and pretty pictures . . . without the rationalizations of psychology and sociology . . . to give in finally, to bow, to scrape, to grin, and to hate one's self for one's servility and weakness and blackness . . . "

ELEMENT OF HOPE

Yet the element of hope springs up almost miraculously and in the most unsuspected people and places.

Roger Thompson, 63, a retired carpenter at Ole Miss, laid aside his saw and stepped gingerly off the splintery porch he was repairing to talk to a reporter.

"I'm so glad there's a black face over there," he said in kind of a squeal with a fling of his arm toward the campus. "I'm proud of it and I hope there'll be more. I'm not afraid. And you can use my name."

An Oxford businessman who didn't want his name used said change was on its way, led by men like Meredith and by young Negroes he hoped would return to the state.

"We have that inward feeling that progress is being made, but we don't talk about it much around here," he said.

In Mississippi the saying is reversed: Talk is expensive.

Medgar Evers, NAACP field secretary, thinks Meredith's move will ignite voter registration again and spur other educational gains all over the State. "Petitions are pending to desegregate local schools in Jackson and Leake County," he said.

"And we're going to make it known to high school and college students that Meredith's suit was designed to break down barriers in all institutions of higher learning," he said, "but we don't expect to win without a fight."

A home economics teacher at Oxford's only Negro high school said several students told her they were going to study real hard so they, too, could go to Ole Miss.

While Meredith is no knight in shining armor, he appears to be pretty close to it to a people too long without hope.

Yet some Negroes refuse to lift him onto a pedestal because they believe it gives the impression that he is a freak, a Mississippi accident, as it were.

"Meredith," said Sugarman, the Memphis lawyer, "is just a Mississippi boy who went home."

But fear follows closely on the heels of hope. Fear of physical violence, of economic repercussion, of change itself, Negroes say.

Some soft-pedal this. Like the youngish businessman in Jackson who said Mississippi is "hell for Negroes," but stoutly insisted that the Negro is more fearless these days and won't stand for any white folks' guff or be scared off.

But he was afraid to give his name.

Medgar Evers thinks there is fear. "I don't know to what degree, but it's greater in the rural areas where you cannot count on local police protection."

During our interview, Evers' phone rang. The caller reported that eight Negro homes had been strafed by shotguns, allegedly held by youthful whites.

Evers immediately called the Justice Department in Washington and asked for Federal protection for the families. There was not any need to bother with local officials, he declared.

Jackson's Dr. Albert B. Britton, a member of the Civil Rights Committee, thinks the fear on both sides is a fear of change. But he thinks the moderates can quiet the rabble—if enough of them speak out.

Oxford's only Negro funeral director, G. W. Bankhead, doesn't put much stock in a flare-up of violence.

"If it comes, it'll come from only the sorriest folks. And we've got enough law and order here to take care of it."

In the wake of the bloody riots, NAACP State President Aaron Henry, a Clarksdale pharmacist, wired President Kennedy to declare marshal law and fan marshals over the state to act as registrars for six months.

"With the Negro vote," said Henry, "will come a liberation to Mississippi of thousands of both white and Negro citizens who are now caught up in the web of static politics."

Yet, said R. Jess Brown, a Jackson lawyer, "there's a little ray of light" from white moderates.

"Was it not inevitable that Federal bayonets would lay a shadow across the heart of Mississippi?

"Anyone—workingman or banker—should know that when he walks into a court of law of the United States of America he is walking into an atmosphere of congealed experience that has fashioned the strongest government and the finest nation that man has ever placed on the map. It revolves around one word—freedom.

"Mississippians have found the 'Law' hard to stomach within the past two weeks.

"But the menu was inevitable, citizens. It had become abundantly clear since the Supreme Court decision of 1954—and even further back—the ratification of Section One of the 14th Amendment in 1868—that the dish was on its way. It was piping hot, and tinged with ingredients that sting the palate. . . ."

In addition to the obvious fears, there is the psychological warfare, as it were, the subtle repercussions.

A home economics teacher at Oxford's only Negro high school said two whites trailed her as she drove from Oxford to Batesville, their headlights glaring down her neck. She said she didn't know what to expect.

Finally they pulled out, shouted obscenities, and sped past.

Notably missing is the humor among Negroes about the present state of affairs. The Southern white press was having a field day with Bobby and the rest of the Kennedys.

The Oxford businessman who couldn't give his name explained it this way: "At this point, we're too concerned to find much that is funny."

Lerone Bennett (b. 1928)—A native of Clarksdale who grew up in Jackson, Bennett became a journalist after graduating from Morehouse College in Atlanta, Georgia, and became an editor for *Ebony* magazine in 1953. He began writing articles on black history, and in 1962 published his best-known book, *Before the Mayflower: A History of Black America, 1619–1962* (Chicago: Johnson Pub. Co., 1962).

CHAPTER VII

I SPEAK AS
A NATIVE
MISSISSIPPIAN

Documents 70–81
(November 7, 1962–June 10, 1963)

"Ain't gonna let nobody turn me 'round,

turn me 'round, turn me 'round,

Ain't gonna let nobody turn me 'round,

I'm gonna keep on a-walkin', keep on a-talkin',

Marching up to freedom land. . . .

Ain't gonna let no jailhouse turn me 'round,

turn me 'round, turn me 'round,

Ain't gonna let no jailhouse turn me 'round,

I'm gonna keep on a-walkin', keep on a-talkin'

Marching up to freedom land.

Ain't gonna let no injunction turn me 'round,

turn me 'round, turn me 'round,

Ain't gonna let no injunction turn me 'round,

I'm gonna keep on a-walkin', keep on a-talkin',

Marching up to freedom land."

"Ain't Gonna Let Nobody Turn Me 'Round,"

Black Freedom Movement Song, 1960s, in
Manning Marable and Leith Mullings, eds.,
Let Nobody Turn Us Around: Voices of Resistance,
Reform and Renewal, An African American
Anthology *(Lanham, MD: Rowman and Littlefield,*
2000), 397–398.

MEDGAR WILEY EVERS had become a marked man throughout the entire state of Mississippi by 1963—the "mastermind" behind the successful effort to place James Meredith at Ole Miss, the chief investigator that brought to national attention the lynchings of Emmett Till and Mack Charles Parker, the coordinator of the "subversive" NAACP. Now when he drove into rural counties or into the Delta, police officers immediately recognized him and his automobile. So did white vigilantes and Ku Klux Klansmen who sought to murder him. Salter recalled leaving Greenwood, Mississippi with Medgar around midnight. Medgar was "casually talking about a rumor he'd heard to the effect that a segregationist killer outfit in Leflore County had installed infrared lights on the cars," which permitted them not to be detected. Throughout this conversation, "we were going about 100 mph! But he was driving easily and well and his talk was calm," Salter comments. "But Medgar did not take chances, and no one could seriously accuse him of consciously or unconsciously seeking martyrdom."[1]

Evers sought to prepare Myrlie and their three children, Darrell, Rena, and Van, for what he believed was an inevitable attack on his home, property, and even quite possibly himself and his family. The children were instructed that if they heard "strange noises" outside after dark, they should crawl, low to the floor, to the bathroom. When leaving their car in the carport adjacent to the house, the children and Myrlie were supposed to exit from the passenger side because it was much closer to the side-door entrance to the house. According to one family friend, Minnie White-Watson, "the carport light was supposed to be lit only if the whole family was home at night. They were virtually prisoners in their own home."[2]

Evers continued to grow in prominence as a sought-after speaker and representative of the Southern civil-rights struggle outside of Mississippi. In early November 1962, Evers engaged in another West Coast tour, speaking out on such issues as James Meredith and various discrimination cases, and raising donations for the NAACP's "Freedom Fund." During this trip Medgar was interviewed by more than twenty television, radio, and newspaper outlets [see Documents 71 and 73]. From November 24 to December 5, 1962, Evers traveled again to the Midwest and East Coast, with lecture appearances including Brooklyn and Newark, New Jersey. On December 15, 1962, Evers was a principal speaker at the NAACP branch conference in Dallas, Texas [see Document 73]. Throughout this intense period of public outreach, Evers maintained his extensive responsibilities in rural Mississippi and in small town meetings throughout the state: as documents in this chapter discuss, on January 18, 1963, Evers visited Pascagoula to investigate the conditions of black workers and charges of job discrimination, which violated Equal Employment Opportunity mandates. On January 27, 1963, he helped to organize an "Emancipation Day Rally," featuring NAACP leader Daisy Bates of Little Rock, Arkansas, as the keynote speaker. On January 30, 1963, he appeared at a press conference in Jackson with James Meredith, who announced his intention to continue his education at "Ole Miss" [see Document 74]. On March 4, 1963, Evers joined five other families in filing a suit in federal court demanding the immediate end of racial segregation in Jackson's public schools. That same day, in Greenwood, Evers participated in a mass voter-registration drive [see Documents 75 and 76].

Evers was no longer just a "local leader," but had acquired a national reputation for integrity, effectiveness, and courage. He was certainly not an "orator" in the style of a King or Malcolm X, to be sure. Yet his contemporaries expressed admiration for his newfound expressiveness and attractive quality of humility as a persuasive speaker. Salter states that "no matter how discouraged he might feel, Medgar was always able to communicate . . . enthusiasm to those with whom he was working. In the early days of the Jackson Movement, our 'mass' meetings were tiny affairs, yet Medgar always functioned as though the meetings were the last crucial ones before the Revolution broke out in Mississippi: he met each person on an equal to equal basis, smiled, joked, gave them the recognition of human dignity that each human being warrants. . . ."[3] When African American celebrities traveled to Mississippi to express their solidarity and support for the Black Freedom Movement, Evers was one of their principal contacts. Novelist James Baldwin visited the Evers home during a time when Meredith was there; Evers took out his camera to take a photograph of the two men standing in front of his modest home, only several feet from the site where he himself would be killed months later. When comedian and social activist Dick Gregory decided to travel to Mississippi, he already knew that "Medgar Evers was the key man down there, and I called him to ask if I could help," Gregory wrote in his 1964 autobiography. "In many ways, Medgar was the man responsible for my being in the civil rights fight."[4]

The 1961 economic boycott of Jackson's segregated businesses had died out after several dramatic months, and NAACP youth activists in late 1962 were determined to revive it. Advised by Ed King, a white Mississippian who was Tougaloo College chaplain, and Salter, the students pushed the Jackson branch toward greater militancy and the revival of mass, nonviolent demonstrations. In nearby Birmingham, in April 1963, mass demonstrations coordinated by King and the SCLC were directly challenging that city's segregation laws and the police brutality of its notorious police chief, "Bull" Connor. SNCC and CORE members in Mississippi also supported more direct measures to confront Jackson's entrenched segregation. More moderate NAACP supporters in Mississippi, especially the black clergy, favored instead concentrating on voter registration, rather than mass arrests. The national NAACP officials were also extremely cool toward direct actions, and according to Salter, began curtailing bail bond money to nonviolent protestors. "There was very sharp internecine warfare between our militant group and the conservatives," Salter states. "Medgar was caught in the middle. As a staff employee of the National office, he was under their direct control; as a Mississippian, he knew that only massive demonstrations could crack Jackson. . . . The stakes were high and everyone—our militant faction, the conservative group, the segregationists, Federal government—knew it."[5]

On May 9, 1963, Evers publicly denounced the arrests of Bob Moses and other SNCC organizers on false charges of "fire-bombing" a white family's home, declaring in the *New York Times* that the atmosphere across the state had lapsed into a "complete reign of terror." When Jackson's segregationist mayor Allen Thompson went on local television to make an address, calling for an end to demonstrations, Medgar went immediately to the U.S. Justice Department, demanding under FCC guidelines the right to "equal time" for him to speak and rebut Thompson's remarks. On May 20, in an unprecedented media event, Evers delivered an historic, 17-minute televised address, calling for racial integration and equal rights for all citizens—the first such broadcast in Mississippi's bloody history [see Document 77]. Racist whites who had long known the name of Medgar Evers finally had the opportunity to identify the man whom they now commonly perceived as the key figure in the movement they were determined to halt dead.

Events rapidly spiraled almost out of control, as documents in this chapter suggest. On May 21, a mass meeting of blacks in Jackson demanded that Mayor Thompson formally meet with their delegation to negotiate a settlement. Two days later, the NAACP state board caucused in Jackson, and resolved that Thompson had to meet immediately with black representatives. After scores of Tougaloo College students were viciously beaten and jailed by police and racist mobs, Evers led a demonstration of more than two thousand in Jackson on May 28. That same day, speaking at the Pearl Street AME Church, Evers called for a "massive offensive against segregation." On May 30, Medgar sent a telegram to U.S. Attorney General Robert Kennedy, calling for Federal intervention in the arrest of three local ministers who had nonviolently protested at Jackson's post office [see Document 78]. On June 1, with Roy Wilkins, Evers and other NAACP activists picketed the segregated Woolworth's store in Jackson. Both Wilkins and Evers were arrested and freed, each on $1,000 bond [see Document 79]. City officials responded to the crisis by banning NAACP demonstrations. Evers issued a public statement to the press, declaring that this action was proof, contrary to the segregationist media's claims, that the Freedom Movement in Jackson remained "sharp, vital, and inclusive" [see Document 81]. He also contacted the FBI, asking the Bureau to investigate the illegal wiretapping of his residence and offices by local authorities.

Early in the morning of May 29, 1963, a Molotov cocktail firebomb was thrown at the Evers home. The firebomb detonated but caused minimal damage. Medgar was not at home that night. Myrlie was awakened by the firebomb, and she managed to extinguish it before her three children were awakened by the commotion. Evers reported the incident to a *New York Times* reporter; white police insisted that the episode was "staged," and that Evers and his family were in no danger.

Medgar was physically and emotionally exhausted; his family now received dozens of telephone hate calls at all hours of the day and night. On June 10, he received a call from Gulfport NAACP head Felix Dunn, warning him "to be careful, to have someone see him home each night, to arrange for guards around the house." A local white attorney who privately was sympathetic with the movement had informed Dunn that "an attempt was going to be made on Medgar's life." Medgar decided not to inform Myrlie about this most recent death threat. But several days earlier, one evening at home, the tired, dedicated "servant leader" sat down on his living room sofa next to Myrlie and rested his weary head.

"And then, for the first time, he expressed real fear of something happening to him. As we talked about it, he said that if anything should happen to him, I must promise to take good care of the children ... And then I noticed tears in his eyes, and I said, 'Oh, Medgar!' and we both broke down and cried together. We clung to each other as though it were our only hope, and in my heart I felt that time was running out. There was no anger, no bitterness, not even a sense of having been robbed of what other people took for granted. There was just a bottomless depth of hopelessness, of hurt, of despair."[6]

On the evening of June 11, Myrlie and the children were up late watching television, waiting to see President John F. Kennedy's televised address to the nation, which called upon Congress to pass a major civil-rights bill which would outlaw racial segregation in all public accommodations. Kennedy's action was the result of concerted, sustained efforts by tens of thousands of civil-rights activists, and it was viewed as an important step forward. A few minutes after midnight, on June 12, 1963, Medgar's automobile drove into the family's driveway. The carport light overhead was on; Medgar left the car from the driver's side and retrieved some bundles of T-shirts from the rear of his car that were to be distributed at the next NAACP rally. The T-shirts read, "Jim Crow Must Go!" Across the street, obscured by a clump of trees, shrouded in darkness, stood white supremacist Byron De La Beckwith, taking aim with a rifle at Medgar. The shot that struck Evers awoke the entire neighborhood; only hours later, it shocked the entire nation.

70 Monthly Report: "Boycott of Mississippi State Fair for
    Negroes" and "17th Annual State Conference, NAACP"

NOVEMBER 7, 1962

BOYCOTT OF MISSISSIPPI STATE FAIR FOR NEGROES
For the second straight year Negro Citizens have responded favor-
ably to the NAACP's request to boycott the Mississippi State Fair for
Negroes. Again this year, 1962, the boycott was approximately
90–95% effective. Picketing was not necessary; requests from the
Field Secretary for the boycott were sent through the wire services,
radio, television, newspapers, handbills, and placards, which made
picketing unnecessary. We shall ask Negro Citizens to boycott the
fair each year, so long as it is segregated.

17TH ANNUAL MISSISSIPPI STATE CONFERENCE, NAACP
The 17th Annual Mississippi State Conference of NAACP Branches
was by far one of the best conferences held in the State. Workshops
included Membership and Fund Raising, Branch Organization, Desegregation, Registration and Voting, and Employment.

Delegates were in attendance from most of the branches. The
highlights of our program being the presentation of a plaque to
James H. Meredith ". . . for Faith, Courage and determination . . ." at
the Freedom Fund Banquet; at which Mrs. Ruby Hurley, our Southeast Regional Secretary, spoke.

Sunday's mass meeting, which featured Mr. Roy Wilkins, our Executive Secretary, and Dick Gregory, climaxed our State Conference. Mr. Wilkins gave a very stimulating address. He brought
forth statistics germane to Mississippi's dual education system,
and then he said, ". . . Not only did the September episode at Oxford reveal Mississippi's philosophy upon and treatment of the
Negro, but it uncovered to an astonished nation a seat of rebel-

lion against the government of the United States of America. Nearly everyone knew the South was sensitive and emotional over the race question, but hardly anyone suspected any section—even Mississippi—was stark-raving mad over the issue, mad enough to offer rebellion."

After Mr. Wilkins' very stimulating and challenging address, Dick Gregory entertained more than one thousand members of the audience with his extreme talent.

Approximately $1,000 was raised on Sunday during the public offering, with a gross for the Conference of more than $2,250.00.

Dick Gregory (1932–) A native of St. Louis, Gregory became a well-known actor-comedian for his biting satire against racism and stereotypes of black people. He became deeply involved in the civil-rights movement during the 1960s, appearing at numerous rallies and marches, risking arrests and police beatings. See Dick Gregory, *Nigger: Autobiography of Dick Gregory* (New York: Dutton, 1964).

---

71 "'Quarantine' on Segregated States Urged"
Los Angeles Times

NOVEMBER 10, 1962

A field secretary in Mississippi for the National Assn. for the Advancement of Colored People proposed here Friday that federal funds be withheld from Mississippi and Alabama until Negroes can vote there.

"Just as our great country put a quarantine on Cuba," said Medgar Evers, a 37-year-old Negro, "it is just as important to put a quarantine on Alabama and Mississippi and make it possible for Negroes to be able to register and vote."

Evers, here for an NAACP fund-raising rally Sunday, said $591 million in federal funds were poured into Mississippi in 1961, while the state sent back but $290 million.

SPEAKING FOR SELF

He said he particularly favored withholding federal funds for any agencies in Mississippi that practice discrimination, "such as the National Guard, which Negroes can't join."

Evers said he was speaking for himself and not quoting NAACP policy.

His appearance at 3 p.m. Sunday at the New Hope Baptist Church, 5200 S. Central Ave., will be to tell the James Meredith story, he said.

72 Transcriptions of two handwritten notes from Medgar to his family

(1) A HANDWRITTEN NOTE ON STATIONERY FROM THE CLAYPOOL HOTEL IN INDIANAPOLIS

November 27, 1962

My darling wife and children,

I love you dearly and miss you terribly! I am now aboard TWA's #54 for Idlewild Airport N.Y. City and the time is 12:50 PM Eastern Standard time or 11:50 your time. It is a beautiful day with a slight overcast and bright sun coming through my cabin window.

Honey, tell the children daddy will be returning soon and that when Xmas comes, if it is in the Lord's will, we are all going to enjoy Santa Claus and a good Xmas.

You be sweet and take care of yourself. Be assured this trip can't end too soon.

Love, Medgar

(2) A HANDWRITTEN NOTE ON STATIONERY FROM
THE SHERATON HOTEL IN NYC

December 1, 1962

My Darlings,

I am now in N.Y.C. having just arrived by bus from Newark, N.J., after a very successful meeting there and after having received a plaque from Ballantine Brewery.

I love all of you and I will be glad when I get back home one day next week.

Love,
Daddy + Hubby

———————————————————————————— *

73 Monthly Report: "Speaking Engagements," "Selected Buying Campaign," and "Investigation"

JANUARY 4, 1963

SPEAKING ENGAGEMENTS

The Mississippi Field Secretary toured the West Coast speaking in behalf of various branches relating facts surrounding the Meredith Case, as well as other discriminatory conditions that exist in the State of Mississippi as they relate to Negro Americans.

In my tour of the West Coast, I appeared on some 12 different television stations as well as an equal number or more radio stations, which proved to be extremely interesting and apparently informing to large audiences throughout the West Coast. In addition to radio and television, newspaper coverage was extensive. Possibly the one big event was a full hour appearance on the "Tom Duggan Show" on November 10.

The West Coast tour began in Los Angeles on November 5, and ended in Topeka, Kansas, November 18, with appearances in San Diego, Phoenix and Tucson, Arizona; Las Vegas, Nevada; Portland, Oregon; Tulsa, Oklahoma; and Sioux City, Iowa.

Miss Althea Gibson, West Coast Sub-regional Field Secretary is certainly to be commended for the extraordinarily efficient work which she is doing. Not to be overlooked, of course, are many of the fine lay people in some of the branches mentioned under her charge.

After the Thanksgiving holidays, the Field Secretary resumed his tour of branches in the Midwest and East, appearing in Kansas City, Missouri November 24, and ending the tour in Jackson, Tennessee, December 5; meetings with branches in between were South Bend and Indianapolis, Indiana; Chester and Mainline, Pennsylvania; Newark, New Jersey; Rockville Center, New York; Charleston, South Carolina; and Brownsville, Tennessee. On the Eastern tour the Field Secretary appeared on four television stations and several radio stations and in numerous newspapers.

Mr. Leonard Carter, the Regional Secretary in Kansas City, Missouri, along with Mr. Phil Savage, Tri-state Secretary in Philadelphia, Pennsylvania, arranged very informative and, we feel, rewarding meetings, not to mention the very splendid work of many of the lay leaders in the various branches.

We feel our tour gave to a wide area of this nation's population a first hand account of many of the events surrounding the James Meredith case.

The Field Secretary spoke to a very enthusiastic group of Freedom Fighters, members and friends of the Dallas, Texas branch of NAACP, Saturday, December 15, under the direction of Mr. Clarence A. Laws. The meeting was quite successful and apparently enjoyed by many in attendance.

Elaborate press coverage greeted the Field Secretary as he deplaned at Love Field in Dallas. Television as well as newspaper coverage was arranged in one of the terminal suites. It was during this news conference that the Mississippi Field Secretary greatly emphasized the need for more Federal action in the area of Registration and Voting; thereby, making it possible for Negroes to Register and Vote in the State of Mississippi.

SELECTED BUYING CAMPAIGN

NAACP units throughout the Jackson area, along with other allied Civil Rights groups urged Negro Citizens to do selected buying mainly on Capitol Street in an effort to gain more courtesy, jobs, and respect from the downtown merchants. The selected buying campaign is judged to have been 60–65% effective.

Leading the selected buying campaign were members of our North Jackson Youth Council and Tougaloo College chapter of NAACP. Efforts to stimulate and dramatize the campaign came about when some eight (8) pickets were arrested and charged with "obstructing the sidewalks." Included in the pickets were Mr. and Mrs. John R. Salter, advisers to our Tougaloo College Chapter and North Jackson Youth Council, and also, faculty members at Tougaloo College.

Each of the pickets was released on a $500 bond. Lawyers who have aided in the case are: Attorney Jack H. Young, R. Jess Brown, William Kuntsler of New York and others. A petition has been filed in Federal Court for removal of said cases to Federal Court, and said petition also requests that Judge Harold Cox, in whose court the case would be tried, if transferred, disqualify himself, because of bias; contributed to statements made by Judge Cox and others.

INVESTIGATION

The Field Secretary is investigating the murder of one Will Roberts, formerly of Route 3, DeKalb, Mississippi, who was shot to death by one Lyle LeGette, grocery store owner, in the DeKalb (Kemper County) area. Our interest stemmed from the fact that despite LeGette's shooting Roberts four times, apparently without provocation, he was not arrested and no charges have been filed against him by the sheriff of Kemper County, who later (approximately one hour) investigated the course and accused Roberts of pulling a knife (taking the white man's words, since there were no other witnesses in the store at the time). We hope to make a more detailed report in the very near future.

Leonard Carter—NAACP Regional Secretary in Kansas City, Missouri, in the mid-sixties. He advocated the full desegregation of Kansas City's public school systems and the inclusion of African American history in curriculum. See the Finding Aid to NAACP Papers microfilm, Part 25, Series B, Scope and Content note, available online, www.lexisnexis.com/academic/guides/Aaas/naacp2502.pdf.

74 Monthly Report: "Poll Tax," "Meredith Returns," "Labor and Industry," "Clyde Kennard," and "Investigation"

FEBRUARY 7, 1963

POLL TAX

January is the month for paying poll taxes in Mississippi, as a prerequisite to registering in order to vote. During January efforts were intensified by our branches across the state to get Negroes to pay their poll taxes. Branches were called upon to put forth a concerted effort in this endeavor, with the aid of the distribution of some 20,000 handbills. 1963 should prove to be one of our best poll tax paying years.

MEREDITH RETURNS

Mr. James H. Meredith eased mounting tensions Wednesday, January 30, 1963 when he announced at a press conference, conducted by the Field Secretary of NAACP and Mr. Thomas Dent of the Legal Defense Fund, Jackson, Mississippi (Masonic Temple building) that he would register for the second semester at the University of Mississippi. There were more than 50 newsmen and approximately 150 spectators in attendance. The text of Mr. Meredith's statement is below:

I notified everyone concerned that would announce my decision at this time for two reasons. First, newsmen from every area of the news services had requested that they be given sufficient notification so that they could be present, if they so desired. Secondly, I have found in the past that by not giving such notification, I have had to spend too much time answering the same questions for each individual newsman. Therefore, it was suggested by many of them that this procedure would be more advantageous both to them and to me.

It is a great tragedy for America that whether a student will attend a University has become a big news item. For the past several days, I have pondered this question. I have, in various ways, been informed of the feelings and opinions of most of the people in this country, and many throughout the world regarding this question.

After listening to all arguments, evaluations, and positions, and weighing all this against my personal possibilities and circumstances, I have concluded that the 'Negro' should not return to the University of Mississippi. The prospects for him are too unpromising. However, I have decided that I, J. H. Meredith, will register for the second semester at the University of Mississippi.

Many things have taken place in recent months, and I see signs that give me hope that I will be able to go to school in the future, under adequate, if not ideal, conditions.

I want to thank the people of the United States of America for their support. With so many of our Citizens genuinely concerned with this grave racial problem we are bound to find an adequate solution. I also want to thank the many people throughout the world who have shown such a great interest in the struggle of men for the equality of opportunity.

LABOR AND INDUSTRY

Herbert Hill, National Labor Secretary for NAACP, along with Medgar W. Evers, Field Secretary NAACP for the state of Mississippi, visited with members of the Pascagoula Branch of NAACP and other Citizens of the Pascagoula-Moss Point area, January 18, 1963.

The purpose of the meeting was to hear additional complaints from individual Negroes working with the various plants in this industrial area, namely, Ingall's shipbuilding Corporation, the B.V.D. plant and the International Paper Company, as well as, complaints against the various international Unions serving the area.

Attending this meeting were approximately 250 Negroes, many of whom reiterated, verbally, what had already been included in approximately 50 complaints filed with the President's Committee on Equal Employment Opportunity.

After the meeting, Mr. Hill and the Field Secretary drafted a telegram to be sent to the Chairman of the President's Committee on Equal Employment Opportunity, Vice President, Lyndon B. Johnson, protesting the inaction of the committee relative to these complaints which were filed in August 1962. The telegram was sent Monday, January 21, the text of which is as follows: "Numerous valid complaints of job discrimination filed by NAACP with President's Committee on Equal Employment Opportunity against Government contractors and organized Labor in Mississippi has not eliminated pattern of anti-Negro practices.

Complaints filed September 11, 1962 against Ingall's ship yard corporation and AFL-CIO Metal Trade Department, against International Paper Company, and Pulp Sulphite and Paper Mill Workers Union AFL-CIO and against B.V.D., Corporation, have brought no adequate response. Economic Welfare of entire Negro community in Pascagoula and Moss Point, Mississippi is directly affected by inaction of President's Committee. Organized Labor and Industrial management blatantly violate anti-discrimination pledges throughout Mississippi. Respectfully request report on complaints."

There was no immediate reply from the President's Committee to us, however, immediate positive action was commenced at Ingall's ship building corporation, in view of the fact that they (Ingall's) had just come in the knowledge of being low-bidder on a $51 million contract with the United States Government, to construct two ships, and they stood a good chance of losing same.

Immediately, Ingall's opened up the Apprenticeship Program to Negroes; promoted nine (9) Negroes to various positions, which were not previously held by Negroes; opened up the blue print reading class to Negroes, the welding school to Negroes, and hired a Negro girl to work in the Employment office.

I might say that as soon as we learned that Ingall's had been low-bidder on this contract we sent the following telegram, again to the President's Committee: "Respectfully, urge that no Government Contract be let to Ingall's ship building corporation of Pascagoula, Mississippi, until all job discrimination against Negro employees is effectively eliminated."

I hasten to add that it was after the second telegram that these job openings were made known to Negro employees of Ingall's.

There was an attempt made by management to get a committee of Negroes to sign a statement to the effect that everything was "progressing right along." I was immediately informed of this, and I informed Mr. Hill of same. The decision was that Negro employees should not sign such a statement. I am happy to add that none to my knowledge signed.

This action on the part of Mr. Hill and the Field Secretary appears to be well appreciated in the community and our memberships, there, are increasing in number.

CLYDE KENNARD

The long awaited release of Clyde Kennard, the Negro chicken farmer who attempted to desegregate Mississippi Southern College in 1959, came January 28, after Governor Ross R. Barnett of Mississippi used executive clemency and gave him an indefinite suspension for the seven years he was serving for allegedly conspiring to steal less than $25 worth of chicken feed.

The Field Secretary along with Attorney R. Jess Brown was instrumental in having Mr. Kennard transferred from the state penitentiary to the University Hospital (Jackson) for treatment, after receiving reports from his mother that she had visited him on

Sunday, January 20, at which time he had to be assisted (by other inmates) in getting dressed, as well as walking around. After such a report from the mother I contacted Mr. Brown and impressed upon him the urgency of getting medical attention for Mr. Kennard. Mr. Brown immediately petitioned the Mississippi Supreme Court for a transfer of Mr. Kennard to the hospital, pointing out the medical neglect which he (Kennard) had received during his confinement by penitentiary officials. The petition was brought to the attention of the Governor, who immediately ordered, on Tuesday, January 22, that Mr. Kennard be brought to the University Medical Center for treatment. On January 23, the Field Secretary along with Attorney Brown visited Mr. Kennard and we indicated to him that we would put forth every effort possible to get a speedy release. The Field Secretary suggested to Attorney Brown the opportuneness of the time to request that Mr. Kennard be released; an appeal was made to the Governor by Attorney Brown and executive clemency was granted January 28, 1963.

Mr. Kennard was permitted to leave the hospital on January 29 for his home in Hattiesburg, Mississippi, while diagnostic tests were being analyzed, relative to his condition.

Comedian Dick Gregory, learning of Kennard's condition, personally flew Mr. Kennard to Chicago on Saturday, February 2, where he was immediately admitted to Billings Hospital, at the University of Chicago, where he remains.

INVESTIGATION

The Field Secretary made an investigation into the death of Sylvester Maxwell, a Negro, who was killed in Madison County, on the night of January 4, 1963.

While the body bore markings of that of a person having been lynched (including castration) a Negro is being held in connection with the killing. We are in serious doubt that this act was committed by the Negro in question. The Negro in question is Thomas William Campbell of Madison County.

We shall continue to investigate this case until we get to the bottom of it.

Thomas Covington Dent (1932–1998)—Dent is known for his poetry and plays, but he also worked as a public information director for the NAACP Legal Defense Fund and an assistant to Thurgood Marshall, from 1961 to 1963. During that period, he established the Umbra Workshop, a legendary black writers' collective in New York. He also funded in 1967 the Free Southern Theater Writing Workshop and BLKARTSOUTH. His works include *Blue Lights and River Songs* (Detroit: Loctus, 1982) and *Southern Journey: A Return to the Civil Rights Movement* (New York: Morrow, 1997). "In Memoriam," *Mississippi Quarterly*, spring 1999, Volume 52, Issue 2, pg. 213.

Herbert Hill (1924–2004)—Hill, who had been a steel-labor organizer, became the NAACP labor director in 1951, and throughout the fifties and sixties Hill worked tirelessly to pressure both large corporations and labor unions to accept black workers. After resigning from the Association in 1971, he began teaching Afro-American Studies at the University of Wisconsin. He wrote *Black Labor and the American Legal System* (Madison: University of Wisconsin Press, 1985, 1977). See "Herbert Hill, 80: NAACP Official Fought Union Bias," *Chicago Tribune*, August 22, 2004, pg. 9.

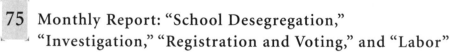

75 Monthly Report: "School Desegregation," "Investigation," "Registration and Voting," and "Labor"

MARCH 6, 1963

SCHOOL DESEGREGATION

A suit was filed Monday, March 4, 1963 by the Legal Defense and Educational Fund of NAACP, representing ten Negro children, and seven parents who are asking a Federal Court to order the first public school integration in Mississippi, on the Elementary and High School level. This was the first such suit filed by Negro residents of Mississippi.

Mississippi's Attorney General, Joe Patterson, has already pledged the "entire resources" of his office to the city of Jackson and its attorneys, in defense of the suit.

The plaintiffs in this suit are: The Field Secretary and his wife, Mrs. Myrlie B. Evers, Mr. Samuel Bailey, Mrs. A.M.E. Logan, Mrs. Kathryn Thomas, Mrs. Edna Marie Singleton and Mrs. Elizabeth White, all members and officers of the Jackson Branch of NAACP.

Federal Judge Harold Cox was asked by Attorney Jack H. Young to set April 12 as the date for a hearing. Attorney Young is the local counsel in the case.

Leake County (Carthage) and Biloxi, Mississippi are two other areas where litigation for public school desegregation is relatively imminent. In both communities, our local NAACP Branches will be bringing the action to desegregate the public schools.

INVESTIGATION

The Field Secretary investigated the shooting of a Negro Voter Registration worker, Jimmy Travis, in Greenwood, Mississippi, February 28.

According to reports, Travis and two other Negro Civil Rights workers were traveling in a car near Greenwood, when another car containing three white men pulled alongside them and fired a number of shots (believed to have been from a sub-machine gun).

Two white men and a minor have been charged with felonious assault in connection with the shooting. They are: William H. Greenlee and Wesley Kersey.

The sheriff announced Monday that the car which was apparently involved in the shooting was found, abandoned, on a country road in Carroll County.

Immediately after the shooting the Field Secretary contacted our Washington Bureau of NAACP, which in turn requested action from the Justice Department. FBI agents, as well as attorneys from the Department of Justice descended on the Greenwood area and began an intensive investigation which ultimately led to the arrest of the two men and youth.

REGISTRATION AND VOTING

While in the Greenwood area, Monday and Tuesday, March 4–5, the Field Secretary noticed a great amount of interest on the part of the Negro community, in the Voter Registration Campaign which is now being carried on in the area.

Involved in this intensified concentration of effort are: the NAACP, SNCC, SCLC, and CORE. The NAACP was represented in the area by the Field Secretary, and the President of the Mississippi State Conference of NAACP, Aaron E. Henry, and President of the Cleveland, Mississippi NAACP Branch, Mr. Amzie Moore. CORE has in the area Dave Dennis; SCLC is represented by James Bevels, Mississippi Field Secretary and a Miss Ponder, who is connected with the school at Dorchester, Georgia, and a Rev. Andrew Young.

On Tuesday, March 5, the Field Secretary took five persons down to the Circuit Clerk's Office, to register, none of whom passed, at that particular time.

Thursday, March 7, Mr. W. C. Patton, Director of Registration and Voting for NAACP and the Field Secretary for Mississippi will be in the Greenwood area, to work with the Voter Registration project.

The Jackson Branch of NAACP in coordination with Mr. W. C. Patton, has launched a 3 month Voter Registration drive in Jackson, Mississippi beginning March 4. Through this effort, and with the pressure of Justice Department officials checking the records of the Circuit Clerk during this period, it is expected that the registration of Negroes in Jackson and Hinds County will take a sharp curve upwards. This is particularly significant in that under the re-apportionment plan, recently put into effect in Mississippi, Hinds County (Jackson) is entitled to 9 Representatives, with 7 Representatives being elected from the city of Jackson proper. This could mean, with a sharp increase in Negro Voters, a great amount of influence from Negro electors on the Representatives from Hinds County to the State Legislature.

In the meantime, weekly meetings and direct door-to-door contact is being made over the city, also general plans for a massive city wide Door-Knock-for-Freedom-At-the-Ballot-Box Campaign is under way.

LABOR

As a further crack down on Federal Government spending in Mississippi, which in effect supports segregation, the Field Secretary forwarded a telegram to the Secretary of Labor, Mr. Willard Wirtz, complaining of the discrimination which exists under the Man Power Re-development Act of 1962, as administered in Mississippi.

As a follow through, the Washington Bureau of NAACP sent a letter to the Secretary of Labor, relative to the expenditure of Federal Funds in Mississippi on a segregated and un-equal basis. As far as we know, presently, the program is still in effect and positively no change, as to the practice of segregation is in evidence. We shall continue to insist that equal opportunity be made available to all, under this and similar Federal programs.

Federal Judge Harold Cox—Appointed to the Federal bench by John F. Kennedy, Cox was a close friend of Mississippi Senator and segregationist James Oliver Eastland, and his appointment brought complaints to the president by CORE and Eleanor Roosevelt. Cox once referred to African Americans as "chimpanzees." See Meier and Rudwick, 180; and Katagiri, 230.

David Dennis (?)—CORE Mississippi field secretary. Head of the state's voting rights efforts for CORE, Dennis supported the decision to recruit hundreds of middle-class white college students to Mississippi for the Freedom Summer project of 1964. He is currently working with Moses for The Algebra Project. See Meier and Rudwick, 178–80, 259–260, 289–271; and Howell Raines, *My Soul Is Rested: Movement Days in the Deep South Remembered* (New York: Penguin, 1977), 273–278.

W. C. Patton (1913–1997)—As Alabama's NAACP President, Patton played a critical role in the state's voter registration program. After the state illegalized the organization in 1957, he became the NAACP national director of voter education, the post he held for 22 years. See Jimmie L. Franklin, *Back to Birmingham: Richard Arrington, Jr. and His Times* (Tuscaloosa: University of Alabama Press, 1989), 68, 72, 76; and The University of Alabama Center for Public TV & Radio, "I Shall Not Be Moved: The Legacy of W. C. Patton," an episode in "Alabama Experience" series, produced by Dwight Cameron. http://www.cptr.ua.edu/alex/studyguides/patton.htm.

Willard Wirtz (b. 1912)—Secretary of labor under John F. Kennedy and Lyndon Johnson, from 1962 to 1969. Wirtz led Johnson's anti-poverty programs (known as the "War on Poverty") with a focus on job training and labor arbitration, and oversaw the Labor Department's implementation of anti-discriminatory regulations.

"Man Power Re-development Act of 1962"—This probably refers to the Manpower Development and Training Act of 1962. Congress passed the law upon the request of President Kennedy, who feared that a large number of unemployed people at a time of economic prosperity would undercut the nation's economy. The law was to provide job training and vocational education through a combination of federal and state funds. A year before, Congress had passed the Area Redevelopment Act, which aimed to induce industries into depressed areas through financial enticement. See Gladys Roth Kremen, "MDTA: The Origins of the Manpower Development and Training Act of 1962," http://www.dol.gov/asp/programs/history/mono-mdtatext.htm.

76 Medgar Evers, Special Report

APRIL 1, 1963

During Friday and Saturday, March 29 and 30, the Field Secretary worked in the Voter Registration Campaign in Greenwood, Mississippi. While in Greenwood, I participated in the assistance of getting together a mass meeting for Friday night, also, in the transporting of individuals to the Registrar's office.

On Friday afternoon, the Field Secretary's attention was called to the eviction of Rev. Jessie Crain, age 67, of Route 3, Box 209, Greenwood, Mississippi and his family of 14, because he refused to take his name off the registration books. Rev. Crain had no place to go and no money. The Field Secretary immediately called Dr. Aaron Henry, of Clarksdale, realizing the $1000 emergency fund, which the national office had sent into the area and immediately apprised him of the situation. Dr. Henry suggested that $100 be given to Rev. Crain and his family.

The Field Secretary, along with James Farmer, Director of CORE, drove to Clarksdale, whereupon the $100 was secured. We then returned to Greenwood, Mississippi where the mass meeting was in progress, before a capacity crowd of some 500 persons, in the First Christian Church. After our arrival, at the meeting, the Chairman of the Program, Dave Dennis of CORE, recognized the Field Secretary of NAACP, at which time the Rev. Crain who was seated on the platform and who had been mentioned prominently earlier, was asked to stand. Some of the remarks the Field Secretary made were: "We appreciate Freedom Fighters like Rev. Crain and family, and to show our appreciation for his courage for standing up like a man, the NAACP is happy to present to Rev. Crain and his family $100, in an effort to help them to make an adjustment.

This was greeted with thunderous ovations, and when the Field Secretary remarked further, "and there is more where this came from—for those who are willing to stand up for freedom," there was another thunderous ovation.

After presentation of the $100 to Rev. Crain, CORE's Executive Secretary, James Farmer, pledged $100 to be sent in from the national office of CORE on Monday, April 1.

The meeting closed with a number of persons expressing interest in becoming members of NAACP, and with a committee being formed to solicit memberships to re-organize our dormant NAACP chapter there.

Saturday, March 30, there was a deal of activity; moving to new headquarters since having been burned out and evicted from the previous headquarters. Also, on Saturday, numerous newsmen, ABC, NBC, CBS, as well as the two major wire services, along with the Afro-American, were on the scene. The Field Secretary commented to each of the newsmen, as a representative of NAACP as well as the role the NAACP is playing in the campaign.

Comments: there is a deal of confusion since it appears that everyone there (Greenwood) is attempting to give directions, however, on

Friday and Saturday Wiley Branton, was there to help coordinate things.

The Field Secretary will be returning to Greenwood on Monday, April 1, however, in view of the planned Voter Registration Drive which is imminent for Jackson, I will be returning for a conference with Ministers on Tuesday and a campaign strategy meeting for Tuesday night, in Jackson, Mississippi.

Wiley A. Branton (1925–1988)—A prominent civil-rights attorney, Branton first came to national attention when in 1956 he represented black high-school students in Little Rock, Arkansas, to desegregate the city's high school. In 1962 he was named director of the Voter Education Project (VEP) sponsored by the Southern Regional Council of Atlanta, Georgia. He came to Mississippi to defend civil-rights workers, and in February 1962, after a SNCC worker was heavily injured by an ambush, called all COFO voter-registration workers to come to Greenwood to counter violence. After practicing privately in Washington, D.C., in 1977 he was named dean of Howard University Law School. See Dittmer, 147–148; "Wiley Austin Branton: Arkansas Native Son," http://www.arkansasblacklawyers.net/branton.html.

77 Medgar Evers, Televised Address, "I Speak as a Native Mississippian"

MAY 20, 1963

I speak as a native Mississippian. I was educated in Mississippi schools, and served overseas in our nation's armed forces in the war against Hitlerism and Fascism. . . . Most southern white people, whether they are friendly or hostile, usually think of the NAACP as a "northern outside group." . . . At least one-half of the NAACP membership is in the South. There have been branches in Mississippi since 1918. The Jackson, Mississippi, branch was organized in 1926— thirty-seven years ago. . . .

Now the mayor says that if the so-called outside agitators would leave us alone everything would be all right. This has always been the position of those who would deny Negro citizens their constitutional rights. . . . Never in its history has the South as a region, without outside pressure, granted the Negro his citizenship rights. . . . It is also in the American tradition to demonstrate, to assemble peacefully and to petition the government for a redress of grievances. Such a petition may legitimately take the form of picketing, although in Jackson, Negroes are immediately arrested when they attempt to exercise this constitutional right. . . .

We feel that Mayor Thompson will help Jackson if he will consult with a democratically selected bi-racial committee, some of whose members may be members of the NAACP. He would profit from the experience of other southern cities. . . .

Tonight the Negro knows from his radio and television what happened today all over the world. He knows what black people are doing and he knows what white people are doing. . . . He knows about the new free nations in Africa and knows that a Congo native can be a locomotive engineer, but in Jackson he cannot even drive a garbage truck.

. . . Then he looks about his home community and what does he see, to quote our Mayor, in this "progressive, beautiful, friendly prosperous city with an exciting future"?

He sees a city where Negro citizens are refused admittance to the City Auditorium and the Coliseum; his children refused a ticket to a good movie in a downtown theater; his wife and children refused service at a lunch counter in a downtown store where they trade; students refused the use of the main public libraries, parks, playgrounds, and other tax-supported recreational facilities. He sees Negro lawyers, physicians, dentists, teachers, and other professionals prevented from attending meetings of professional organizations. He sees a city of over 150,000 of which 40% is Negro, in which there is not a single Negro policeman or policewoman, school crossing guard, fireman, clerk, stenographer, or supervisor employed in any city department or the mayor's office . . . except those employed in segregated facilities. He sees local hospitals which segregate Negro patients and deny staff privileges to Negro family physicians. The mayor spoke of the twenty-four-hour police protection we have . . . there are questions in the minds of many Negroes whether we have twenty-four hours of protection, or twenty-four hours of harassment. . . .

What then does the Negro want? He wants to get rid of racial segregation in Mississippi life because he knows it has not been good for him nor for the State. He knows that segregation is unconstitutional and illegal. . . . The Negro citizen wants to register and vote without special handicaps imposed on him alone. . . . The Negro Mississippian wants more jobs above the menial level in stores where he spends his money. He believes that new industries that have come to Mississippi should employ him above the laboring category. He wants the public schools and colleges desegregated so that his children can receive the best education that Mississippi has to offer. He believes additional Negro students should be accepted at Ole Miss and at other colleges. He feels strongly about these and other items although he may not say so publicly.

. . . Jackson can change if it wills to do so. If there should be resistance, how much better to have turbulence to effect improvement, rather than turbulence to maintain a stand-pat policy. We believe there are white Mississippians who want to go forward on the race question. Their religion tells them there is something wrong with the old system. Their sense of justice and fair play sends them the same message.

But whether Jackson and the State choose change or not, the years of change are upon us. In the racial picture things will never be as they once were. History has reached a turning point, here and all over the world. Here in Jackson we can recognize the situation and make an honest effort to bring fresh ideas and new methods to bear, or we can have what Mayor Thompson called "turbulent times." If we choose this latter course, the turbulence will come, not because of so-called agitators or presence or absence of the NAACP, but because the time has come for a change and certain citizens refuse to accept the inevitable.

Negro citizens want to help all other good citizens bring about a meaningful improvement in an orderly fashion . . . the two races have lived here together. The Negro has been in America since 1619, a total of 344 years. He is not going anywhere else; this country is his home. He wants to do his part to help make his city, state, and nation a better place for everyone regardless of color and race.

Let me appeal to the consciences of many silent, responsible citizens of the white community who know that a victory for democracy in Jackson will be a victory for democracy everywhere.

Allen Cavett Thompson (1912–?)—A five-term mayor of Jackson (starting in 1949), he was an unapologetic segregationist known for condoning excessive police force against civil-rights demonstrators in the city. After his retirement in 1969, he founded a group called FOCUS, which demanded "freedom of choice" in public schools, and became a spokesperson for a movement to ban the airing of *Sesame Street*. See "Mississippi Agency Votes for a TV Ban on 'Sesame Street,'" *New York Times*, May 3, 1970, 54.

78 Telegram to President John F. Kennedy

June 1, 1963

The President
The White House

Please, mistreatment of Negro children and their parents reported behind hog wire confines of Jackson Concentration Camp. City, county, and State Law officers involved. Medical attention being denied. Injured in some cases. Urge immediate investigation by Department of Justice agents of these denials of constitutional rights to peaceful demonstrations and protests.

NAACP, Medgar Evers, Mississippi Field Secretary
1072 Lynch St., Jackson, Miss.

John F. Kennedy (1917–1963)—A former Navy pilot and thirty-fifth president of the United States, Kennedy apparently believed in the general goals of desegregation, but until the summer of 1963, consistently refused to put any major civil-rights bill to Congress. Kennedy feared alienating one of his major electoral bases, white southern Democrats. He gave a televised address announcing his intent to pursue what would become the Civil Rights Act of 1964 on the evening Medgar was assassinated. See Herbert S. Parmet, *JFK: The Presidency of John F. Kennedy* (New York: Dial Press, 1983); and Carl M. Brauer, *John F. Kennedy and Second Reconstruction* (New York: Columbia University Press, 1977).

79 "Roy Wilkins Is Arrested at Jackson: NAACP Official Accused of Felony; D.C. Man Seized," Associated Press
Washington Post and *Times Herald*

JUNE 2, 1963

JACKSON, Miss. (AP)—Police seized a national Negro leader, Roy T. Wilkins, when he started picketing in front of a downtown variety store today.

They booked him on a felony charge and released him on $1000 bond. Wilkins, 61, is executive secretary of the NAACP.

A few hours later, police swooped down on a Negro mass march and arrested truckloads of the demonstrators.

The sidewalk march, with Negroes walking in pairs, many carrying American flags, started from NAACP headquarters.

About 100 Negroes joined in the March. Others trailed in cars.

Police blocked the march with a line of officers across their path, forcing the Negroes to swerve into a side street. Motorcycle officers then blocked off both ends of the side street and began loading the Negroes remaining in the march—about 40 of them—into trucks for the trip to a special detention center. Part of the crowd had dispersed as the march veered into the side street.

AGREE TO 3 DEMANDS

A little earlier, in a move to ease the rising tension, Mayor Allen Thompson and the City Commission agreed to three of eight Negro demands.

They agreed: 1. to hire Negro policemen for patrolling Negro sections; 2. to hire Negro school crossing guards for Negro schools; 3. to upgrade Negro city employees.

The Mayor flatly rejected a key proposal—that the city join in forming a biracial committee to work toward easing racial problems.

However, Thompson said there would be further negotiations on some of the demands. As for school desegregation, he said the city would abide by court decisions in pending suits.

Wilkins was charged with restraint of trade. Released with him were Medgar Evers, 37, of Jackson, State head of the NAACP, and Helen Wilcher, 37, of Jackson. They were arrested on the same charge.

Police also arrested Thelton Henderson, a Negro attorney with the Justice Department. Officers took Henderson to Police Headquarters, where he was released almost immediately.

Henderson, 29, of Washington, was picked up while observing the picket demonstration that led to Wilkins's arrest.

Wilkins arrived here from New York Friday. He assumed his picket role in front of a downtown store where violence flared last Tuesday during a sit-in that kicked off the drive.

In a telegram to President Kennedy, Evers asked for a Justice Department investigation of the treatment of Negroes arrested during demonstrations.

Evers accused police of mistreating children and said medical treatment was denied when 327 juveniles and 94 adults were arrested yesterday.

The 421, transported in a variety of city trucks, were placed in special detention compounds at the fair grounds. Evers called it a "concentration camp."

Police said special medical supplies were taken to the compound last night.

Mayor Thompson said the special detention quarters—converted exhibition halls—were nice "but those demonstrators nearly tore it down last night."

"This is a tense time with us," he said. "We're trying to keep from having real trouble. It doesn't matter if 100,000 people are sent in by the pressure groups, we will maintain law and order and arrest lawbreakers."

The Mayor added that city voters will be asked to approve a bond issue of $500,000 to $1 million to build additional detention facilities for racial demonstrators.

Thelton Henderson (1933–)—In 1962 Henderson became the first African American lawyer to serve in the Civil Rights Division of the Justice Department and traveled the South extensively for investigations. Henderson has authored many legal articles on civil rights and legal professions. He is currently a US District Judge in San Francisco. See "Judge Who Blocked Prop. 209 Has Made His Mark in Civil Rights," *USA Today*, November 29, 1996, A3.

*

80 "Negroes' 'Awakened Militancy' Now Centers on Mississippi," Wallace Terry

Washington Post

JUNE 7, 1963

JACKSON, Miss.—"You're itching for freedom but you won't scratch," the dark-skinned minister told some 500 Mississippi Negroes jammed into a hot, steaming church auditorium for an NAACP rally one night this week.

It is true that in this capital city of what generally is regarded as the most segregated state in the Union, Negroes are itching for freedom as they never have before. But it also is true that daily a larger number of them are beginning to scratch.

One of them is Marvin Wilson, 13, who stuffed his hands in his jeans and, without hesitation, explained why he was arrested and jailed for picketing against segregated lunch counters.

"Christ died on the cross for our freedom—white and colored. But we colored down here got none anyway, that's why I went to jail. And when I grow up and go to college, I don't want no white folks pushing a mop in my hands when I get out."

MILITANCY AWAKENED

The arrests of more than 300 Freedom Riders here in 1961, the enrollment of James Meredith at the University of Mississippi in the midst of a bloody riot last year, and the anti-segregation campaign just ended in Birmingham awakened this new militancy among Jackson's Negroes, NAACP leaders believe.

"Ten years ago you couldn't pay a Negro to go downtown and challenge the law the way he's doing here now," according to Jacob L. Reddix, president of all-Negro Jackson State College. "And these Negroes now are even unafraid of guns staring them in the face."

The NAACP is channeling this new militancy into a four-pronged attack on discrimination in public facilities and city employment.

The attack calls for a boycott of white merchants, demonstrations by a few persons each day to publicize the Negro's plight here before the rest of the Nation, legal action in the courts and build-up of the Negro's voting strength.

ENCOURAGEMENT IS AIM

If successful, the NAACP hopes this campaign will encourage Negroes elsewhere in the country to hasten their efforts to end segregation and discrimination.

"After all, this IS Mississippi," one Negro leader said, "and if Negroes here can get their rights, no one should be waiting around in New York or anyplace else."

In addition, the NAACP would like a victory in this hard-core center of segregation to answer the charges leveled by some top Negroes that its methods of ending segregation have been outdated by the non-violent direct action techniques used by CORE and the Southern Christian Leadership Conference.

But the NAACP is faced with many problems.

At the start of the drive a few weeks ago, that organization faced the reticence of many Negroes from both the upper and lower classes.

'CONDITIONED' BY WHITES

"The white man has very shrewdly conditioned us down here," a Negro insurance executive said. "He has let the upper class Negro do whatever he likes so long as he stays out of the white man's way. The lower class Negro has to fend for himself."

"But now we are enjoying support from both levels in the community," Negro attorney Carsie Hall said. "Even the old-line ministers, who 10 years ago wouldn't dare to venture out on these problems, are now in the forefront of this struggle."

Medgar Evers, Mississippi field secretary directing the drive, points out that Negroes on the city's payroll have given their financial support, though not openly. One anonymous contribution to the movement was accompanied by a note reading, "Don't keep talking about teachers not supporting you, because we're in it too."

OBSTACLES IN THE NAACP'S WAY

NAACP officials are complaining of "Uncle Toms" who are in league with the city fathers, wiretapping telephones at the movement's headquarters, and leaks to police by newspaper reporters of their plans for demonstrations.

The movement also has given the appearance of petering out. The NAACP explained that it may have reached an early peak in the drive when on May 24 some 400 students were arrested.

A controversy between the NAACP and some workers for CORE in this area has been brewing over whether or not to launch massive demonstrations to fill the jails here as Negroes did in Birmingham.

"I think if we continue to send four or five people down to get arrested every day this movement will peter out," Charles Smith, a CORE field secretary said. "We must get masses. We need more numbers to impress our determination on the power structure."

The NAACP traditionally has taken the position that demonstrations should be limited to a small number, since only one arrest is necessary to test the police action in the courts.

And here, the NAACP further tied up $64,000 in bond money which "we don't really have to spare," one NAACP lawyer said.

"I don't believe the sizes of the demonstration should be controlled by the NAACP or any other organization because of financial considerations," said Robert Carter, chief counsel of the NAACP. "But at some point we must indicate to the local leadership what our resources are."

Wallace Terry—Award-winning journalist and commentator, he covered the Black Freedom Movement for *Time* magazine. Terry won wide-spread recognition for his remarkable reporting on African American soldiers during the Vietnam War. He edited the bestseller *Bloods: An Oral History of the Vietnam War by Black Veterans* (New York: Ballentine, 1984).

Jacob L. Reddix (1897–1973)—Fifth president of Jackson State University, 1940–1967. Reddix is credited with enhancing the faculty and school buildings and known for the philosophy of black economic independence through cooperation. In 1948, Reddix traveled to Liberia to work as a consultant to the Booker T. Washington Institute at Kakata. He founded the State Mutual Savings and Loan Association, which became the First American Bank of Jackson, the only black-owned commercial bank in the state. See George Alexander Swell, *Mississippi Black History Makers* (Jackson: University Press of Mississippi, 1977), 143–154.

81 Medgar W. Evers, Press Statement

JUNE 10, 1963

IN RESPONSE TO JUNE 6, 1963 INJUNCTION
AGAINST DEMONSTRATIONS

Jackson officials once more documented their unique capacity for speaking from two sides of their mouths today by seeking to enjoin NAACP sparked demonstrations and selective buying activities currently being executed to expose Jackson's rough and rigid racial abuses. Why spank a tottering infant? Why enjoin a "faltering" movement, as they describe it?

White leaders in Jackson gave the world the answer today. Their injunction proceedings have proven that our movement is sharp, vital, and inclusive. They are hurting inside. This is their outcry.

Our attorneys are studying the language of the injunction papers and will advise us of what action to take.

CHAPTER VIII

AFTER
MEDGAR,
NO MORE FEAR

"Freedom has never been free. . . . I love my children and I love my wife—with all my heart. And I would die, die gladly, if that would make a better life for them."

Medgar Wiley Evers, June 7, 1963. Quoted in Barbara Harris, "Forty Years After Medgar Evers the Struggle Continues," Jackson Advocate [Mississippi], June 12, 2003.

"Someone said . . . that Medgar did more in death than he accomplished in life. Now, I don't know whether that's so. But his death did accomplish a lot. And when I met with President [John F.] Kennedy and the children and Charles [Evers] . . . the president signed a draft copy of the civil-rights bill . . . he said to me, 'Your husband's death will make this possible.'"

Myrlie Evers-Williams, interviewed by Manning Marable, August 21, 2004.

M EDGAR WILEY EVERS was officially pronounced dead at the University of Mississippi Medical Center at 1:14 a.m. on June 12, 1963. He was only thirty-seven years old. Medgar's funeral was set for June 15.

This was the first political assassination of a major leader of the modern Black Freedom Movement: it would not be the last. Perhaps the thousands of women, men, and children who gathered in Jackson to honor their servant-leader understood this, that Evers's death had changed everything. By mid-morning on June 12, Meredith released a press statement, declaring that Evers had been "one of my best and most beloved friends. . . . [For]18 years he devoted his life to making America truly the land of the Free. We must not fail him now," Meredith vowed. "This system under which we live in Mississippi, and throughout the South, must be changed at any cost."[1] Over 6,000 people came to Medgar's funeral, including King and other prominent civil rights leaders. The vast majority of mourners, however, came from hundreds of tiny towns and rural areas from all over Mississippi, to honor their fallen son. They solemnly marched the three miles from the Masonic Temple to the Collins Funeral Home on North Farish Street. Many wept; others defiantly chanted, "After Medgar, No More Fear!"

In 2003, Myrlie reflected:

"I can recall wanting very badly to get out of the car that we were in, the family members . . . and joining those people. It was a turning point . . . because people had been so fearful of losing their lives, their jobs, their homes, as many people did. And Medgar's death just appeared to give them a strength and a determination that they never had before. It was like, 'Our leader is gone, and we aren't going to take it anymore.' And I know that it would have been so gratifying to him because I recall times when Medgar would come home and he would say, 'My people, my people—will they ever be ready?' And then he would answer that, and say, 'Yes.' I remember times he would come home and sit in a chair and weep, because he did not have the support that he wanted to have, and he knew it was only because of fear that people had of losing their homes and their lives and livelihoods."[2]

Following the formal funeral march, several thousand demonstrators proceeded down North Farish Street toward Capitol Street downtown. The Reverend Ed King, Salter, and other local civil-rights activists were quickly identified by police and were arrested. Hundreds were clubbed and stampeded, and shots were fired over their heads.[3] On June 19, Evers was laid to rest at Arlington National Cemetery. Approximately 25,000 mourners had viewed Evers's body at a Washington, D.C., funeral home. As the funeral procession made its way toward Arlington, Myrlie became "amazed at the thousands of people who lined the streets, black and white people sharing grief." In death, Medgar Evers had become "a hero not only to Mississippi but also to the entire nation."[4] President Kennedy sent a letter of condolence to Myrlie, expressing the "deepest sympathy" of both his wife Jacqueline and himself "on the death of your husband. Although comforting thoughts are difficult at a time like this, surely there can be some solace in the realization of the justice of the cause for which your husband gave his life" [see Document 82].

Following Medgar's efforts, CORE accelerated its voter-registration campaign in Mississippi's fourth congressional district. COFO then launched the ambitious "Freedom Vote Project," to demonstrate to the nation that thousands of Mississippi blacks would indeed vote if they were enfranchised. The project organized a mock election for governor, running an interracial progressive ticket headed by Aaron Henry and the Reverend Ed King. Statewide, 93,000 African Americans cast ballots in the mock vote.[5] In the Freedom Summer of 1964, about 1,000 idealistic white college students traveled to Mississippi to assist local civil-rights workers in directing Freedom Schools and engaging in voter education and registration efforts. There were more sacrifices: three young civil-rights activists—James Chaney, Andrew Goodman and Michael Schwerner—were brutally murdered by white supremacists. By late August, 1964, white racists were responsible for firebombing or attacking thirty-seven black churches and thirty black-owned homes and businesses. Eighty civil-rights activists were seriously injured by beatings, and about 1,000 people in all were jailed. But with the courageous leadership of Fannie Lou Hamer, Aaron Henry, and Charles Evers, who had replaced his late younger brother as the NAACP field secretary, there could be no turning back.[6] In August 1964, with President Lyndon B. Johnson's endorsement and support, Congress passed the 1964 Civil Rights Act, outlawing racial segregation at all public accommodations—hotels, restaurants, and every public establishment for the first time in U.S. history. The following year, Congress approved the Voting Rights Act, guaranteeing that all American citizens would have the inalienable right to the franchise. American racism was certainly not yet dead, but "Jim Crow segregation" in its nearly century-long, terrible existence, was now gone.

After the passage of the 1965 Voting Rights Act, by 1967 61.8 percent of Mississippi's black electorate was registered to vote—a stunning achievement. Yet the struggle for multicultural democracy still continued. In 1966, the Mississippi state legislature passed House Bill 911, redistricting five overwhelmingly black districts in an attempt to limit the potential number of African American elected officials from the area.[7] In 1968, Mississippi made a list of what it described as "heavy crimes," including murder and rape, as "disqualifying factors" for voter registration.[8] Before the 1972 National Democratic Convention, Mississippi Governor Bill Walter led an effort to deny seats to black district delegates. It was only in 1975 when a court-ordered redistricting permitted the election of three African American representatives from Hinds County.[9] In 1979, federal courts ordered Mississippi to redraw districts to permit more African Americans to be elected.[10] By 2005, the largest number of African American elected officials of any state was in Mississippi. Medgar Evers's vision had partially come true.

Achieving racial justice for Medgar Evers in Mississippi's court system would also prove to be an elusive goal. Despite his fingerprints found on the murder weapon, Beckwith was released after two mistrials by all-white juries in 1964. Through the relentless determination of Myrlie, the murder case was reopened in 1989. Finally, more than three decades after Medgar's assassination, a jury of eight African Americans and four whites convicted Beckwith of murder and sentenced him to life in prison, on February 4, 1994. A new generation of Mississippi leaders in government, business, and higher education now celebrates the life and legacy of Evers. In 2002, Myrlie agreed to donate her late husband's papers to the Mississippi Department of Archives and History in Jackson. On April 25, 2002, in a public ceremony held at the Old Capitol Museum to mark the donation of Evers's papers, Myrlie received a standing ovation. Former Governor William Winter proclaimed that Medgar Evers was "a true hero. He is why we are here today." Winter also observed about Myrlie: "This lady has a right to be the bitterest and angriest person in America because of what's happened to her. Yet she has reconciled the tragedies of her life and become a leader for future generations." Mississippi Governor Ronnie Musgrove stated: "Medgar once said, 'You can kill a man, but you can't kill an idea.' Because of his bravery, because of his focus and desire to bring about change, because of his ideas, the idea of a better Mississippi has come to light."[11]

The documents in this final chapter represent fragments of speeches and notes Medgar drafted during the period 1954–1963, and related materials that post-date his assassination. Taken together, the entire volume represents only one small part of the intellectual output and creative legacy of a man of uncommon courage. This work cannot by any measure represent the full complexity of the Freedom Movement in Mississippi, much less that which occurred across the American South in the decade following the *Brown* decision. Our purpose as editors and interpreters is to document the legacy of one individual who was shaped by the times in which he lived, and who selflessly strove to make a critical difference, both to society as a whole, and to his people. Myrlie reflected in 2004: "I believe . . . that this book will help not only enlighten people about the man, but to give them different twists to that period of time that will delve deeper into the heart of it than what we have already done as a nation. And on a personal basis, it will probably shed new information on him and his work, and me and our adult children. It will certainly be a document for his grandchildren to embrace. . . . It will lend to discussions about strategies that young people, young adults, will be able to know his name, and perhaps find something in this book that will inspire them to follow suit. Not that we would ever want anyone to go through the tragedy of being hunted and killed. We don't want that. Certainly we don't need that. But to inspire them [toward] that kind of leadership."[12]

82 President Kennedy to Myrlie Evers

June 13, 1963
The White House
Washington

Mrs. Medgar Evers
2332 Gynes Street
Jackson 3, Mississippi

Dear Ms. Evers:

I extend to you and your children my sincerest condolences on the tragic death of your husband. Although comforting thoughts are difficult at a time like this, surely there can be some solace in the realization of the justice of the cause for which your husband gave his life. Achievement of the goals he did so much to promote will enable his children and the generations to follow to share fully and equally in the benefits and advantages our nation has to offer.

Sincerely,

[signed by President Kennedy]

Mrs. Kennedy joins me in extending her deepest sympathy.
[handwritten by the president at the bottom of the letter]

83 Bill Peters, "A Talk with Medgar Evers"
New York Post

Transcript of an interview of Medgar by CBS reporter Bill Peters, given in the summer of 1962, but aired in full in the days immediately following his assassination on June 12, 1963, and June 16, 1963.

In a TV interview filmed last summer, the NAACP leader told of the violence that was to take his life.

Medgar W. Evers, the NAACP official who was murdered this week in Jackson, Miss., had been interviewed last summer by CBS-TV reporter Bill Peters on the voter-registration drive in Mississippi. The following is a condensation of that interview, a portion of which was rebroadcast earlier this week.

Peters: I'm speaking with Mr. Medgar W. Evers, Mississippi Field Secretary for the National Assn. for the Advancement of Colored People. Mr. Evers, can you tell me how long you've had this job?

Evers: I've been Field Secretary for the National Assn. for the Advancement of Colored People going into my eighth year.

Peters: And during these eight years, has there been an NAACP effort towards getting Negroes to vote and register?

Evers: Yes, there has been all over the state—an effort to get Negroes registered to vote in most of the counties where we're organized, and even in a number of counties where we're not organized. We think now in terms of back in 1954 and '55, when up in Belzoni, Miss., which is in Humphrey's County, we had a very active chapter getting Negroes registered to vote.

The president of our branch there was Rev. G. W. Lee, and of course, Rev. Lee was putting out a little handbill urging Negroes to go down to the registrar's office and he got a message from some unidentified person telling him to cease his activities, and of course he refused to cease these activities, and as a result of his refusal to not let people intimidate him, one Saturday afternoon as he was driving home from the cleaners from downtown—a car drove up beside him with two men in it and shotgunned him to death. A little later on Rev. Courts, who was active in getting people registered to vote—was told to cease his activities in this same town of Belzoni and he was shot down as he made change in his store.

Peters: Looking back over the eight years that you've been engaged in this work, would you say that it has become more or less difficult for Negroes to register in Mississippi?

Evers: Well, I would say that it has become in some instances more difficult for them to register, and in other instances possibly less difficult. I think in terms of some of the counties that I've mentioned— since 1954 they passed a literacy bill which requires all persons to fill out a form consisting of some 21 questions and they make it most difficult for Negroes to register. For example, if you fail to cross your T or dot an I, in a number of instances, Negroes are refused the right to register. In other instances we find Negroes not even given the application form to fill out.

Just recently, down in Forest County, it was mentioned that one fellow was asked how many bubbles in a bar of soap, which was most difficult for anybody to answer. These are some of the questions that are asked Negroes when they go in, and some of the obstacles— some of the problems that we face in trying to register to vote here in Mississippi.

Peters: Would you say that there is less violence now in connection with it?

Evers: Well, we have not had violence in connection with voting that we had in 1955, not recently that is, and I'd say that we are thankful for the role the federal government is playing in this regard. The federal government has gone in and filed a number of suits to make it possible for Negroes to register and vote in Mississippi. And this, of course, we are very proud of and we're most cooperative with the federal government in making affidavits available to them from Negroes who have been denied the right to register and vote.

Peters: In your work, Mr. Evers, in the state of Mississippi, have you personally been subjected to any difficulties or problems?

Evers: Yes, I have. I've suffered some personal difficulties. Number one, I'm a native of the state, lived here all my life, but in 1958, as I came from a regional meeting in North Carolina, I boarded the bus in Meridian, Miss., on the front seat where I sat and was told to move by the police. I, of course, refused. I refused to move to the back of the bus after being ordered to do so by the driver. And after I refused, of course—of course he got off the bus and went and called the police in Meridian and they conferred. And after having conferred with one another, two came on the bus and asked to see my identification. I showed them my identification. And after having done that, they asked me to get off the bus and come over to the police station with them—which was across the street. I went over there with them and they asked me what I was trying to do—stir up trouble? I told them, no, I was merely going home to my wife and children. Of course I had two children at the time. And they said, well, you know how things are done here. I said, yes, I was born 30 miles from here, which was Decatur, Miss. And after some 15 or 20 minutes of interrogation they permitted me to go back to the bus.

I went and got back on the bus and, of course, I sat back on the front seat. And having refused to move again, the bus driver pulled off. I heard as we moved away—a number of people say that, "We should go on and pull him off." Of course I sat there and some three blocks from the bus terminal a white man boarded the bus and struck me in the face. This was about 3 o'clock in the morning. I was alone. Of course I refused to move and I came all the way to Jackson without any further incidents.

That along with many others—I've had a number of threatening calls—people calling me saying they were going to kill me, saying they were going to blow my home up and saying that I only had a few hours to live. I remember distinctly one individual calling with a pistol on the other end, and he hit the cylinder and of course you could hear that it was a revolver. He said, "This is for you." And I said, "Well, whenever my time comes, I'm ready." And, well, we get such pranks pretty frequently. But that does not deter us from our goal of first-class citizenship and getting more people registered to vote and doing the things here that a democracy certainly is supposed to espouse and provide for its citizenry.

Peters: Why do you feel that it is important for Negroes to vote?

Evers: Well, I think it's necessary for all people to vote, and Negroes especially, with the conditions as they are here. For example, in Mississippi, we have police brutality galore. We have bad roads. We have a number of things that we don't get simply because Negroes do not vote. For example, here in Jackson there is not one single Negro policeman. There are some 60,000 Negroes who live in Jackson, Miss., with no Negroes represented on the police force. This, of course, is the result of the fact that Negroes are not voting. And once we become registered voters in the numbers that we should be, then, of course, we should get these Negro policemen and other individuals in good positions that will benefit all the people.

And I think another thing, too, and that's the fact that we're not interested in making Mississippi better or this country better for Negroes, we're interested in making this country better for people, for all of us, and we feel that only through voting, like we should—everyone voting—are we going to be able to do this. We would hope that everybody would be able to register and vote and be able to elect those officials who are going to best serve the community. And then we would not have, for example, many politicians who get on the stands and—and of course, they appeal to prejudice and bigotry as a result of the fact that Negroes are not registered to vote. Once we are voting in the numbers that we should be voting, then we're not going to have these politicians getting on the soapboxes, making his first speech on the Negro, using the Negro to climb into office, and that's what we have here in Mississippi, and that's what we have in many other Southern communities where Negroes are not voting. So these are some of the reasons why Negroes, as well as white people, should be permitted to register and vote.

Peters: Do you feel that in campaigns where the question of race is a paramount issue that perhaps some of the more important issues don't get discussed?

Evers: Well, that's quite true. Many a candidate who runs for office and gets into office on the Negro question fails to really bring out to the constituency that he's supposed to represent what quality of man he really is. Because what he has done has been more or less to appeal to the emotions of the people rather than give them some concrete platform or some concrete plans that he intends to institute for the community or for the state that he represents. What he does—what he normally does is get into office on emotionalism and, of course, race emotionalism which is very paramount here in the state.

Peters: Are there places in Mississippi where the presence of a significant number of Negro voters had resulted in some progress?

Evers: Yes. There is one that I remember right off hand and that's Washington County, which is Greenville, Miss. In Greenville, Negroes comprise a large percentage of the total vote for the county. As a result of this large vote, you have Negro policemen. You have detectives and you have fairly good schools and you have a number of different things that we don't have, for example, here in Jackson. You have certainly no police brutality of any consequence in Washington County. I think now in terms of a coastal town. Gulfport—Negroes vote freely and they have a large number of voters there. They have Negro deputy sheriffs and they have Negro policemen. And, of course, you don't have the brutality that you have in areas where Negroes are not voting in large numbers. So, certainly, where they are voting, then, of course, you get better results all the way around.

Peters: In other words a Negro without a vote really has no appeal, no power to appeal for anything in his local government?

Evers: That's quite true. I think it's often said that a voteless people are a hopeless people. And I think that's true with us or true with anybody or any group of people. So it's necessary that we try to get our hands on the ballot and use it effectively. We're just not interested in voting so that conditions will be improved for Negroes. We want conditions improved for everybody. We feel that in this country that all persons should have an opportunity to register and vote and do the things that the Constitution guarantees them. That's all we're interested in.

Peters: Thank you very much, Mr. Evers.

Evers: Thank you, sir.

84 "He Said He Wouldn't Mind Dying—If . . . ,"
Myrlie Evers
Life

JUNE 28, 1963

At Arlington National Cemetery, Medgar Evers, murdered Mississippi field secretary for the N.A.A.C.P., was buried with a dignity he had been denied in life. In the tribute below, Evers's widow pays her own respects to the man who was her husband.

We all knew the danger was increasing. Threats came daily, cruel and cold and constant, against us and the children. But we had lived with this hatred for years and we did not let it corrode us.

Medgar was a happy man with a rich smile and a warmth that touched many people. He was never too busy to listen or too tired to help. But beneath that gentle sympathy lay strength that could not be intimidated. Lord knows, enough people tried. But it never worked and that, I suppose, is why they killed him.

I don't know what makes one man feel so passionately the needs of his people. It began for Medgar when he was a little boy in Decatur, Miss., where he was born. A family friend was lynched, and years later Medgar could still recall the shock with which he had turned to his father.

"Why did they kill him, Daddy?" he asked.

"Well, just because he was a colored man," his father said.

"Could they kill you, too?"

"If I did anything they didn't like, they sure could."

Medgar never forgot that blunt statement of the facts of Negro life in Mississippi. When I met him in 1950, at Mississippi's Alcorn College, I did not know or care much about civil rights. But Medgar and his brother Charles were already members of the N.A.A.C.P. and deeply involved in racial affairs. After a while we began to date. He was a veteran and seemed quite polished. I found him fascinating. After perhaps a year of going together, he told me one day that he couldn't go on. I thought he was breaking off with me and my heart nearly stopped. Then he smiled and said we were getting married. He had a ring in his pocket and he pulled it out and put it on my finger. He never asked me to marry him—he told me what he wanted me to do.

After college Medgar sold insurance for a couple of years but he spent at least as much time with an organization for Negro rights which he helped form. They issued bumper stickers all over the state that said in big letters, "Don't buy gas where you can't use the rest room." It was the first of many campaigns for economic boycott that Medgar would run.

Meanwhile, entirely on his own, he was organizing N.A.A.C.P. chapters wherever he could. At this point he became the first Negro to apply for admission to the University of Mississippi. He was turned down, but his mere application created a furor. I suppose it was natural that later, when the N.A.A.C.P. wanted a statewide field secretary, it should turn to Medgar.

We knew the job was dangerous. From the beginning we accepted the possibility that any of us might be killed. But he loved the work and I loved him, and whatever made him happy pleased me. I was frightened, especially when he traveled. But in time it changed. There was always the knowledge of what could happen, but it was not fear. The mind adjusts to such things. Medgar told me one time, "Sure, you're scared at first, but then you get mad. You think 'When it comes, I'm ready.' You know that if you stay scared, you can't do anything."

In a funny way, the constant threat of death made life richer and more meaningful—it made us more aware of each other, and it brought us closer together. When he left in the morning, I never knew if I would see him again. We never parted in anger, because we couldn't afford to.

As soon as Medgar took the N.A.A.C.P. job, the threats began. During crisis times the phone would ring all night. At first I tried to talk to the callers, but that was hopeless. Then I started hanging up, but they just called right back. Finally—and I've done this for years now—I began putting the phone quietly down on the table and letting them talk to the empty wall. So much hatred has been poured out on that wall.

Every time a Negro was jailed or beaten or killed in violation of his civil rights, Medgar investigated. At the time of the Emmett Till murder in 1955, he dressed as a field hand and rounded up evidence and witnesses. These investigations usually took him to small towns where justice is primitive and the Negro is hated.

Men who went with him said the trips were hair-raising, but Medgar never seemed disturbed. Still, he took precautions. When he left these little towns he drove swiftly, scanning the highway behind for followers. Once he was trailed out of a little Mississippi town and he drove better than 100 mph to escape.

At home, we learned to stay away from the windows at night lest we become a target. Recently he taught the children to fall to the floor, infantry fashion, if they heard a sharp noise outside.

Until recently Medgar wasn't really worried. All over the state he worked furiously on the two approaches he always believed are keys to the southern Negro's future. The first is the ballot box, the second is economic boycott.

"If we can get rid of our sense of inferiority," he always said, "we can begin to win our equality peacefully." This conviction that the Negro was not inferior—this was the thing, above all else, that he was trying to get across.

When the last series of demonstrations began in Jackson, the other side seemed to realize the seriousness too. The threats against all of us intensified. Then about a month ago the first attack on our home came in the form of a fire bomb. Late one night when I was waiting for Medgar and the children were already in bed, a car came slowly by the house and a moment later there was the crash of a bottle breaking and a whoosh of fire. It bathed the carport in flames. I was afraid someone was waiting outside to shoot at us, but as the flames billowed up I forgot my fear and ran out to douse them with a garden hose.

Perhaps this incident began to prey on Medgar's mind. By the week before he was killed, he was nearly exhausted. He had been working 20 hours a day for months. I think that on that last Sunday we spent together he knew something was going to happen.

It was the first time in months that he spent even a part of a day at home. That night we had a long talk. He asked me to massage his temples, which relaxed him, and while I did we talked about death. He said that he wouldn't mind dying if dying was necessary; he only feared what it would do to me.

Somehow we had a feeling that night that we'd never had before. There was a closeness, a oneness that you almost could reach out and touch. We had always been close, but this sense was new.

On Monday he was very busy. He mentioned death again that day, I remember, and again on Tuesday morning before he left. He kissed each of the children that morning, and he held me in his arms a long time.

He called three times from his office that day. I laughed and asked how he found time, and he said he wanted to hear my voice. The last thing he told me was that he loved me and he loved the children. "I'll see you tonight," he said.

For some reason I let the children stay up all hours that night. They had learned the sound of his car and, as he turned into the driveway about 12:20 a.m., they said, "Mama, there's Daddy," and they all scrambled to meet him.

We heard the car stop and the door open and then we heard the shot. It made a horrible noise. I knew instantly that Medgar had been shot, and as I ran for the door I prayed that he was just wounded, that it would not be fatal.

When I jerked open the front door, he had staggered from the car to the steps with his keys in his hand, trying to come home. He fell face downward and there was blood everywhere—everywhere. I screamed and screamed and, even as I did, I fell on my knees and lifted his head.

The children ran out of the house and surrounded me, and they kept crying, "Daddy, get up, please get up." After a while the neighbors came and they put Medgar on a mattress. His heart was laboring and his mouth was moving as if he was trying to talk. He seemed to be struggling, perhaps to speak, or perhaps just to live. Then they took him to the hospital.

I went inside with the children and fell to my knees. I prayed as Medgar had taught me, not that he would be saved, but that God's will would be done, and that He would give me strength to bear up under what must be. After a time someone called from the hospital and said Medgar had died. I think from the time I saw him taken away that I knew.

The next day when the police and other white people came, I looked out and saw them, and for a moment I hated everybody with a white skin. But that didn't last. Medgar taught me not to hate, and today I feel no hate for anyone, not even the man who killed him.

But it is still hard for me to realize that he is gone. Mornings are the worst time. He always came home late, and he often came to bed without awakening me. Every morning, automatically, when I awakened, I would reach out and touch him, and he always would be there. Now, in the mornings, I still reach out.

So I grieve, but I do not regret. We had a wonderful 11 years together. Some people are left with nothing; I have magnificent memories. Medgar didn't belong just to me—he belonged to so many, many people everywhere. He was so willing to give his life that I feel his death has served a certain purpose. When I find myself in pits of depression, I remind myself that fulfilling this purpose is what he really wanted.

✳

85 Myrlie Evers, Remarks in Acceptance of the 48th Spingarn Medal for Medgar Evers (posthumously) at the 54th Annual NAACP Convention

THURSDAY, JULY 4, 1963
CHICAGO, ILLINOIS

I accept this Spingarn Award for my deceased husband, Medgar Evers, as he would have personally accepted it—with a deep sense of humility and gratitude. He had more than a strong feeling about his work and the NAACP, he loved both dearly—he loved his people, city, state, and country to the extent he worked seven days a week and up to 23 hours a day to help America be the type of democracy she should be.

He stood for justice and freedom for all equally under the law of man and God. To be fully aware of the dangers in store for you from the hands of your fellow man and yet continue with the work that has produced this very danger shows how important he felt this work to be.

He did not consider his job as Field Secretary of Mississippi for the National Association for the Advancement of Colored People merely a means of making a livelihood but a job that made it possible for him to work at his best, and doing what he could to help make this a better place in which to live for us, our children, and generations to come; to help make this a country that is really free, where people can walk, and sit, work and pray, and vote, and be elected in the dignity which citizens of this great nation are entitled—and, yes, a place to live and die in dignity.

He felt that these are times that try men's souls, faiths and hopes and desires. These are not times for men with faint hearts, but times when men should pray, run, fight for their rights and not get weary, but rather hold out with determination to the end, for surely the end is in sight—and we are on the side of right.

I cannot accept this award without paying tribute to the many people in Jackson and throughout Mississippi who have worked, prayed and given of their time, money, assistance, encouragement, and part of their lives to help bring us closer to our goal. One man cannot do the job alone. It takes many dedicated people. In a sense this award belongs to so many.

I would like to quote a favorite prayer of Medgar's from St. Francis: "Lord, make me an instrument of Thy peace. Where there is hatred, let me sow love; where there is doubt, faith; where there is despair, hope; where there is darkness, light; and where there is sadness, joy."

If all of us put forth a great effort to do these things and everything else in our power to make America a real democracy—we shall overcome some day and soon.

The Evers family will forever cherish this award and try to live up to the standards, ideals, and goals it stands for. Thank you.

--- *

86 Medgar W. Evers, Address, "Our Need for Political Participation"

NO DATE
TOUGALOO COLLEGE
JACKSON, MISSISSIPPI

Under the American system of government, the vote is the basic tool for all citizens who would "promote the general welfare, and secure the blessings of liberty," set forth in the preamble to the Constitution.

In recent years, with increasing attention directed to the American ideal of equality for all, the access of Negro citizens to the ballot has assumed new importance.

The ballot is one of the keys to the solution of the myriad problems of segregation. Through our vote, the Negro citizens can be heard, and given equal consideration along with other groups representing business, labor, veterans, and farmers.

Due in large part to the power of the Negro vote, both major political parties have included in their platforms stronger resolutions aimed at improving the lot of the Negro citizen.

This is not to imply that only practical considerations will focus attention on the plight of the nation's 18 million non-white citizens. A kind of national soul-searching began with World War II. While fighting a war against forces proclaiming a doctrine of racial superiority, it became increasingly difficult to justify racial discrimination at home. Since then, the difficulty has mounted as questions about discrimination have been raised with each new court case, whether involving school desegregation or other efforts to obtain civic justice, with each publicized case of violence against Negro citizens.

At the same time, there has been a new awareness of the threat to all citizens in denial of individual liberties to some.

During the same period, as the United States became the leader of the free world, racial injustice at home has been an ever-growing source of embarrassment. In emerging areas of Africa and Asia, it is one of the greatest liabilities.

No one has understood this better than the Negro citizens of the United States. World opinion, as well as individual rights, have been stressed repeatedly in their demands for political equality.

Any study of the political behavior of the Negro voter must begin with the recognition that he is an American citizen first and is basically influenced by the same kind of political considerations which motivate other American voters. But because of disabilities peculiar to the Negro as a racial group, there are additional factors which condition his voting habits. Other groups, of course, are also influenced by considerations affecting their special interests. Each believes that a government that gives due consideration to his special interests is good government for the whole American people.

Race is no factor in registration or voting in many states and in some counties in Mississippi, but, as is the case, Negroes have been slothful in asserting the privilege that is theirs. Registration and voting have lagged to some extent because we have no political machines to herd voters to the registrar or to the polls. That task must be assumed by organizations interested in the welfare of Negro citizens.

The enhanced position of the Negro in the political life of the nation is bound to sharpen up competition for our vote. Politicians with little or no personal concern with civil rights want our vote in order to use public office to cope with other pressing problems.

The future of the Negro is very largely in the hands of the Negro citizen and voter. The burden of improvement rests primarily with the Negro himself. Negro citizens must prepare to present themselves in numbers to be qualified, and that preparation is their responsibility. There is no attempt here to underestimate the forces of resistance, the ignorance, trickery, fear, threats, and physical assaults that have been employed and will continue to be employed. But their eradication will not be accomplished by some miracle out of the sky, some wished-for relief from a far-off place; it will be done primarily through the intelligence, diligence, persistence, and courage of the population presently disfranchised. This population as a whole must be like the lone colored woman who presented herself on seven successive Saturday mornings to be registered and was finally enrolled. Let no man say that it is somehow unfair or unethical for Negro citizens to push politically for their rights as citizens. If it is legitimate to lobby and use political pressure to secure wider markets and fatter profits, what is so wrong with using political power to secure human rights? The answer is "nothing" and Negro Americans should proceed on that basis.

All the effort will have been wasted in a sense, if, after the battle has been won and the right to vote freely has been secured, the Negro citizen uses his ballot in a purely selfish and narrowly racial manner. To the degree that Negro Americans use their ballot for the maintenance for all citizens of the constitutional guarantees of liberty, i.e., for the preservation and strengthening of the American ideal, they will demonstrate the maturity which must be the end product of citizenship in a democratic society.

87 "Ingratitude vs. the NAACP"

NO DATE, NO LOCATION

"That man may last, but never lives
Who much receives, but nothing gives."

In our modern society, no man is sufficient unto himself. All mankind is dependent upon other people for survival. The most disgusting of all God's creatures are those who are puffed up with their own conceit. Those who have achieved a semblance of success and cry out in a great loud voice, "Look what I have done all by myself," are the world's biggest fools. Somewhere, somehow, in some manner, a helping hand has been extended to ease the burden and smooth the way for those who have risen a little above the crowd.

People who take and never give, who receive and never contribute may exist but never live. Those who remove everything from the pot and put nothing back deserve to be scorned by their fellow men, for they are like hogs under an oak tree who fill their bellies with acorns but never look up to understand from whence their blessings come.

Negroes in America are enjoying greater freedom and financial security than ever before in history. They hold higher and better positions both in government and private industry. Ministers, doctors, lawyers, school teachers, insurance agents, small business people, in fact all classes of Negroes have a higher standard of living because of the efforts of organizations like the National Association for the Advancement of Colored People to remove the restrictions which prevented Negroes from working and enjoying their rights as American citizens.

It now appears that many of those who have been able to improve their positions as the direct result of the NAACP refuse to support its present struggle to remove the restrictions which hold down the masses of their people, especially in the Deep South.

They assume that since they have better jobs, educational facilities, homes, and the privilege of voting, they have no responsibility to contribute anything to elevate others to a higher standard of living. If they would reflect for a minute and remember the money and time spent to smooth the way for their improved conditions there is little doubt that they would give to and work with the NAACP and similar organizations until every semblance of segregation and discrimination is destroyed.

Those who think that the battle has been won and everything is peaches and cream on the racial front are mistaken. There remains much to be done. The NAACP has achieved much with the support of a comparably few members. The opposition to equality for Negroes is fighting desperately. This organization needs and deserves the support of all Negroes and men of good will, and especially those who have attained higher standards of living because of the NAACP should make substantial contributions. The time to do it is right now!

"That man may last . . . "—The quotation is attributed to Thomas Gibbons (1720–1785) *When Jesus Dwelt.* The complete stanza reads:

That man may last, but never lives,
Who much receives, but nothing gives;
Whom none can love, whom none can thank,—
Creation's blot, creation's blank.

See http://yahooligans.yahoo.com/search/ligans_bfq?lb=q&p=num%3A690. 30.

88 "Life Challenges for Today's Youth"
[Draft is similar to a second talk, "Life Challenges for Today's Men."]

NO DATE, NO LOCATION

Today we are witnessing a great transition, things that were unimaginable fifteen years ago are realities today. The cotton picking machine was hardly thought of as being a remote possibility, spaceships were fantasies only to be found in Buck Rogers cartoons or some other unrealistic place. Transmitting a live program from Broadway in New York City or Sunset Strip in Hollywood, California to the backwoods of Amite County, Miss. could only be that of a miracle to happen once in a lifetime.

But ladies and gentlemen, we have seen these things and many others come to pass and doubtless there will be many, many others during your life span and mine. For example, man has been successful in landing an object on the moon while during the same period descending to an ocean depth never before equaled by man. The fact that man travels faster than sound is history. It is no wonder then that the meaning [title] of our subject "Life Challenges for Today's Youth" [this is crossed out and "Today's Challenge for Today's Man" penciled in, apparently for a later address] bears [holds] such a great significance upon our youth of [for us] today.

Why do we say this? Because it is true. Why is it true? Simple [we want] our young people will [to] be the ones to operate the spaceship, the rock launcher, jet planes, television cameras, submarines, bathyspheres and many of the other wonders of our times. All that I am trying to point up, ladies and gentlemen, is that there is a great challenge before us. Are we going to accept it with confidence, courage, and know how, or will we blunder through life contributing little or nothing to make our living here worthwhile?

You know, as Negro Americans living in Mississippi [today] it is imperative that we put forth extra effort to accomplish our desired goals [of freedom for all]. Doing just enough to get by is obsolete [no food. We must do our best] It is necessary that we become a part of this world-wide struggle for human dignity, for the world now recognizes the rights of those men and women who are willing to make a sacrifice for human dignity. Some of the things that encourage me most are the demonstrations in Africa which are bringing about the independence of many of the hither-to subjected Africans and placing them beside men and nations as equals.

Yes, and it is heartening indeed to see how young Negroes [Amen] throughout the south today are willing to go to jail for a principle rather than to accept as a "way of life" the old out-dated philosophy of "white supremacy" as is practiced in the south today [we have known it in the south]. Many people may not altogether agree with the method used, but certainly the principle involved should never be compromised and we encourage the very splendid work of these young people in their struggle for justice and equality.

89 Address, "The Challenge Is Ours"

NO DATE, NO LOCATION

Today we face the greatest challenge that has ever been before us. The Supreme Court, on May 17, 1957, made an historic ruling. It laid the legal foundation on which we may stand and fight for the rights which have been so long denied us. In 1957 the United States Congress passed a Civil Rights statute, the first since Reconstruction. The Interstate Commerce Commission has ruled that segregation in interstate transportation is illegal.

The challenge is ours and we must continue in the struggle with patience and courage, lest we be like the children of Israel, who were permitted to behold the Promised Land, but because of their fear of the new and untried, continued to wander in the wilderness. We can either move forward into the great "Promised Land" of freedom or because of our fear and lack of faith, continue to wander in the wilderness of racial discrimination, educational inequalities, political apathy, and economic servitude.

There are still far too many Negroes who would sit in the seat of the scornful and take counsel with the ungodly. They have been blinded by their own insecurity, frightened by their insufficiency, and have been unable to see that their position ultimately results in a situation where they have neither freedom nor respect.

[Following handwritten]

So politicians, who for years have thrived upon ignorance, hate, superstition, and fear are once again upon the beaten paths seeking spurious and fallacious ground for the perpetuation of a system which is a travesty of democracy.

"a Civil Rights statute . . . "—Medgar refers to the 1957 Civil Rights Act, which provided African American voting rights, and the 1961 Interstate Commerce Commission ruling against racial segregation in bus stations, a concern that had been sparked by the Freedom Rides.

NOTES

Introduction

1. General sources on the extraordinary sacrifices, courage, and leadership of African American women in the Black Freedom Movement include Bettye Collier-Thomas and V.P. Franklin, eds., *Sisters in the Struggle: African American Women in the Civil Rights–Black Power Movement* (New York: New York University Press, 2001); Vicki L. Crawford, Jacqueline A. Rouse, and Barbara Woods, eds., *Women in the Civil Rights Movement: Trailblazers and Torchbearers* (Brooklyn, NY: Carlson Publishing, 1990); Arlyn Diamond, "Choosing Sides, Choosing Lives: Women's Autobiographies of the Civil Rights Movement," in Margo Cully, ed., *American Women's Autobiographies: Feasts of Memory* (Madison, Wisc.: University of Wisconsin Press, 1992), pp. 218–231; Cynthia G. Fleming, "Black Women Activists and the Student Nonviolent Coordinating Committee: The Case of Ruby Doris Robinson," *Journal of Women's History*, Vol. 4 (Winter 1993), pp. 64–82; and Belinda Robnett, *How Long? How Long? African American Women in the Struggle for Civil Rights* (New York: Oxford University Press, 1997).

2. Important sources on African American women's leadership in the Montgomery desegregation boycott include Rosa Parks, with Jim Haskins, *Rosa Parks: My Story* (New York: Dial Books, 1991) and Jo Ann Gibson Robinson, *The Montgomery Bus Boycott and the Women Who Started It* (Knoxville, Tenn.: University of Tennessee Press, 1987).

3. See, in particular, Lea E. Williams, *Servants of the People: The 1960s Legacy of African American Leadership* (New York: St. Martin's Press, 1996) and Ken Blanchard, Larry Spears, and Michele Lawrence, eds., *Focus on Leadership: Servant-Leadership for the 21st Century* (New York: John Wiley and Sons, Inc., 2001).

4. On Septima Poinsette Clark, see Cynthia Stokes Brown, ed., *Ready from Within: Septima Clark and the Civil Rights Movement* (Navarro, Calif.: Wild Trees

Press, 1986) and Septima Poinsette Clark with LeGette Blythe, *Echo In My Soul* (New York: E. P. Dutton and Company, 1962).

5. The best single scholarly study of Ella Baker is the wonderfully rich and theoretically engaging biography by historian Barbara Ransby, *Ella Baker and the Black Freedom Movement* (Chapel Hill, NC: University of North Carolina Press, 2003). Also see Charles Payne, "Ella Baker and Models of Social Change," *Signs*, Vol. 14 (1989), pp. 885–899; Joanne Grant, *Ella Baker: Freedom Bound* (New York: John Wiley and Sons, Inc., 1998); and Shyrlee Dallard, *Ella Baker: A Leader Behind the Scenes* (Englewood Cliffs, NJ: Silver Burdett Press, 1990).

6. An excellent presentation of Baker's views is her short yet important article "Bigger Than A Hamburger," *Southern Patriot*, Number 18 (June 1960), reprinted in Manning Marable and Leith Mullings, eds., *Let Nobody Turn Us Around: Voices of Resistance, Reform and Renewal, An African American Anthology* (Lanham, MD: Rowman and Littlefield, 2000), pp. 398–400.

7. August Meier and Elliott Rudwick, *From Plantation to Ghetto*, third edition (New York: Hill and Wang, seventeenth printing, 1994). Charles Evers, Medgar's brother, is briefly mentioned in the text (page 348).

8. Jeffrey O. G. Ogbar, *Black Power: Radical Politics and African American Identity* (Baltimore: Johns Hopkins Press, 2004), p. 47.

9. Ransby, *Ella Baker and the Black Freedom Movement*, pp. 186, 313.

10. Grant, *Ella Baker: Freedom Bound*, p. 3.

11. Chana Kai Lee, *For Freedom's Sake: The Life of Fannie Lou Hamer* (Urbana, Ill.: University of Illinois Press, 1999), pp. 60, 118.

12. James Farmer, *Lay Bare The Heart: An Autobiography of the Civil Rights Movement* (New York: New American Library, 1985), pp. 14, 351.

13. Myrlie B. Evers with William Peters, *For Us, The Living*, first edition (Garden City, NY: Doubleday, 1967).

14. John R. Salter, *Jackson, Mississippi: An American Chronicle of Struggle and Schism* (Hicksville, New York: Exposition Press, 1979).

15. Michael Shultz, dir., and Ossie Davis, screenplay, *For Us, The Living: The Story of Medgar Evers* (Charles Fries Productions, 1983).

16. Brochure, "The Medgar Evers Statue Fund, Inc., 1987–1993," copy in possession of the author.

17. The Civil Rights Research and Documentation Project, ed., "Remembering Medgar Evers . . . For A New Generation" (Oxford, Miss.: Afro-American Studies Program, University of Mississippi; distributed by Heritage Publications, 1988), pp. 2, 17.

18. Beckwith died at age eighty while serving his life sentence in the Central Mississippi Correctional Facility, in January 2001.

19. See Adam Nossiter, *Of Long Memory: Mississippi and the Murder of Medgar Evers* (Reading, Mass.: Addison-Wesley, 1994); Jennie Brown, *Medgar Evers* (Los Angeles: Melrose Square Publishing Company, 1994); Reed Massengill, *Portrait of a Racist: The Man Who Killed Medgar Evers?* (New York: St. Martin's

Press, 1994); and Maryanne Vollers, *Ghosts of Mississippi: The True Story* (Boston: Little Brown, 1995).

20. Paul Hamann and Sheila Nevins, prods., *Southern Justice: The Murder of Medgar Evers* (Ambrose Video for Home Box Office, 1994).

21. Rob Reiner, dir., *Ghosts of Mississippi* (Columbia Pictures and Castle Rock Entertainment, 1996).

22. Literature on the Medgar Evers Institute, 2003–2004, in possession of the author.

23. The 2003 fortieth-anniversary Evers commemoration at Arlington National Cemetery was initiated by three high-school students from Illinois, who were upset over the lack of public recognition of the civil-rights martyr.

24. Mark V. Tushnet, ed., *Thurgood Marshall: His Speeches, Writings, Arguments, Opinions, and Reminiscences* (Chicago: Lawrence Hill, 2001), pp. 510–511. The quoted interview of Marshall was conducted in 1977 by Ed Erwin for Columbia University's Center for Oral History Research.

Chapter 1

1. "Go Down, Old Hannah," recorded in the Texas Prison System between 1964 and 1966, in Bruce Jackson, *Wake Up Dead Man: Afro-American Worksongs from Texas Prisons* (Cambridge, Mass.: Harvard University Press, 1972), p. 2.

2. See Winbourne Drake, "The Mississippi Constitutional Convention of 1832," *Journal of Southern History*, vol. 23, no. 3 (August 1957), pp. 354–370.

3. See Vernon Wharton, *The Negro in Mississippi, 1865–1890* (Chapel Hill, NC: University of North Carolina Press, 1947), pp. 199–200.

4. Wharton, *The Negro in Mississippi, 1865–1890*, pp. 238–239. An excellent and more recent source on convict-labor exploitation is Mathew Mancini, *One Dies, Get Another: Convict Leasing in the American South* (Columbia, SC: University of South Carolina Press, 1996).

5. See William Mabry, "Disfranchisement of the Negro in Mississippi, *Journal of Southern History*, vol. 4, no. 3 (August 1938), pp. 318–333, and Michael Perman, *Struggle for Mastery: Disfranchisement in the South, 1888–1908* (Chapel Hill, NC: University of North Carolina Press, 2001), pp. 70–90.

6. Walter White, *Rope and Faggot* (New York: Arno Press, 1969), pp. 254–256. A total of 3,513 African Americans were lynched in the United States from 1882 to 1927.

7. V.O. Key Jr., *Southern Politics* (New York: Vintage Books, 1949), p. 229.

8. Charles M. Payne, *I've Got the Light of Freedom: The Organizing Tradition and the Mississippi Freedom Struggle* (Berkeley: University of California Press, 1995).

9. Civil Rights Research and Documentation Project, ed., *Remembering Medgar Evers . . . For A New Generation*, p. 1.

10. Author's interview with Myrlie Evers-Williams, August 20–21, 2004.

11. Ibid.

12. Ibid., and Civil Rights Research and Documentation Project, ed., *Remembering Medgar Evers . . . For A New Generation*, pp. 2–3.

13. Author's interview with Myrlie Evers-Williams, August 20–21, 2004.

14. Charles Evers and Andrew Szanton, *Have No Fear: The Charles Evers Story* (New York: John Wiley and Sons, 1996).

15. Interview with Myrlie Evers-Williams, August 20–21, 2004.

16. Ibid.

17. Ibid.

18. Ibid.

19. Ibid.

20. Ibid.

21. Ibid.

22. Evers and Szanton, *Have No Fear*, pp. 75–76.

23. Interview with Myrlie Evers-Williams, August 20–21, 2004.

24. Payne, *I've Got the Light of Freedom*, pp. 32–38.

25. Interview with Myrlie Evers-Williams, August 20–21, 2004.

26. Evers and Szanton, *Have No Fear*, p. 77.

27. Interview with Myrlie Evers-Williams, August 20–21, 2004.

28. Ibid., and Myrlie Evers with William Peters, *For Us, The Living* (New York: Doubleday, 1967), pp. 133–136.

29. Bettye Collier-Thomas and V.P. Franklin, *My Soul Is A Witness: A Chronicle of the Civil Rights Era, 1954–1965* (New York: Henry Holt and Company, 1999), pp. 6–10.

30. Evers and Szanton, *Have No Fear*, p. 81.

31. Numan V. Bartley, *The Rise of Massive Resistance: Race and Politics in the South During the 1950s* (Baton Rouge: Louisiana State University Press, 1969), pp. 55–56.

32. Ibid., pp. 85–86, and Collier-Thomas and Franklin, *My Soul Is a Witness*, pp. 11–12.

33. Payne, *I've Got the Light of Freedom*, pp. 41–42.

34. Ibid., pp. 36–39.

35. Evers and Szanton, *Have No Fear*, p. 86.

36. Howard Spence, interviewed by Hardy Frye, 1968, in Bob Blauner, *Black Lives, White Lives: Three Decades of Race Relations in America* (Berkeley: University of California Press, 1989), pp. 33–34.

Chapter 2

1. Collier-Thomas and Franklin, *My Soul Is A Witness*, p. 41.

2. Ibid., p. 45.

3. Payne, *I've Got the Light of Freedom*, p. 43.

4. Interview with Myrlie Evers-Williams, August 20–21, 2004.

5. Evers and Szanton, *Have No Fear*, pp. 92–93.

6. Ibid., p. 93.

7. "NAACP Opens 47th Meeting," *Washington Post*, June 27, 1956; "NAACP Studies Resistance Move," *New York Times*, July 1, 1956; and Michael D. Davis and Hunter R. Clark, *Thurgood Marshall: Warrior at the Bar, Rebel on the Bench*, Revised Edition (Citadel Press, Carol Publishing Group, 1992), pp. 200–203. In King's speech before the NAACP convention, he largely focused on his religious convictions as being central to his protest strategy. He also argued that the desegregation campaign in Montgomery had created a "new Negro," and that "I have no doubt that by 1963 we will have won the legal battle" against Jim Crow. See David Garrow, *Bearing The Cross: Martin Luther King, Jr. and the Southern Christian Leadership Conference* (London: Vintage, 1986), pp. 78–79.

8. Evers and Szanton, *Have No Fear*, p. 92.

Chapter 3

1. Collier-Thomas and Franklin, *My Soul Is A Witness*, pp. 67, 89.

2. Barley, *The Rose of Massive Resistance*, pp. 274–275, 288–289.

3. Collier-Thomas and Franklin, *My Soul Is A Witness*.

4. Payne, *I've Got the Light of Freedom*, pp. 59–60.

5. Medgar Evers, "Monthly Report," April 11, 1958.

6. See Jack Dougherty, "'That's When We Were Marching for Jobs': Black Teachers and the Early Civil Rights Movement in Milwaukee," *History of Education Quarterly*, Vol. 38, no. 2 (Summer 1998), pp. 121–141.

7. Address by Medgar Evers, May 18, 1958, Milwaukee, Wisconsin.

8. Medgar Evers, "Why I Live in Mississippi," as told to Francis H. Mitchell, *Ebony* magazine (November 1958).

Chapter 4

1. Medgar Evers, "Monthly Report," May 21, 1959.

2. See Cabell Phillips, "Lynch Case Prosecution Is Now up to Mississippi," *New York Times*, May 31, 1959; Robert E. Baker, "Special Lynch Jury Illegal, Coleman Says," *Washington Post*, May 29, 1959; "FBI Finds Body of Negro in River," *New York Times*, May 5, 1959; and Howard Smead, *Blood Justice: The Lynching of Mack Charles Parker* (New York: Oxford University Press, 1986). As Myrlie commented in *For Us, The Living* (pp. 204–205): "Everyone in town knew who did it. The FBI turned over names and evidence to Governor [J.P.] Coleman. There were no arrests. Some years later, a Mississippi judge, speaking in Connecticut about the wonders of our state, was asked if he thought the lynchers of Mack Charles Parker would ever be caught and tried. He said he didn't think so and then added, without thinking, 'Besides, three of them are already dead.' *Everyone* knew who did it."

3. Evers, with Peters, *For Us, The Living*, p. 205.

4. Interview with Myrlie Evers-Williams, August 20–21, 2004.

5. Ibid.

6. Medgar Evers, speech, Los Angeles Branch, NAACP, May 31, 1959.

7. Interview with Myrlie Evers-Williams, August 20–21, 2004.

Chapter 5

1. Collier-Thomas and Franklin, *My Soul Is a Witness*, p. 123.

2. Ibid., pp. 120–126.

3. Interview with Myrlie Evers-Williams, August 20–21, 2004.

4. Collier-Thomas and Franklin, *My Soul Is a Witness*, p. 123.

5. Interview with Myrlie Evers-Williams, August 20–21, 2004.

6. Payne, *I've Got the Light of Freedom*, p. 55; and "Evers v. State," Supreme Court of Mississippi, No. 41960, 241 Miss. 560; 131 So. 2nd 653; 1961 Miss Lexis 374.

7. John R. Salter, Jr. [Hunter Bear], "Medgar W. Evers: Reflection and Appreciation," January 15, 2004, at http://www.hunterbear.org/medgar_w.htm.

Chapter 6

1. Interview with Myrlie Evers-Williams, August 20–21, 2004.

2. Salter, "Medgar W. Evers: Reflection and Appreciation."

3. Interview with Myrlie Evers-Williams, August 20–21, 2004.

4. James Meredith, *Three Years in Mississippi* (Bloomington: Indiana University Press, 1966), pp. 56–57.

5. See Claude Sitton, "Meredith Decides to Complete His Education at Mississippi U," *New York Times*, January 31, 1963.

6. See "23 More Riders Fined and Jailed," *New York Times*, June 27, 1961.

7. Evers with Peters, *For Us, The Living*, p. 252.

8. Ibid., p. 254.

9. Ibid., p. 253.

10. Payne, *I've Got the Light of Freedom*, pp. 61–63.

Chapter 7

1. Salter, "Medgar W. Evers: Reflection and Appreciation."

2. Emily Wagster Pettus, "Mississippi Marks 40th Anniversary of Evers Slaying," Associated Press, June 6, 2003.

3. Salter, "Medgar W. Evers: Reflection and Appreciation."

4. Dick Gregory with Robert Lipsyte, *Nigger: An Autobiography* (New York: E. P. Dutton and Company, 1964), p. 197.

5. Salter, "Medgar W. Evers: Reflection and Appreciation."

6. Evers with Peters, *For Us, The Living*, p. 295.

Chapter 8

1. Meredith, *Three Years in Mississippi*, p. 305. Meredith added with great anger that responsibility for Evers's murder "clearly rests with the governors of the Southern states and their defiant and provocative actions; it rests with the blind courts and prejudiced juries—it is known both by blacks and whites that no white man will be punished for any crime against a Negro, especially if it is one of the controversial areas." Meredith called for "a general boycott on 'everything possible' by 'all Negroes within the boundaries of the state of Mississippi.'"

2. Myrlie Evers-Williams, interview with Tavis Smiley, June 12, 2003, National Public Radio broadcast, transcript.

3. Salter, "Medgar W. Evers: Reflection and Appreciation."

4. Harris, "Forty Years After Medgar the Struggle Continues."

5. Juan Williams, *Eyes on the Prize: America's Civil Rights Years, 1954–1965* (New York: Penguin, 1987), p. 228.

6. See John Rachal, "'The Long Hot Summer': The Mississippi Response to Freedom Summer," *Journal of Negro History*, vol. 84, no. 3 (Autumn 1999), pp. 315–339.

7. See Frank Parker, *Black Votes Count: Political Empowerment in Mississippi After 1965* (Chapel Hill: University of North Carolina Press, 1990), pp. 34–77.

8. See Andrew Shapiro, "The Disfranchised," *The American Prospect*, vol. 8, no. 35 (1997), pp. 60–62.

9. See E. C. Foster, "A Time of Challenge: Afro-Mississippi Political Developments Since 1965," *Journal of Negro History*, vol. 68, no. 2 (Spring 1983), pp. 185–200.

10. Ibid., pp. 190–191.

11. Jerry Mitchell, "Miss. Thanks Evers Family," *Clarion-Ledger* [Jackson, Mississippi], April 26, 2002; and "Papers of Medgar, Myrlie Evers Donated to Department of Archives and History," News Release, April 25, 2002, at www.mdah.state.ms.us.

12. Interview with Myrlie Evers-Williams, August 20–21, 2004.

BIBLIOGRAPHY

Medgar Evers, Voting Rights, and the Black Freedom Movement in Mississippi

I. BOOKS AND ARTICLES:

Belfrage, Sally. *Freedom Summer* (New York: Viking Press, 1966).

Brown, Jennie. *Medgar Evers* (Los Angeles: Melrose Square, 1994).

Burner, Eric. *And Gently He Shall Lead Them: Robert Parris Moses and Civil Rights in Mississippi* (New York: New York University Press, 1994).

Carson, Clayborne. *In Struggle: SNCC and the Black Awakening of the 1960s* (Cambridge: Harvard University Press, 1981).

Civil Rights Research and Documentation Project, ed. *Remembering Medgar Evers . . . For A New Generation* (Oxford, Miss.: Black Studies Program, University of Mississippi, 1988).

DeLaughter, Bobby. *Never Too Late: A Prosecutor's Story of Justice in the Medgar Evers Case* (New York: Scribner, 2001).

Dittmer, John. *Local People: The Struggle for Civil Rights in Mississippi* (Urbana: University of Illinois Press, 1994).

Doyle, William. *An American Insurrection: The Battle of Oxford, Mississippi, 1962* (New York: Doubleday, 2001).

Evers, Charles. *Have No Fear: The Charles Evers Story* (New York: John Wiley & Sons, 1997).

Evers, Mrs. Medgar Wiley, with William Peters. *For Us, The Living* (Garden City, NY: Doubleday, 1967).

Foster, E. C. "A Time of Challenge: Afro-Mississippi Political Developments Since 1965." *Journal of Negro History*, vol. 68, no. 2 (Spring 1983): 185–200.

Henry, Aaron. *Aaron Henry: The Fire Ever Burning* (Jackson: University Press of Mississippi, 2000).

Holt, Len. *The Summer That Didn't End: The Story of the Mississippi Civil Rights Project of 1964* (New York: Da Capo Press, 1964).

Jackson, James E. *At the Funeral of Medgar Evers in Jackson, Mississippi: A Tribute in Tears and a Thrust for Freedom* (New York: Publishers New Press, 1963).

Lee, Chana Kai. *For Freedom's Sake: The Life of Fannie Lou Hamer* (Urbana: University of Illinois Press, 1999).

Lindsay, Beverly. "The Role of African-American Women in the Civil Rights and Women's Rights Movements in Hinds County and Sunflower County, Mississippi." *Journal of Mississippi History*, vol. 53 (August 1991): 229–239.

Mason, Gilbert. *Beaches, Blood and Ballots: A Black Doctor's Civil Rights Struggle* (Jackson: University Press of Mississippi, 2000).

Massengill, Reed. *Portrait of a Racist: The Man Who Killed Medgar Evers* (New York: St. Martin's Press, 1994).

McAdam, Doug. *Freedom Summer* (New York: Oxford University Press, 1988).

McMillen, Neil. *The Citizens' Council: Organized Resistance to the Second Reconstruction* (Urbana: University of Illinois Press, 1971).

Meier, August, and Elliot Rudwick. *CORE: A Study in the Civil Rights Movement, 1942–1968* (New York: Oxford University Press, 1973).

Metcalf, George R. *Black Profile* (New York: McGraw-Hill, 1970).

Mills, Kay. *This Little Light of Mine: The Life of Fannie Lou Hamer* (New York: Dutton, 1993).

Mitchell, Dennis, and Nancy D. Hargrove. "Trial for Honor" and "A Question of Honor" (Jackson: Mississippi Humanities Council, 1986).

Moody, Ann. *Coming of Age in Mississippi* (New York: Dial Press, 1968).

Morris, Willie. *The Ghosts of Medgar Evers: A Tale of Race, Murder, Mississippi, and Hollywood* (New York: Random House, 1998).

Nossiter, Adam. *Of Long Memory: Mississippi and the Murder of Medgar Evers* (Reading, Mass.: Addison-Wesley, 1994).

O'Reilly, Kenneth. *Black Americans: The FBI Files* (New York: Carroll & Graf, 1994).

Oshinsky, David M. *Worse Than Slavery: Parchman Farm and the Ordeal of Jim Crow Justice* (New York: Free Press, 1996).

Parker, Frank. *Black Votes Count: Political Empowerment in Mississippi After 1965* (Chapel Hill: University of North Carolina Press, 1990).

Payne, Charles M. *I've Got the Light of Freedom: The Organizing Tradition and the Mississippi Freedom Struggle* (Berkeley: University of California Press, 1995).

Perman, Michael. *Struggle for Mastery: Disfranchisement in the South, 1888–1908* (Chapel Hill: University of North Carolina Press, 2001).

Rachal, John. "The Long, Hot Summer: The Mississippi Response to Freedom Summer, 1964." *Journal of Negro History*, vol. 84, no. 3 (Autumn 1999), 315–339.

Salter, John R. *Jackson, Mississippi: An American Chronicle of Struggle and Schism* (Hicksville, NY: Exposition Press, 1979).

United States Commission on Civil Rights, Mississippi Advisory Committee. *Administration of Justice in Mississippi: A Report to the United States Commission on Civil Rights* (Washington, D.C., 1963).

Vollers, Maryanne. *Ghosts of Mississippi: The Murder of Medgar Evers, the Trials of Byron de la Beckwith, and the Haunting of the New South* (Boston: Little, Brown, 1995).

Voting in Mississippi: A Report of the U.S. Civil Rights Commission (1965), collected in John Hope Franklin and Isidore Starr, eds., *The Negro in Twentieth Century America: A Reader on the Struggle for Civil Rights* (New York: Vintage, 1967), 321–347.

Walker, Margaret. *Prophets for a New Day* (Chicago: Broadside Press, 1970).

Wharton, Vernon. *The Negro in Mississippi, 1865–1890* (Chapel Hill: University of North Carolina Press, 1947).

Williams, Juan. *Eyes on the Prize: America's Civil Rights Years, 1954–1965* (New York: Penguin, 1987).

II. RECENT NEWSPAPER AND MAGAZINE ARTICLES ABOUT MEDGAR EVERS, 2002–2004

"Alcorn Names Auditorium after Alumnus and Civil Rights Leader, Medgar Evers." *Black Issues in Higher Education*, April 10, 2003, vol. 20, no. 4, 11.

"A Tribute to Medgar and a Hand to Lott." *Tri-State Defender*, July 2, 2003, vol. 52, no. 25, 4A.

"A Tribute to the Memory of Medgar Evers." *New Pittsburgh Courier*, July 5, 2003, vol. 94, no. 54, A6.

Harris, Barbara. "Forty Years After Medgar Evers the Struggle Continues." *Jackson Advocate*, June 12, 2003–June 18, 2003, vol. 65, no. 34, 1A, 12A.

Joiner, Lottie L. "The Nation Remembers Medgar Evers." *The Crisis*, July–August, 2003, vol. 110, no. 4, 8.

"Legacy of Medgar Evers Maintained." *Jacksonville Free Press*, June 25, 2003, vol. 17, no. 21, 5.

Lynch, Adam. "Maryland Lawmaker Proposes Adding Medgar Evers' Name to Airport." *Mississippi Link* 4, May 2004, vol. 12, no. 18, A1.

"NAACP Celebrates 40th Anniversary of the Legacy of Medgar Evers." *Atlanta Inquirer*, June 28, 2003, vol. 42, no. 48, 6.

"Profile: Mississippi 40 Years after the Killing of Civil Rights Leader Medgar Evers." *All Things Considered*, June 10, 2003, 1.

"Teens Create Ceremony Honoring Slain Rights Leader Evers." *New York Beacon*, June 25, 2003, vol. 10, no. 24, 16.

Pettus, Emily Wagster. "Medgar Evers' Widow Tries to Keep Her Husband's Legacy Alive 40 Years after his Assassination." Associated Press, June 16, 2003.

"Slain Activist's Legacy Lives On: Evers' Work for Civil Rights Honored 40 Years After His Killing." *Houston Chronicle*, June 11, 2003: 10.

Wade, Courtney K. "Project Puts Students in Touch with Legacy of Medgar Evers." *Chicago Sun-Times*, June 19, 2003, 20.

Witte, Griff. "Civil Rights Project Turns Personal: Students Celebrate Medgar Evers in Documentary, Arlington Ceremony." *Washington Post*, June 17, 2003, B01.

III. DISSERTATIONS

Murrain, Ethel Patricia Churchill. "The Mississippi Man and His Message: A Rhetorical Analysis of the Cultural Themes in the Oratory of Medgar Wiley Evers, 1957–1963." Ph.D. diss., University of Southern Mississippi, 1990.

Tisdale, John Rochelle. "Medgar Evers (1925–1963) and the Mississippi Press." Ph.D. diss., University of North Texas, 1996.

INDEX